The Heart of
Simple Living:
7 Paths to a Better Life

Wanda Urbanska

Host of the TV series,
Simple Living With Wanda Urbanska,
on *PBS* stations nationwide

©2010 Wanda Urbanska

Published by

krause publications
A division of F+W Media, Inc.

700 East State Street • Iola, WI 54990-0001
715-445-2214 • 888-457-2873
www.krausebooks.com

To order books or other products call toll-free 1-800-258-0929 or visit
us online at www.krausebooks.com or www.Shop.Collect.com.

Library of Congress Control Number: 2009937590

ISBN-13: 978-1-4402-0451-7
ISBN-10: 1-4402-0451-9

Designed by Wendy Wendt
Edited by Candy Wiza

Printed in United States of America

Make the change to a sustainable lifestyle using expert advice and know-how
garnered from our Simple Living books. We'll provide you with the knowledge
to develop long-term self-sufficiency that will save you time and money.

Mission Statement: *Enjoy the simple things in life while you reduce, reuse and recycle.*

" 'The Heart of Simple Living' says it all — no one has more heart than Wanda Urbanska, and no one is better able to take you on an enchanted Simple Living journey. Follow her clear pathways to a sustainable lifestyle and you will not only 'grow flowers for your body and soul,' you will find that your entire life is a bright bloom for the planet. It happened to me."

- Carol Holst, director, Postconsumers

"Wanda Urbanska has done it again. This carefully crafted, inspiring and practical journey down the path of simple living is bursting with real life examples gained through years of personal experience and practice. 'The Heart of Simple Living' is an easy-to-follow road map for learning to do more — and live more fully — with less."

- Dave Wampler, founder, The Simple Living Network,
www.simpleliving.net

"Wanda Urbanska has turned her years of research about simple living and the highlights of her popular PBS television series into a wonderful guide for the rest of us. She's been a remarkable writer since she wrote her first front page story for the Bangor Daily News while still in high school and has only gotten better with each book. Her ideas separate real wealth from the glitter of American over-consumption, and they are sure to enrich every reader."

- John de Graaf, co-author, "Affluenza: The All-Consuming
Epidemic"

"Wanda is a dynamo of good sense and goodness who, with wit and wisdom, invites us to explore a life of sanity and satisfaction. 'The Heart of Simple Living' offers a treasure-chest of ideas and suggestions for growing a life of creative and compassionate simplicity."

- Duane Elgin, author of "Voluntary Simplicity," "The Living
Universe," and "Promise Ahead"

"I love Wanda, and I love Wanda's new book! No phoniness or self-righteousness here, which reminds me of something I've always known — simplicity people are wonderful people! My conclusion? Read this book, and you'll be wonderful too!"

- Cecile Andrews, author of "Slow is Beautiful" and
"Circle of Simplicity"

"Wanda Urbanska is a spokeswoman for a phenomenon known as the simplicitty movement."

- The New York Times

Dedication

To my cherished sister, Jane, who personifies so many lessons of
simplicity, in thought, word and deed.

Acknowledgments

This book is the brainchild of Candy Wiza, a talented, caring, and visionary editor for Krause Publications who has been a pleasure to work with and to know.

In addition, I want to thank key members of "my community" without whose support this work would not have been possible:

My mother, Marie Olesen Urbanski Whittaker.

My friends (many of whom appear in these pages): Ann Vaughn, Ann Williams, Ann Belk, Hattie Brintle, Bonni Brodnick, Carol Holst, Cecile Andrews, Kay Taylor, Leonard Kniffel, Irene Tomaszewski, Eve Krzyzanowski, Laura Bruzas, Marion McAdoo Goldwasser, Liz Brody, John Wear, Nancy Murray, Pat Woltz, Cathy Stevens, Ellen LaConte, Pilar Gerasimo, Ruth Olesen Kelley, Charlotte Sheedy, Scott Kelley, Hallie Gay Bagley, Allen Paul, Grzegorz Urbanski, Monika Malcher, Tad and Ola Tuliszka, Thurman Williams, Margaret Olesen Raley, Mondee Tilley, Linda Brinson, Reed Bunzel and many more.

To my son, Henry, thank you for the person you are … and are becoming!

Contents

Chapter Five: Back Into the Kitchen ...165

Chapter Six: Beating a Path to the Garden ...189

Chapter Seven: Reclaiming Ritual and Community for Life ...211

Introduction

Drawing on the wisdom of my remarkable parents — iconoclasts who lived simply — I've been able to distill their lessons about money, work, meaning, service to humanity, and following your own drummer into a cohesive philosophy for myself and others. My father, Edmund Stephen Urbanski, experienced privation, tragedy, and ultimately triumph during his life journey. A Polish Roman Catholic whose name was on a Nazi death list, Daddy managed to escape war-torn Europe in 1939, leaving behind his family and country, but gaining the chance to start over. He married my American-born mother and began a new chapter, in which he was able to maintain his sterling work ethic, gregarious spirit and innate curiosity. After retiring from Howard University in Washington D.C., Daddy remained active with his scholarship and international correspondence until his death at 87. Although he was a naturalized American, I like to joke that my father was a Pole teaching Americans how to speak the Spanish language.

My mother, Marie Olesen Urbanski Whittaker, grew up in Texas and Oklahoma during the Great Depression and invented herself several times over. In her 20s, she was an idealistic rebel with an adventurous spirit who worked for the United States Air Force in North Africa. In her 30s and 40s, she morphed into a wife and mother, moving frequently with my father to different college campuses around the country; in mid-life, she forged a successful career as a university professor. Then, at age 74, she fell in love again and married Col. Joseph Whittaker, a widowed World War II airman who flew missions over Europe with Jimmy Stewart. In fact, Joe Whittaker comes as close as anyone I've ever met to resembling the earnest, good-guy persona that Jimmy Stewart portrayed on screen. Heck, Joe was even a Pennsylvanian (like Jimmy) with a droll voice eerily reminiscent of the famous actor's. Joe had a kind word to say about almost everyone. On the rare occasions he was put off, the closest he ever came to sounding critical was to say, "He sure was a *different* one."

From both of my parents and my stepfather, the lessons of common sense and frugality — when applied to money, life and thinking for yourself — took hold. In this book, I set out to pass along to you their wisdom, along with nuggets I've gleaned from the many people and resources I've encountered during two decades of simplicity advocacy, including four seasons producing America's first nationally syndicated public television series promoting sustainable, eco-friendly living, "Simple Living With Wanda Urbanska" (*www.simplelivingtv.net*).

It is my wish to help you on your journey to the good life, which is not "the goods life" or a life centered on material acquisition, but rather a life in which consciousness reigns supreme. Reclaiming the good life starts with bringing *you* back into your own life. By bringing you back, I mean inviting your thoughts, dreams, and inner life to the driver's seat of your existence rather than somewhere on the trivialized sidelines. Reclaiming the good life means deciding your objectives in life, rather than accepting some prefab version of that life, props and all, delivered by the marketers on Madison Avenue. The good life involves knowing who you are, doing work you love — or at least making yourself fully present in the work you have — and bringing awareness and direction to your actions, finances and planning for the future.

My prescription involves rethinking choices for housing, food, clothing, and cleaning, generally moving you in the direction of common-sense, good-for-you choices. And, it invites you to take a new look at the concept of ownership to understand what things you really *need* to live well. Whatever you don't need is excess. What simplicity wisdom teaches is that excess is *not* a good thing; excess possessions are like carrying oversize baggage on a trip, or extra pounds on your frame. Rather than giving you more options, *excess* actually weighs you down. By inviting you to join me on the path to the good life, I invite you to creatively construct your daily rituals, your annual celebrations, and significant rites of passage. Finally, the good life cannot be "good" without connecting you to community in ways that are both meaningful and life-enhancing. For all of these paths, I provide myriad examples of how I and others have adapted the American lifestyle to invent the kind of lives in which we have become most vibrantly alive. I offer these life lessons as a way for you to become most fully yourself.

Following are my seven paths to the heart of simple living, around which this book is organized:

1. Live frugally; save money; retire debt as fast as you can.

2. Find work that sparks your flame and colleagues whom you respect and enjoy.

3. Rethink the American way of housing, and focus your direction on small, green, and paid-for.

4. Personalize and simplify your decorating choices; adopt non-toxic cleaning strategies to save money and create a healthful home environment; green your clothing, wardrobe and laundry.

5. Cook healthful food at home and in bulk. Rediscover your kitchen, source your food with an emphasis on local fare, and establish the ritual of regular, sit-down, family meals.

6. Plant a new victory garden with fresh fruits, herbs and vegetables, and allow its growth to spur on your own. Grow flowers for your body and soul.

7. Infuse your rituals and celebrations — daily, annual and life-passage — with meaning not money. Plan in advance and be original! Engage in community life as one primary ritual.

Taken together, these paths will send you on your way to the good life.

We start with frugality because money and money management have been foremost on our minds during the last two years. Many people have seen their net worth erode or even collapse. Others have lost homes and jobs. Still others are up to their eyeballs in debt. How can you pursue a life of contentment and peace — how can you seek to establish a vital connection to your inner self — if you're up nights trying to figure out how you're going to pay your bills? But even in times of relative financial prosperity, frugality always represents the first best means of gaining control of your life. Once you get started on the road to financial sanity, the simple life — the good life — will be easier to achieve.

The second path — finding work you love — represents another fundamental purchase on the life worth living. As Sigmund Freud famously opined, "Love and work ... work and love, that's all there is." While it may not be quite that simple, the work we do and choose to do represents the focus of our life energy. For most of us, our work is our largest contribution to the world. If you hate your job and dread going to work in the morning, if you find no redeeming qualities in what you do for a living, you need to find another source of livelihood.

The third path leads us home. We need only look at housing trends over the past 40 years to see alarming trends. House size has expanded while family size has contracted. During that period, the often flimsily built "McMansion" displaced the solid brick rancher as the home destination of choice. But the way back to the good domestic life is found by scaling down our housing-size ambitions, by seeking out homes that are greener, more energy-efficient, and affordable. At the end of the trail to the good life, the adjectives "healthy" and "paid-for" should be at the top of the list.

The fourth path to the good life — finding comfort living in your body and your home — is through decorating your home with your personality and "greening" your clothing and cleaning practices. On this path, I'll recommend scaling back your wardrobe and offer pointers for what to consider when you do add something new. I'll suggest ways to adopt green cleaning practices in your home. Too often, over-the-counter cleaning products contain toxic substances, even known carcinogens. (I can just hear my friend, simplicity advocate Cecile Andrews saying, "*Lower* your standards. Clean only when absolutely necessary.") Not only can you make your own ordinary household cleaning agents yourself, but through green cleaning techniques you can start to transform your home into a nurturing, healing — not to mention eco-friendly — environment.

The fifth path brings us to the kitchen and dining room, sacred spaces which we need to reclaim. Too many of us have designer showroom kitchens but no knowledge of how to put them to work in the preparation of our sustenance. Rediscover the art of food preparation; learn to cook, bake, and make a good meal. And finally, I'll urge you to reclaim the family, sit-down meal.

The sixth path invites us to beat a path to the yard to reclaim the multiple and overlapping benefits of gardening. When you grow some of your own food, you reduce your grocery bills, you eat more healthful fruits and vegetables, you know where your food is coming from and are acting on behalf of the environment. Gardening also puts you in touch with nature and the seasons. While home-grown vegetables are hard to beat, nurturing and enjoying flowers runs neck in neck on the enjoyment scale.

The seventh path to the heart of simple living involves community, connection and ritual. We as human beings vitally need connection with others, yet forces in our society — such as automation, the accelerated pace of life, and the Internet age — seem to be conspiring to separate us more rapidly and effectively than ever before. Connecting with community adds value to your life, your health, and your worth as a human being. Connecting with community involves ritual: meetings, organizations, religious community, social clubs, organized activity. We'll cover the importance of rituals in your daily routine: your meals, exercise program, eating, cleanup, and sleeping habits, and invite your more active engagement. Then, we'll move to your annual celebrations and once-in-a-lifetime rites of passage, in which so many Americans have detached from full participation. The path of infusing rituals and celebrations with meaning allows you to orchestrate crucial events surrounding such life changes as birth, coming of age, marriage and death.

Your Journey to the "Good" Life

Each of these paths will guide you toward a simpler life. All seven, taken in aggregate, provide a road map for sending you on your journey toward a more fulfilling reality, a world filled with less stuff, but more connection and meaning. An existence where you live in the present, consciously connected to others and the natural world. A world in which you have the chance to be fully alive — maybe for the first time.

In an ideal world, you would take each of these paths sequentially, like seven legs on a journey of exploration. However, as we all know, this is not an ideal world, and it's unlikely that your journey will be that ... shall I say it? ... simple. More than likely, you'll start down one, and then skip to another. Or you may gallop to your destination on one path, but struggle with the next, taking two steps forward and one back. Or, you may wish to cherry-pick changes from one area while proceeding on another. That's okay, too. You're getting started. Remember, you're the lead dog blazing the trail. If you look at what I present and decide to modify it, argue with it, change it, that works for me. My wish is for *you* to create your life. Not Madison Avenue. Not even a simplicity advocate like me.

Speaking of being a simplicity advocate, you may wonder how I came by these chops? Who am I to be dispensing this advice, you may ask. I'm neither a trained psychologist, counselor, nor credentialed academic. Instead, I've always been an inquisitive on-the-job learner. While still in high school, I started my career in journalism as an intern and stringer for the Bangor Daily News in Maine; in college, I interned at Newsweek magazine in New York, and decades later became an on-air television host without having taken a single course in film or television. In fact, everything I've accomplished in life has come from trying my hand at things, setting goals, and learning from my triumphs and stumbles. That and listening to others.

In fact, in childhood, my curiosity about others earned me the nickname "Miss Hypothetical" because I couldn't seem to stop asking questions.

Like most of us who reach middle age, I've endured bumps along the way, including a lengthy and painful parting from my former husband and long-time collaborator. But I have moved forward, working hard to bring my life into alignment with my values, all the while seeking to live with as much integrity as possible in a world where it often seems in short supply. All the while, I've tried to live by the maxim that no experience is a bad experience if you can make it a learning experience.

While the seven paths I'm presenting to you are by no means the only routes to achieving the good life, given our collective cultural experience, given our cultural strengths and weaknesses, they represent the best routes I know for most Americans circa 2010. From growing up with two parents who thought for themselves, who tended to non-conformity, who fought hard for their accomplishments and place in the world, I know that life is rarely a cakewalk.

"Who said life was easy — or fair?" my Mother often says. But once you adopt the attitude that life is an adventure and you're blazing the trail, once you retool your habits and your attitudes and start to define success on your own terms, life can become a grand adventure. As Mother used to say, "Jump onboard, hold on, and don't look back!"

Chapter One

The Path to
Financial Independence

*Live frugally; save liberally;
retire debt as fast as you can.*

These words of wisdom represent the first, most basic path to the good life. It's hard to live well when you're worried about paying your bills or knowing where your next meal or mortgage payment is coming from. By the same token, seeking the good life through the accumulation of wealth alone can actually undermine your future well-being. Once you temper your material desires and adopt a frugal mind-set and sensible approach to money management, saving will become second nature. The money you set aside will help retire debt and build security.

The Lesson of The Table

My mother, sister and I were strolling around Quebec City one lazy summer afternoon more than three decades ago when a bear-tooth pendant in the window of a jewelry store caught Jane's eye.

This weekend vacation was Jane's high school graduation present from Mama, and Jane had some gift money to spend. After stepping inside to examine the pendant up close, sticker shock set in. We sisters glanced idly at several other items on display — all out of our price range — then looked around for Mother. What had become of her?

Finally we spotted her, at the back of the store, admiring ... a table. Granted, it was no ordinary table, but a lovely, hand-crafted coffee table made from an old-growth elm tree. A section of the trunk — the kind where you can count the concentric rings from the center to determine the tree's age — formed the tabletop. A thick coat of clear polyurethane protected the wood, giving it a glossy patina. No doubt about it, the piece was stunning but not exactly cheap. Mama just gazed.

"Why don't you buy it?" I suggested. I was 16 and the risk-taker of the trio. A weathered footlocker had served as our coffee table for the seven years since my parents' divorce. In fact, most of the furniture in our rented duplex in Orono, Maine was grad student stuff — bricks and boards for bookshelves, thrift-store and yard-sale finds.

Mother gave me a strange look. *"Buy it?"* she said. The thought had never crossed her mind.

"Sure, Mom," Jane joined in. "You've saved some money. Treat yourself."

The opposite of an impulse buyer, my mother has always been all about "basic necessities" when it comes to money. If it's not groceries on the list or an oil change for the car, she doesn't spring for it.

Well, you guessed it. Mama surprised us that afternoon by pulling out her credit card, signing on the dotted line and transporting The Table across the Canadian border back home into Maine. Though she has moved four times since, The Table remains among Mama's most cherished possessions, a testimony to her hard work, fiscal discipline, and that rare summer's whim.

The larger lesson of The Table is the story of the frugality that undergirds it, the frugality that made its acquisition both possible and memorable, the frugality that enabled Mama to dream large and reach for the stars — at an age and in a day when the culture wasn't exactly cheering on the professional ambitions of a single, 40-something woman with two young daughters to raise.

In her approach to money and dreaming — and, boy, are the two ever connected — Marie Olesen Urbanski Whittaker has always been my role model. Lack of money never stopped her from anything. Like the big-dreaming, do-what-I-please Scarlett O'Hara, Mama followed her own stars, never caring much about what society thought. Back in the 1940s, when respectable, young, middle-class women were supposed to pursue matrimony (rather than careers or self-fulfillment), Mama decided to have her fun and play the field. "I'll get married when I'm 30," she vowed. And she did.

Watching as her two sisters married well, Mother set her sights on traveling the world. Setting a goal and saving up allowed her to decorate her suitcase with sticker pendants from hotels in French Morocco, Tangier, Spain, and Portugal; it allowed her to fill her memory bank with exotic experiences like camel rides in the desert outside Marrakesh and haggling for souvenirs at the famed Djemaa el Fna Square marketplace amidst the legendary Moroccan snake charmers and musical performers.

Given her unorthodox choices, one might expect my mother to be a reckless spender. On the contrary, her legacy — when it comes to money — is one of fiscal restraint, sensible spending and conservative money management. Dream big, but be sure you can afford to pay for the ballet slippers. So after the Great Recession of 2008, when a friend pronounced that everyone he knew was worth half of what they had been 18 months earlier, I begged to differ. Mama's net worth was down — but not by that much. She never played the stock market. Her condominium was paid for and her money tucked safely away in the bank.

Be "Resourceful" When Young

Another lesson from Mother's life is this: Many Americans have it backwards. Too many of us spend out our dreams in our youth (think extravagant weddings, late-model cars, fancy vacations, and state-of-the-art electronics). Sometimes the young lovebirds are divorced before the wedding's paid off, and may be forced into penury in old age. Much better to reverse this order: Live modestly and sensibly while young — when youth is a priceless privilege — and salt away your money for old age when it will matter more.

I often reflect on the philosophy of my niece, Teresa Miriam Van Hoy, who is not yet old but no longer young. I recall the tremendous energy she expended in her salad days back in the 1980s to save money for her later years. "I may not be rich," she told me back then, when she was in her 20s, "but I'm resourceful." Who wouldn't be impressed with the sum she managed to amass in just a few short years working as a foreign language teacher at a private school in Connecticut? It came to a staggering $90,000. Teresa, who taught French and Spanish while putting her husband through graduate school, used every resource at her disposal to feather their nest egg. In addition to her full-time teaching job, she tutored and baby-sat for students, house-sat for their wealthy families when they were away, and furnished their own small apartment with their cast-offs. What she couldn't use, she unloaded at tag sales. For a time, she even waitressed on weekends.

Today, 20 years later, she and husband, Roberto Hasfura, are both tenured university professors in San Antonio, Texas with two teenage sons and a small home that's long since been paid for. While frugality remains part of her core identity, today Teresa loosens her billfold a bit more often. She recently purchased a high-end Bianchi road bike for her commute to her classes at St. Mary's University. And she enjoys pampering her special pets, like my son, Henry, when she comes to the family home place in Southwest Virginia in June to pick cherries and camp out under the stars. She's not counting pennies when she treats Henry and her own two boys to pancake breakfasts, fixings for campfire cookouts, and rents inner tubes for rafting on the New River. "I'm happy to be living a moment where I don't have to be so Spartan," she says.

My own prescription for the good life involves rethinking work, housing, food choices, wardrobe, cleaning and community. It asks you to do the hard thinking about, and advance planning for, your daily life and rituals, your annual celebrations and rites of passage. And, finally, it involves connecting with community in ways that add value to your life, health, and net worth. All of these important paths to the good life involve the management of money: acquiring and dispensing it, as well as saving and investing it. The fundamental challenge facing you is: How can *you* — like Teresa Van Hoy — set aside more greenbacks so you can retire your debt as quickly as possible, build your own nest egg and get on with the business of the good life?

"I Buy; Therefore, I Am"

If finding your way to the good life is so simple, why has it been so hard for so many?

Until its recent resurgence, a whole set of skills revolving around thrift and common-sense money management had faded into obscurity during the two generations of increasing prosperity in the United States. During that period, we went from being a nation of citizens, who by and large practiced fiscal restraint, to a nation of consumers who went on an extended consumer binge. We bought into the notion that to live well was to consume, or more precisely, to buy.

"I buy; therefore I am," was the motto of the gilded age of consumerism, recently ended. We were told that a product exists for whatever ails us. If you're too tired to cook, there's always takeout. If you're having a bad day, go pamper yourself with a spa treatment or pick up some deliciously packaged personal-care product that promises to neutralize the forces against which you're struggling. Just charge it. And so we spent … and spent … and spent, engaging in a decades-long buying spree that has only recently ended — statistics tell us, in 2009. As recently as 2006, for every $100 Americans under the age of 35 earned, they spent about $117, according to The Wall Street Journal. Those in the next age cohort up — people from 35 to 55 — displayed a negative savings rate nearly as large.

But, in less than a year, these spenders did an about-face and entered into a race to *out-save* the Joneses, competing to see which person or family was thriftier than the next. Indeed, in the first half of 2009, the rate of personal savings shot up to five percent, from less than one percent in August 2008. Martha Olney, a professor of economics at the University of California, Berkeley, who specializes in the Great Depression, consumerism and indebtedness, told The New York Times that this rapid consumer shift was all the more noteworthy because generally in recessions consumers save *less* money. "It implies a re-emergence of thrift as a *value*."

Before personal finance columnist MP Dunleavey found her inner thrifty self, she admits to being one of those overextended younger Americans, "living on income and credit cards." For her, the line between income and credit had blurred. You could say that many of us, like Dunleavey in her earlier, more profligate days, learned a system for extravagance, which was backed up by the easy credit practically handed to us by financial institutions and with the surfeit of credit card offers that would stack up in the mailbox. Back in the 1990s and mid-2000s, MP didn't give a lot of thought to money; she had "more important" things on her mind, such as her writing career and her personal life.

"I entered the adult working world completely devoid of money skills," she says now, looking back. "I didn't even balance my checkbook. My mother tried to show me how. I was like 'yeah.' I had one giant blind spot." When it came to handling her money, MP muddled through with what she describes as "one hand over my eyes and the other hand with my fingers crossed." The fact is, she was living beyond her means with a bravado that fostered carelessness. "My phone would get turned off periodically. I had one of those kooky responses: 'Has it *really* been that many months since I paid the phone bill?' " In hindsight, she says, she had effectively "disconnected" herself from her own financial truth.

Interestingly, a number of factors converged to bring MP to her financial senses. One was the creation of her column on women and finance, "Women in Red," for the MSN Money Web site; another was getting a contract to write her first book, "Money *Can* Buy Happiness: How to Spend to Get the Life You Want" (Broadway Books: 2007). The rejection of her extravagant self is complete. Today, if she doesn't have cash on hand to pay for something, she doesn't buy it. Dunleavey, 43, and her husband, Matthew, recently pulled themselves out of debt, in part accomplished by moving out of pricey New York City with their son, Connor, now 2 years old, to less-expensive Delaware County in upstate New York.

"Stop blowing your money. There is no such thing as disposable income. Take 'disposable income' out of your vocabulary. Could you burn any of the money you make? If not, why do you treat so much of your income as disposable?"
— Michelle Singletary

"We try to adhere to a cash-only, no-debt-but-the-mortgage way of life," she says. This "way of life" poses challenges, given the continual maintenance needs of their 95-year-old house, located in the postage stamp-sized town of Margaretville. "We are much better savers than we used to be," she says, "but life just seems to eat up our cash reserves, which probably means we need to save more."

"New-Found Frugality"

Dunleavey is in the forefront of a great wave of the newly frugal. In January 2009, The Wall Street Journal heralded an era of "new-found frugality" in America, calling it "a particularly profound shift" and predicting that the current downturn would not end any time soon. Long-time simplicity advocates like me are more than happy to declare the over-consuming, "Biggie-Size-Me" era over. At last!

Ever since the financial meltdown and the Great Recession of 2008 and 2009, Americans have been reconsidering our culture of extravagance, of easy lending and spending, our culture of entitlement. Is everyone really entitled to a vehicle of her own? What about a cell phone? An MP3 player? Does every American household deserve a flat screen TV? Do we all have some divine right to cable and Internet access? What about eating out at the drop of a hat? As we ask these hard questions about equal-opportunity high-end living for all — a culture defined by convenience, disposability and easy credit — many of us are beginning to view our way of life as a blight rather than a blessing. As it was recently configured, our culture has been struck with an epidemic of "affluenza," the tongue-in-cheek name for the disease of our affluence. Its definition should it appear in a dictionary, coauthors John de Graaf, David Wann and Thomas H. Naylor, write playfully in their book, "Affluenza: The All-Consuming Epidemic," might read: "affluenza, *n.* a painful, contagious, socially transmitted condition of overload, debt, anxiety, and waste resulting from the dogged pursuit of more."

Indeed, the turnaround from this era of excess — what some of us might call a national reckoning or a coming to our senses — has been dramatic and rapid. It is as if collectively we Americans were like kids with our hands in some mammoth cookie jar, feeding from a seemingly limitless supply, borrowing from some future account with only the vague sense that reckoning day would ever come. We were just waiting to be caught. If we hadn't known all along — somewhere deep in our subconscious — that our behavior was out of line, how else could you explain the rapid turnaround? In a matter of *months*, we reversed the negative savings rate of those 55 and younger, moving it in a positive direction, despite widespread falling economic barometers. For the first time in decades, *new home size has begun to contract,* and it appears that our love affair with the SUV is at last over, as smaller, gas-sipping hybrids and other low-carbon-emissions models gain ascendancy.

The recession has turned high-flying Wall Street bankers into Wal-Mart shoppers and has status-conscious teens considering second-hand prom dresses, used cars, and picnicking (instead of restaurant dining) for the first time in decades. Even those firmly entrenched in the super-wealthy camp find that it is no longer fashionable to flaunt their riches. In short, living large no longer seems quite right. It's certainly not right from an environmental point of view, never has been, nor even from an economic point of view. A combination of the mortgage crisis, cascading job losses, industry failures, and the economy teetering on the brink — not to mention environmental calamities — have caused us to look for new answers, new paradigms and new ideals.

The Frugal Mind-Set: A Mental Transformation

As it turns out, the answers we're seeking are right under our noses. Some come from the past, from elders like my mother, who lived through the Great Depression and other economic downturns. Others are popping up in the popular culture, on talk shows, Web sites, blogs, and Twitter®. The concepts may be dressed up with fancy new words, like "transumerism," a neologism describing a new class of transient consumers for whom experience trumps ownership. ("Transumers" are non-traditional consumers who seek out rental, leasing, barter, swapping, group ownership, and other collective solutions to satisfy individual and occasional needs.)

Some answers are commonsensical. People are ratcheting down spending, scaling back on all manner of things: large homes, oversized vehicles, vast wardrobes, and lavish vacations. For the first time, many are evaluating even small purchases, making cautious decisions, one at a time. Sure, these 400-count percale sheets are on sale and I could use another (read: better) set, but could I live another year without them? Another decade? The rest of my life? Still others are freezing plastic spending altogether, and like MP Dunleavey, going on "cash-only" diets.

The first and most important step on the path to financial independence involves making a mental transformation, re-visioning the person you are in relation to your spending. It involves revising your definition of success to be based on financial security and solvency rather than some high-flying appearance of affluence; it involves a degree of restraint, even sacrifice. If our recent downturn taught us anything, it is that the person driving the paid-for car, or living in the low-mortgage payment home, is on more solid footing than the one in the luxury SUV for which the resale market has dried up, or living in the "McMansion" that is repossessed by the bank.

Claiming a thriftier self involves shutting down those little voices that egg on mindless consumption, urging you to treat yourself to that cappuccino or designer handbag, to go for the bigger house, the more luxurious handbag, and even, the most expensive item on the menu. These voices — which, surprise, resemble so much of the commercial messaging to which you've been exposed — are like termites eating away at your financial foundation. As MP Dunleavey put it, "We have to do daily battle with our culture." The fact is, it's difficult — if not impossible — to achieve the good life if you harbor grandiose fantasies of living large or, even worse, if you attempt to finance some faux version of the good life by borrowing money you don't have in order to pay for it.

In order to create a new self, you must construct a new set of voices and values to replace the ones with which you previously lived. When stifling the urge to splurge, remind yourself about the greater goal for which you are saving your money: financial independence so you can live the life you want; saving for your daughter's college education; investing in your home or your retirement. Even giving to such worthwhile causes as charity is a legitimate rationale for a new, higher set of values.

The Power of Financial Affirmations

If you're having trouble tapping into your inner frugal self, an approach that absolutely will work if you give yourself to it fully is tapping into the powers of your mind. One of the most effective ways to do this is to create your own personal affirmation to reduce your spending, pay off debt, or save for the future. Give thought to your specific situation, taking into account your goals, and naming your greatest obstacles to frugality and money balance. Then, write an affirmation that applies to you.

Keep your affirmation short (no more than a dozen words), sweet, and upbeat, such as, "I am gloriously debt-free." Remember, even if you're *not* debt-free at the moment, the point of this exercise is to create a vision of your future reality, as you choose it to be, not a statement of where you are today.

Or, you may choose to construct a situational affirmation, such as, "I own my beautiful home, free and clear."

Or, if you want to wean yourself from credit cards and go to a cash-only basis, try this: "I pay for everything life-sustaining with cash."

When composing your affirmation, always phrase it in the present tense, as if what you are wishing for has already happened. Be sure to include a positive word or phrase, such as, "gloriously," "beautiful" or "life-sustaining" into your affirmation.

Write out your affirmation in longhand. Then make several copies. (You also can enter it into your computer and print out copies.) Tape copies where you often will see them throughout the day. You might place one on your computer monitor at work, another over the kitchen sink and a third above your bathroom mirror. If you spend a lot of time in the car, tape a copy to the dashboard. Then, set aside three minutes every morning before your day gets going and three minutes in the evening (more if you can swing it) and repeat it to yourself, over and over. Own your affirmation as your personal mantra. Say it in the shower, as you wait in line, and as you're out walking your dog. By fully embracing this exercise, you're reprogramming your powerful unconscious to go to work for you.

My Journey Toward Frugality

In high school, I landed my first "real" job, working at a drugstore in Orono, Maine, in a job that used to be referred to as a "soda jerk." Even then, in the early 1970s, that term and the job it described were already antiquated. But at Nichols Drugstore downtown, we made fountain drinks the old-fashioned way, by squirting thick Coke syrup from a special dispenser and mixing in soda water. When I added ice cream to the sodas, I had to be careful about portion size. If I served an overly generous scoop, I could feel the wrathful eyes of my boss, Old Man Nichols, upon me while he maintained constant surveillance of lunch counter doings from behind the swinging door to the pharmacy in the back.

When payday came, Old Man Nichols would hand me an envelope containing my earnings in cash. I remember liking the feeling of having cash — my *own* cash (though I used to wonder why he didn't pay with a check — was he trying to avoid the IRS?). When I got home, I would divide that money up into three piles: one for immediate use; the second for the little extras I planned to buy soon, like the pair of Dr. Scholl's® exercise sandals I'd been eyeing in Seventeen magazine for months (and kept for more than 30 years); the third went into my passbook savings account. It didn't take long to see that the money I spent on pizza and ice cream vanished quickly, whereas what I deposited in the bank added up, with interest, in a hurry.

My interest in frugality as a teenager was reinforced by the environmental movement that was gaining traction in Maine and nationally. In 1975, as an intern at the Bangor Daily News, I attended the 23rd annual World Vegetarian Congress on the campus of the University of Maine at Orono. Scott Nearing received a standing ovation from an overflow crowd at Hauck Auditorium as this rock star of the simplicity movement — a magnificent specimen at 92 — strode with his charismatic wife, Helen, to the podium. Scott talked about the couple's commitment to "vegetarian homesteading," including the division of their day into four-hour blocks: the first for physical "bread labor" (harvesting food and raising cash crops); the second segment for personal pursuits, such as meditation and music; and the third block for service work, writing, receiving visitors, and giving back to humanity. He made the case for why it was imperative for humanity to live lightly on the Earth. Though at the time I didn't feel that I could possibly do everything he suggested, the Nearings' approach struck me as an ideal to which I could aspire — the highest and most principled way for us to live at that moment in history.

I decided then and there that I did not want to use more than my share of the world's resources; being frugal rather than frivolous with my earnings made sense. I vowed then to live *below* my means, spending only on things that were essential. After college, first living in New York City and later in Los Angeles, I did live simply, never earning much but not spending a lot either. But it was not until 1986, when I moved with my then-husband from Los Angeles to the rural South, that I began to study simplicity in earnest: its philosophical and religious underpinnings, as well as how a simple lifestyle could be adapted to late twentieth century America. At that time, Frank and I devoted a tremendous amount of time and energy to thinking through and defining how we wanted to live, resulting in the book we coauthored, "Simple Living: One Couple's Search for a Better Life" (Viking/Penguin/Blair: 1992).

The Frugality Mentality

In the nearly two decades since that first book was published, I continue to follow many of the strategies developed then and have incorporated a few more. Following are some of my strategies that can work for you as well in establishing financial independence:

• *Pay your credit card(s) in full every month.* Make this a habit. If you still have a way to go with large credit-card balances you owe, put yourself on an immediate "pay-with-cash-only" diet until you have paid off all of your credit cards *completely*. Then, reduce your credit cards to one — or two, at most — and pay them off *in full* each month. If you cannot manage the discipline of this, try this zany trick. Insert your credit card(s) into a zip-lock bag full of water and stow in the freezer. I'm not kidding. This technique will quite literally put a freeze on your spending. If your credit card is encased in ice, you must make a conscious decision in advance to use it (i.e. thawing it out the night before). If you try sticking it in the microwave, the plastic will melt … which might not be a bad thing for some.

• *Pay your bills as quickly as you can.* Some penny-pinchers put off paying bills until the last possible moment in order to maximize interest payments from the bank (even if it's only a matter of a few dollars and cents). I am from the other camp. I derive my pleasure from paying bills quickly. The minute a bill arrives in my mailbox, I'm raring to write the check and send it on. If you pay immediately, you eliminate the danger of accruing late fees. You eliminate the danger of forgetting. What's more, I have come to believe that paying bills early helps keep money moving, helps create a flow of money energy into your life that somehow attracts more money to you. Also, referencing what's left in your checkbook, *after* you've written out your bills, serves to make you feel *poorer* rather than richer, hence less likely to spend. Remember, a basic lesson when trying to adopt the frugality mentality is to reinforce a feeling of having less — *less is more.*

• *Carefully consider any purchases that involve recurring charges.* When I began fund-raising for the "Simple Living" television series, I met with Jim Frye, a wise and generous banker in Pilot Mountain, North Carolina. We had a wide-ranging conversation, as you do when you ask people for money. But one of the points he made then that has always stuck with me is this: On your way to solvency and wealth, you need to closely scrutinize any and *every recurring charge*, no matter how small. "I'd much rather give you a one-time gift of $3,000 than sign onto giving you $25 a month for an indefinite period," he told me. I've never forgotten that wise counsel. It's easy to lose sight of the smaller charges, but they add up in a hurry, and if you don't watch it, they'll get away from you.

• *Delay purchases.* This one is one of the most fundamental concepts for people to employ when traveling the path to frugality. If you want something — whether it's something "small," like a new pair of shoes, or something larger — like a new computer or new vehicle, almost always the best strategy is to put it off. Delay spending. If you do curb the impulse to buy something you want, one of several things will happen:

1. You may forget all about it. In this case, you discover you didn't really want (or need) it that much to begin with and you've saved yourself the money of buying it.
2. You continue to fantasize about it, developing new scenarios in your mind about how owning this thing will enhance your life. If this desire persists over time and you can figure out how to pay for it without borrowing to do so, go for it!
3. You've delayed buying it but when you go to purchase it, guess what? It's gone. There's a silver lining to this scenario, too. The cosmic forces in the universe have conspired to make the decision for you. You can live without it. And, you've saved money!

• *Quash impulse buying.* The merchants will hate me for this but a corollary to my directive to delay purchasing is to *quash, squelch and stamp out impulse buying.* When you buy on impulse, by definition, you have not carefully considered the purchase in advance. It's rarely something that you've budgeted for (unless you have a "mad money" category in your budget). Impulse spending is likely to go for one of those "feel-good" purchases that give you an artificial high but at the end of the day (or month or year) leave you feeling low. Impulse purchases are usually the ones that deliver a nasty case of buyer's remorse once the reality of having to pay — or having paid — the bill settles in.

• *Rule out recreational shopping.* Do you go out shopping when you're bored, hungry, sad or tired? Is shopping a habit for you, or your major form of entertainment? In your journey to frugality, it's essential that you come to view this habit as dangerous and set out to break its back. I never had a bad shopping habit (though I admit to enjoying shopping more in my younger years than today). Nowadays, shopping simply cannot compete with such pleasures as gardening, swimming, reading or visiting with my friends. But I don't dread it either. To me, shopping remains one of life's necessities like clipping my toenails or cleaning up after dinner. It's something you need to do on occasion. In pursuit of frugality, it's *out* with recreational shopping and *in* with conscientious shopping.

• *Learn to say "no" to your children and your friends.* Have you ever noticed how people are always trying to tell you how to spend your hard-earned money? If it's not your child wanting you to buy him a new computer game, it's your friend inviting you to a household products or specialty jewelry party, or out for a night on the town at a pricey restaurant. Just learn to say no.

• *Celebrate small infusions of cash.* I've been an environmentalist since grade school (long before the word entered the popular parlance). So when I can do good by the earth and put a few dollars in my pocket at the same time, that's an exciting synergy. One of my pet frugality exercises is saving aluminum cans, which I sell to Mount Airy Iron & Metal here in town. This outfit — run by a good-natured man named David Pearce, who also happens to be my neighbor — pays you on the spot for what you bring in. The price of aluminum is always fluctuating but I may get $2.20 for a groaning garbage bag full of cans. Or, I may pull in $3.45 or $1.90. David always writes a ticket and delivers it with cash and coin and some droll comment, such as, "Don't spend it all at once." Or, "I'm sure you're reporting this to the IRS."

I look forward to my quarterly visits to Mount Airy Iron & Metal. Once, when a well-meaning intern inadvertently carted off a box full of aluminum cans to the recycling center in town — where you discard plastic, glass, newsprint and, yes, aluminum for *free* — I was fit to be tied. I could have *sold* those cans for money. I did manage to get over it, but my emotion brought home how important my little money-saving ritual had become.

Find and identify those places in your own life where you hold the line on spending (washing your own car, parking on the street and walking rather than springing for paid lots), where you are resourceful rather than extravagant, or where you pick up what used to be called "pin money." Then give yourself a pat on the back.

Yard Sales Are Good for the Soul ... and the Billfold

One of the best ways to generate a little extra cash is through holding an old-fashioned yard sale, garage sale, tag sale or rummage sale. You know what I'm talking about.

Though I'm a lifelong yard-sale aficionado, it had been years since I'd actually had one. Last summer, when I went in with my friend, Molly, on a yard sale, I was reminded once again what delightful, uplifting enterprises they can be. Yard sales offer what I like to call the multiple and overlapping benefits of every red-blooded, simplicity-oriented enterprise: they allow you to de-clutter your home while recycling items (that might otherwise be sent to the landfill); they build community, offering a place for neighbors and strangers to interact around a recreational activity that is light on the pocketbook; and they generate cash.

Since Molly was moving out of town and wanted to lighten the load on her moving truck, she was the catalyst for the sale. I was an enthusiastic participant, and offered to hold the sale in my well-to-do neighborhood where such sales are uncommon. My elderly mother, who lives in a condo downtown, had a few items for sale, but primarily joined in for the opportunity to mix it up with the public.

From my observation through the years, the best yard sales are not those held by regular yard-salers who drag out the same tired stuff every other weekend. Rather, your primo sales are the once-in-a-blue-moon events like the one Molly and I held where you put out big pieces at small prices. The day is auspicious when you're blessed with good weather, early buyers, and an attractive, intriguing mishmash of merchandise. In these, you send seldom-used, dust-gathering items (some of which may have some age on them) down the pike and into the hands of others. An enormous part of the fun is the creation of a festive community happening — almost like a theatrical production — which brings together strangers, neighbors, friends and acquaintances who bond while combing through your cast-offs for treasures. At the end of the day, you have a few more dollars in your pocket than you did when you started and that sense of lightheadedness that comes with clearing unnecessary clutter out of your home.

On our big day last June, we sold potholders and pictures, rocking chairs and trinkets. We moved faded towels, an antique telephone and buckets full of books. I sold a stand-up mirror and most of a free-standing clothes rack (it was missing a critical central pole). Molly sold an antique sewing machine, a Thomas train table and children's clothing galore. I sold a few items that came with my house: a chipped particleboard microwave rack, an old shower head (which I'd replaced with the water-saving type), an oversized, faded pink planter. Mother easily managed to sell the sturdy metal frame lawn chairs she'd held onto for years in the hopes of getting them re-strapped. At the end of the day, I had earned $338; Molly pulled in $280; and Mama was $8 richer.

Guidelines for a Dynamite Yard Sale

1. Arrange a group sale, if possible. Invite your friends, neighbors, or church group to go in with you. Volume adds to the attractiveness of a sale and the sellers have more fun. (Plus, having someone there to mind the shop allows you to take bathroom breaks.)

2. Big things bring buyers. If you have any furniture, lawn chairs, wheelbarrows, bicycles, put them out. Bookshelves always go and so do occasional chairs. Someone may come in looking for a chest of drawers and go out with a potholder.

3. Price objects the day before. If you're having a multi-family sale, pick up a package or two of multi-colored stickers and give each seller a color. Then stick 'em on. Price items as reasonably as possible.

4. Get the kids involved. This is a great way to get children working on de-cluttering their closets and toy collections. Get them involved in deciding what toys to part with. When it comes to the thorny issue of who gets the proceeds (your child will doubtless contend that it's her toy so *she* should get the money, even if you bought it), why not compromise. Give her a percentage of the sales (half or a quarter) and put the rest in her college fund.

5. Place an ad the local newspaper or online posting. If you can manage it, tape up a few flyers at community center bulletin boards, supermarkets, laundromats and schools a few days in advance of the sale. But remember to put out signs on the street the night before the sale clearly stating the street address and sale hours. Include an arrow pointing toward your destination.

6. Start-up money and your cash stash. Begin your yard sale with $55 in cash, in the following denominations: 2 - $10's; 3 - $5's; 15 - $1's; $5 in change. (Be sure to deduct your start-up money at the end of the day when you tally your receipts.) And finally, never, *ever* leave your money pouch unattended. I highly recommend my method of wearing a fanny pack or an apron throughout the day with a deep front pocket into which you stuff the money. This way, your money is always with you.

(continued)

7. Remember to round up pens, pencils, scratch paper and a pocket calculator. This will help with figuring tabs, jotting down people's names and phone numbers in case they want to come back later to pick something up, or if you take a backup bid on an item. Let's say it's still morning and someone offers you $2.50 for a lamp you'd priced at $12. If you haven't had any interest by 3 o'clock, you may want to give that person a call.

8. If you have a bunch of small things, put them in a grab-box or bag. Mark the items to move. You might pull together a bag of baby bibs, rattles and sippy cups, or a box of T-shirts for 4-year-olds. You may even consider a grab-bag of miscellaneous items.

9. No object is too insignificant to put out. People invariably buy stuff that amazes even you. The seller can never guess what will go first. So put out broken, beat-up items, partial sets, stained carpets, even an old pair of tweezers. Prepare to be surprised.

10. Realize that what you believe to be a surefire seller may disappoint. Molly was flummoxed that no one bought her top-quality car seat. I couldn't believe no one wanted my Drexel end tables in mint condition. But don't despair. Other items will move. Develop a Zen-like feeling of detachment. What was meant to go will go.

11. If you have lots of clothing, find (or devise) a temporary rack on which to hang items. People are less likely to buy when garments are laid out — or stacked — on the ground (even if on blankets), and they get messy in a hurry.

12. Let go of what you paid for it — especially as the day progresses. When you stop calculating what you spent on something, you've really gotten into the rhythm of the sale. Let it go: $3, $2 — whatever the buyers offer. It's the transaction that counts. Seen in that light, a quarter is as valuable as a $10 bill. Move it on down the pike. What counts is recycling the item, letting it get carted off so it can find new life elsewhere.

13. If you're doing a group sale, shop and swap in the other person's stuff. Rather than shelling out cash for items, swap things. In our sale, I got Molly's plates; she got some of Henry's old cleated shoes for her 5-year-old son.

14. After the sale's over, load the remaining stuff into a truck and haul it off to a charity. This will clean out your house, basement or garage. Clearing out your space is almost as much cathartic as counting your earnings.

15. Don't forget to remove your signs when the sale's over. If you forget, you could get some "surprise" visitors when you're least expecting them.

Destination: Financial Independence

Being debt-free was near the top of the list of commitments I made back in my early adulthood. Though I've not yet reached the goal of being debt-free, or stating it more positively, becoming *financially independent*, I have managed to pay off my credit card balances in full religiously every month since my move to the South in the mid-1980s. And I've managed to retire (or help retire) several significant financial obligations during that time, including two homes and one piece of land.

I'm not here to tell you that my record is without blemishes, however. The largest, costliest mistake I ever made was of startlingly recent vintage. It involves the purchase of the home in which I now live. I took out a mortgage in 2007 for a place that was larger than I really needed and pricier than I could really afford. (My FICO score was so high and my financial balance sheet so strong that I had no trouble obtaining the loan.) This purchase occurred in the aftermath of my breakup with my long-time business partner and former spouse. You might say I acted rashly. You might say I made a financial decision to handle an emotional need. You might say I was looking for a healing environment for myself and my son, a place to lick my wounds, pull myself together, and get on with my life. If you said all those things, you'd be right. I've been preaching the gospel of financial prudence for two decades now, telling people to guard against throwing money at problems that money cannot solve, nonetheless, I made the mistake myself.

This mistake — investing in real estate — wouldn't have been so bad if the housing market hadn't crashed and burned. In short, I overbought. Oddly, even though it was doubtless a financial mistake to purchase my "Sunflower House," I'm not knotted over with regret. I've now lived in it for two years, as of this writing. Not only has it provided a nurturing environment for me and Henry and a canvas on which to paint the next phase in my life, but I see this mistake as offering me a chance to relearn the fundamental lessons of frugality and wise money management that will carry me through the rest of my life. (More in Chapter 3.)

Avoid Debt Like the Plague; Retire What You Have

There is no more crucial component on your path to frugality and financial well-being than getting a handle on debt. As of 2007, according to numbers provided by the Federal Reserve, consumer debt stood at nearly $2.6 trillion, which works out to around $8,500 for every adult and child living in America. Bear in mind that this figure covers *consumer* credit, not including debt secured by real estate. A number of factors have been driving consumer debt in recent years. They include the easy accessibility of credit, low interest rates, and an increase in Internet shopping, which drives customers to pay by credit card.

Having so much debt poses multiple problems as our recent crisis has shown us. As my dear friend and CPA, Hattie Brintle, put it, "The hardest part of getting out of debt is you have to pay for yesterday, today, and save for tomorrow." In other words, it's twice as hard to get out of debt as to get into it. Taking on a large amount of debt — with no plan about how to pay it off — only serves to consign you to a lower standard of living in the future.

Any prescription for the good financial life must include the directive to do four things: 1. Avoid debt like the plague. 2. Retire the debt you do have as quickly as possible. 3. Once you're out of debt, resolve to stay out. 4. Save as much money as you can.

Seven Debt-Dousing Strategies

The following ideas can provide some guidance on the path to debt retirement:

1. Make a list of all your debts, from largest to smallest, on a legal pad. Include mortgage payments, car payments, student loans, credit cards and anything else you owe. In the right-hand column, write the total amount you owe. Next to it, note the size of your monthly payment and its due date. Beside that, jot down the interest rate.

2. Identify those debts with the highest interest payments (generally these belong to credit cards) and make it a priority to pay these off as quickly as possible. If you can't pay them off completely, double or triple payments here until you retire them. (If a windfall, such as a tax refund, stimulus check or some other extra money comes your way, use it to pay as much off, if not the entire amount on your high-interest obligations.)

3. Make it a policy to meet all minimum payments for all your obligations on time.

4. Once you retire any of these debts, transfer the amount you were paying on those bills to the next target on your list of debts. Take aim and fire, going for the bull's eye.

5. If you have multiple credit cards, once you pay them off, try going cold turkey, and stop using them.

6. Some financial counselors suggest that you simply cut up the credit cards and stash the plastic pieces in a drawer because canceling credit cards may adversely affect your credit score. However, my suggestion is that it's best to actually cancel the card. This way, you avoid the temptation of using it, while at the same time protecting yourself from identity theft.

7. Unless you are truly compulsive and can't control your credit card spending, do keep at least one card for use for travel and Internet shopping. But remember, once you've paid down the balance, make it a habit to pay it off in full every month.

Hattie Brintle: "Wisdom" Is Knowledge Gained the Hard Way

One of my favorite frugality gurus happens to be the person who has a closer eye on my finances than any other human being besides myself — namely, my CPA, Hattie Brintle. Though she is tactful and maneuvers gracefully in our Southern culture here in North Carolina, Hattie never sugarcoats reality. She works hard for her clients, subjecting their finances to the keen scrutiny she gives to her own. To that end, she does not hesitate to speak her mind, even if that means telling people things they may not want to hear. When one of her clients, a man with a small farming operation, recently confessed his desire to purchase a new, $80,000 tractor with an air-conditioned cab, Hattie looked at him hard: "I wonder if the IRS would recognize that as a deduction," she said. Her comment effectively put an end to his fantasy.

Hattie's personal journey to frugality is unlike any I've ever known. She came up by the school of hard knocks. Her father died when she was 7, and when Hattie got pregnant at age 14, she chose to get married and keep the baby. Another baby followed at 16. "Fertile Myrtle," she jokes today about her younger self. Hattie dropped out of school in ninth grade and went to work at a textile manufacturing plant in town. She recalls handing her paychecks over to her male-chauvinist husband who, in turn, doled a dramatically reduced portion back to her. "When you're 14 and pregnant, everyone treats you like you're stupid."

But, even then, Hattie knew better. With two baby daughters to raise, a domineering husband to contend with, and a demanding factory job, she set her sights on improving her lot: by completing her education and biding her time until she could end her marriage. At age 21, she took the GED test for her high school equivalency. When she called the state office to find out if she had passed (she couldn't wait for the letter to come), the person on the other end asked her to hold the line as she checked something. When she came back on she said, "Ma'am, I just want you to know that you received the highest score in the State of North Carolina." The year was 1985. Hattie was off and running. She went on to get her college degree from High Point University, and her CPA credentials followed.

Today, Hattie has created a life that anyone would envy. She's happily settled into a stable, fulfilling, long-term relationship with fellow CPA, Luke Horton. Hattie and Luke live in a 1,500-square-foot home that they paid off in four years. Hattie's financial stability allows her to help her older daughter obtain her graduate degree as a neo-natal practitioner at Duke University, while saving for her own retirement and growth experiences, such as foreign travel. Her grown daughters are now successful nurses; both are married and each has produced a son, giving Hattie — at the ripe old age of 44 — two grandsons.

In her younger years, Hattie recalls with a chuckle, she used to spend an hour a day fussing with her hair and makeup, and spending every extra dollar she could find on fashionable clothing and high-dollar cosmetics. At that point, her financial cushion was non-existent.

"There was a time when I couldn't be sick; I couldn't miss a day of work. Because everything I was making was already spent." Wisdom, Hattie likes to say, "is knowledge gained the hard way. ... I had to have been at a place in my life where I owed everyone for everything and wanted more (in order) to come out the other end, knowing what I know now." The financial security she enjoys today is all the sweeter because of her starting point. Today it is her pleasure to draw on her memory bank of experiences to counsel friends, family, and clients about sensible money management. When Hattie speaks, you better listen. Because what she says — and who she is — conveys the authenticity that comes from having arrived the hard way, of knowing herself.

Hattie and Her Car

Back in 1991, Hattie's then-husband came home with a car — that panacea on wheels that he was convinced would put an end to their marital woes, while boosting his young wife's status in the community. This dream car was a gleaming white 1988 Acura Legend with just 40,000 miles on it. "I remember when we bought it, I told him, 'I will not pay more than $300 a month for the car.' " It turned out, the monthly payment came to $400, but at that point, it was too late to renege on the deal. It was a stretch, Hattie recalls, making the car payment each month. "I remember saying at the time, 'When I pay this off, I will drive it till the wheels fall off.' "

If her former husband or anyone else thought Hattie was exaggerating, they didn't really know her. Hattie Brintle did exactly what she said she'd do. She drove that 1988 Acura Legend for another 18 years, until it had 254,000 miles on it. "I would pat her every time she flipped another 1,000 miles," she says. In fact, she developed such a loving relationship with the car, dubbed "Miss Hattie," that her devotion to her aging car became a statement of who she was in the world.

Long after her financial condition had improved to the point where she easily could have handled paying for a new — or newer used — car, Hattie held onto a car that others might consider a clunker. Sure, the driver's side electric window wouldn't roll up once you put it down, so you had to remember to always leave it closed. So what if the roof leaked occasionally? And, it's true, the transmission would grind and sometimes smoke. Hattie's grown daughters were a tad embarrassed about their mother's vehicle. Once, in jest, they threatened to put a DNR (do not resuscitate) bumper sticker on the fender. The car, in short, became Hattie's testimony to simple living, an active and public statement about keeping things in use past their date of planned obsolescence.

Hattie had resolved that she would not purchase another vehicle until she and Luke had paid off their home. (See Chapter 3.) This, they managed to do in 2008. The following year, she put out the word that she was looking for ... another Acura. "I had such success with this one, why should I switch models?" she asks. Turns out, the Legend had been discontinued by Acura in 1996 and was replaced by the Acura RL. A friend alerted her when he heard that a 2000 RL model in mint condition with 77,000 miles on it, was coming on the market. The owner wanted $10,000 for it. Hattie snapped it up, this time paying cash.

Hattie's "new," nine-year-old car — also gleaming white — has been so well-maintained that it appears brand-new. That's what I thought the first time I spotted it when driving by her office one day. At that moment, seeing the Acura RL occupying old "Miss Hattie's" spot in the parking lot, I felt a pang of sadness, as if looking for the face of an older person who is no longer among the living. Hattie Brintle is struggling with the change, too.

"To this day, I'm having a hard time adjusting to this newer, more luxurious car," she says. "I miss 'Miss Hattie.' This newer car is not my testimony." Its day is coming, though, I tell my friend, the frugal CPA. Give it 10 years.

Hattie's Used Car-Buying Protocol

Hattie has developed a protocol for buying cars for her daughters, friends, and whoever else is listening. She shared it with me on camera for one of our early episodes of "Simple Living With Wanda Urbanska."

1. If at all possible, set your sights on a used car. Remember, a new car depreciates in value the minute you drive it off the lot. If you can buy a good used car, why not let the previous owner take the hit?

2. Once you've found the vehicle you desire, go to the dealer and ask to be pre-approved for a loan. This will determine what your monthly payment will be. Now comes the hard part. You do not yet buy the vehicle. Instead, you make the monthly payment to your savings account for six months (longer if possible).

3. If you can make the payment comfortably during this time frame, you have given yourself the green light to move forward toward buying a car similar to the one you set your sights on. The beauty of this method is that you not only proved you can handle the payment, but you will have saved a hefty down payment.

(continued)

4. But first, when buying used, always research a vehicle before buying it. Better to do your own independent research than take the seller's word for granted. Ask for the car's vehicle identification number (VIN) through which you can determine if the car has been in a major accident or was ever stolen. You can research your prospective vehicle through the National Motor Vehicle Title Information System (NMVTIS). Go to *www.nmvtis.gov* and follow the prompts. You will pay between $2 and $4 for a report. (You also can obtain comprehensive used-car reports from commercial firms, such as Carfax and Experian's AutoCheck, but expect to pay more for those.)

5. If your car hunt is local, contact the car dealership where the vehicle was serviced, and inquire about its service history. You may also ask the seller for a copy of its service records. Once, Hattie helped her daughter research a luxury car that was priced so low her daughter's mouth was watering, only to learn that it had been in a wreck which the seller had not disclosed.

"Petty Change"

Hattie maintains that frugality can be fun — if you make saving money into a game. One of the core concepts to keep in mind as you move toward frugality is that *even small amounts of money add up to large sums in the end.* Just as those calories start to add up a little bit at a time, so do those coins. One of Hattie's pet practices is to save every coin that crosses her palm. She's been doing this for six years and has saved an estimated $2,400. (At first, she saved only quarters, but, more recently, she expanded her personal version of the adult piggy bank to include all coins.)

Here's how it works. Whenever she goes to the supermarket for smaller purchases, Hattie makes a point to pay in cash. If the tab comes to $4.05, Hattie hands over a $5-dollar bill and deposits into her coin-savings shoe box. "If I buy a postage stamp, I use a dollar and save the change."

Every six months, Hattie takes her heavy, coin-laden box to the credit union and runs the contents through its change-counting machine. This generally nets her around $200. "Instead of 'petty cash,' Luke and I call it my 'petty change,' " she says. These days, Luke has taken a coin out of Hattie's purse, so to speak, and saves his change the same way. Hattie once shared her savings plan with a client who, in turn, told his struggling daughter — let's call her Lissa — about it. Lissa immediately began saving her change. Just a few months later, a tire went out on her car. With no other savings, Lissa was able to dip into her petty change to pay for the new tire. After an experience like this, Lissa appears likely to be well on the way to becoming a life-long saver.

Money and Kids: From Spend-Centricity to Generosity

So how do you start people — even younger than Lissa — on the path to financial health and well-being?

Imprinting children with the benefits of saving while young and impressionable is the best way to set the stage for a lifetime of financial responsibility. Through a national network of simplicity advocates, I had the good fortune to meet and become acquainted with Nathan Dungan, a Minnesotan who has made it his life work to educate young people — and their parents — about wise money choices. Drawing on his background as a financial advisor and vice president of marketing for a Fortune 500 financial services company, Nathan established Share Save Spend®, the mission of which is to help youth and adults achieve Financial Sanity™ by developing and maintaining healthy money habits.

The Minneapolis-based author of "Prodigal Sons & Material Girls: How Not to Be Your Child's ATM" (Wiley: 2003) and coauthor of the high school textbook "Personal Finance: A Lifetime Responsibility" (EMC/Paradigm: 2009), speaker, and media expert presents a marvelous concept that folds both saving and *giving* money into the core formula. "Recognizing now that we are in a society where it's all about *spending* — it just horrifically skews toward spending," Nathan told me while we were taping an episode for "Simple Living;" "the challenge became, 'How can I turn this around?'" Emphasizing sharing first reminds children that they are not the center of the universe and challenges them to develop sensitivities to the needs of others, while countering the relentless cultural message that all that matters is the stuff we accumulate.

Not long after the interview, I put my son, Henry, on Dungan's Share-Save-Spend® program. I'm here to report that the program has been a success. Here's how it works: Using a set of three clear tubes (each configured to resemble the kind of pneumatic tube you insert into a bank's drive-through window), children are asked to divide their money into each of the tubes. The three tubes — which are printed with the words *Share, Save* and *Spend* on the side — are all equal in size to symbolize the importance of each leg of a healthy financial life. A parent, working with his or her child, can modify the proportionate allocation. But the concept is that for every dollar that passes through your child's hands, some portion is allocated into each of the tubes.

So, for example, with Henry's weekly $7 allowance from me, he puts the $5 in the *Spend* tube; the remaining two $1 bills are directed into *Share* and *Save*. Every three or four months, Henry has accumulated enough money to go to Lowe's Foods and buy some staples for our local homeless shelter. After purchasing the flour, margarine, and bleach, we drop it off at the Shepherd's House. "Sharing comes first," says Nathan, "because it offers the most effective counter-rhythm for all the messages on spending."

When the sharing habit is added to the saving habit — and this becomes ingrained in your child's management of money — you have helped to set him or her up for a lifetime of wise financial choices. For more information on Nathan Dungan, go to *www.sharesavespend.com*.

Giving!

For a long time, being frugal carried a bad rap, as if the person who practiced frugality was parched, pinched or somehow frozen. But what I've observed about the genuinely well-balanced, frugal souls I've come to know over the years with my simplicity advocacy work is quite the opposite:

rather than being tight with a dollar, they are actually *more* generous than some of their wealthier counterparts. They're tight-fisted when it comes to frivolous expenditures on such things as fancy furnishings, new vehicles, junk food and meals out. But the truly frugal never hesitate to ante up for worthwhile causes about which they feel a real need exists.

I also have noticed on my own personal journey toward frugality that as my interest in nice clothes and material possessions has diminished, my budget for charity has expanded. This development has occurred independent of my fluctuating financial fortunes. I have simply come to enjoy giving — especially to causes with which I'm familiar and in which I believe. It makes me feel good. And I also mentally reference all those people who donated when I was raising funds. There is no question that, as Peggy Payne puts it in the book she coauthored with Allan Luks, "The Healing Power of Doing Good" (Fawcett Columbine: 1991), being generous and giving freely of your time and money makes you feel better about yourself, increases your sense of self-worth and reduces your stress level. Greed — not frugality — is what makes you parched and pinched. As you move down the path to the good life and adopt the habit of frugality, remember, you will be richer for it.

The Benefits of Frugality

Even if you could go on spending to your heart's desire — even if you could continue to withdraw limitless cookies from that aforementioned cookie jar — would you really want to? After a party of reckless spending, we've discovered what we should have known all along: All that stuff doesn't deliver lasting happiness. Its pleasures are fleeting. What really gives us lasting happiness are intrinsic developments, such as self-exploration and acceptance. Tim Kasser, Ph.D., associate professor of psychology at Knox College and author of "The High Price of Materialism" (MIT Press: 2002), concluded from his research that wealth doesn't bring happiness and that materialistic values are associated with unhappiness.

Genuinely happy people express "intrinsic values," he says, through self-exploration and acceptance, by maintaining close personal relationships and developing "community feeling." By contrast, those who exhibit "extrinsic values" associated with the pursuit of wealth, status and image, tend to display narcissistic behavior, to be less empathetic, have lower self-esteem and engage in lifestyle patterns that are more ecologically damaging. Even at middle-school age, materialistically oriented students are less likely to do relatively simple things for the common good like turn off lights when no one is looking, says Kasser.

The lesson is clear. Once you adopt a frugal mind-set, along with a sensible approach to money management, it will bring consciousness to your spending decisions. This way, saving will become second nature. The money you set aside will help retire debt and build security. You will be, quite literally, setting yourself up for the time of your life — the good life. Once you have established a habit of frugality, once you have put yourself on solid financial footing, even buying can become fun again. Remember the story of my mother's table? When you are selective about what you purchase, you can truly enjoy acquiring investment possessions, even those occasional indulgences that come your way. You can buy them outright, enjoy them, and claim them for the rest of your life. Now that's happiness!

Chapter Two

The Path to Meaningful Work

Find work you love, colleagues you respect, and contribute to the greater good.

When you find work you love — a life calling that means more to you than just bringing home the bacon — you've made enormous strides on your path to the good life. Finding work that sparks your flame — regardless of the financial reward — calls you to express *your* unique gifts rather than merely doing what is expected. Claiming your higher purpose on the job may mean reducing work hours, gaining greater control over your time, and a sense of mastery over your work. Building community adds tremendous meaning.

My Professional Adventure

My professional journey has been marked by accomplishment and adventure, by remarkable diversity, and unexpected twists and turns along the way. It has been characterized by risk-taking, persistence, and a liberal application of elbow grease; it has included some mountaintop moments, along with my share of disappointments. I never cease to mentally reference the comment attributed to Winston Churchill: "Success is going from failure to failure without loss of enthusiasm."

Whenever I speak to school children, I pose this question: "Who do you believe experiences more failure in life — the more successful or the less successful person?" Though the answer may be counterintuitive, it is, of course, the *more* successful person who has taken the greater number of hits because that person has put himself out there on life's firing range. By contrast, the person who cowers inside a shell, too timid to stretch or fail, is unlikely to be slapped back as often, but is, by the same token, unlikely to live life to its fullest.

Without a doubt, I have enjoyed my share of success in more than 30 years as a professional writer, including two decades of simplicity advocacy. I've birthed seven books, several of which have been in print for more than a decade, and which have landed me appearances on "Oprah," the "Today" show and NPR's "All Things Considered"; my articles have run in USA Today, The Washington Post and the Los Angeles Times, and my work has been featured in The New York Times, London's, The Daily Telegraph and Poland's national newspaper, Dziennik.

Doubtless my professional pinnacle has been creating, co-producing and hosting four seasons of America's first nationally syndicated public television series on sustainable living, "Simple Living With Wanda Urbanska," which debuted back in 2004. At that time, some skeptics suggested that sustainability and frugality might be topics of marginal, if not fleeting, interest. Carriage numbers for the series have fluctuated, but reached a high of 75 percent of U.S. TV households in the fourth broadcast season. This media platform has helped open many doors, allowing me to rub elbows in Plains, Georgia with former President Jimmy Carter and First Lady Rosalynn Carter; manage a brief exchange in Polish with former Polish President and Nobel Prize-winner Lech Walesa; and visit Denmark's Samso Island to evaluate the success of that national experiment in energy self-sufficiency. Dreaming up ideas — whether for books, television segments, or applied to my own life — and watching them blossom into reality is among the most creative and satisfying parts of my professional life and core identity.

Through it all, though, one striking aspect of my work is that it has *never been about making money.* Though I've always managed to pay my bills, and my work has always generated income, going after the big bucks was never the end goal. Don't get me wrong. I'm not adverse to doing well financially, and would be delighted if one of my projects were to hit pay dirt. But the choices I've made have always come down on the side of taking work that intrigues and stretches me rather than going for the gold. Unlike my sister, who has worked most of her life for major corporations and who faces retirement with a substantial financial cushion, I have never invested much in the stock market or amassed large sums. When I retire, there will be no pension checks in the pipeline or annuities rolling in. Instead, my "wealth" is invested in my network of friends, supporters, and activists in my field, as well as in the fruits of my labor.

When pursuing creative work like mine, the conventional wisdom has always been, *don't quit your day job.* If you're an aspiring Broadway actor, don't give up bartending to pay the bills. If you are writing "the Great American Novel," keep teaching fourth grade until your book is published *and* has hit the best-seller list. For a number of years my "day job" was *retail* — selling cherries and peaches at my former husband's successful family orchard. I used to relish the mix of my glamorous creative pursuits (writing and media) and the gritty, real-world work of selling fruit. Sorting through unsold inventory for soft cherries to discard; scrubbing buckets sticky with cherry juice at the end of each day; and interacting with a devoted clientele of locavores and fruit fanatics all kept me grounded in life's fundamentals. Selling fruit was an excellent touchstone for being a writer.

Today, without benefit of that steady stream of orchard money, like many Americans, I have to work harder to pull together my income. But I am fortunate to have developed the life-long habits of thrift, saving, and keeping my overhead as low as possible. These financial habits have enabled me to face my own personal financial downturn without panic or having to veer from my course. Will I have to seek another "day job" in the future? Perhaps. If I do seek paid employment in the future, I'll look for something for which I am suited, where I can make a contribution, and work diligently to secure my financial future.

In middle age, looking back on my career up until this point, I see my work life as an extended search for meaning, fulfillment, and community — for my place in the world. I have learned lessons from every job I have ever held and every assignment I have completed. I never see myself as having "arrived," but as someone in transit, a soul on a mission. In fact, my quest for meaningful work parallels my search for the good life.

"Real success is finding your lifework in the work that you love."
— David McCullough

How I Found "The Work of My Life"

Like those happily married couples who meet in high school and stay true for a lifetime, finding "the work of my life" was an uncomplicated thing. The year was 1974. It was the Watergate era, and President Richard Nixon and his operatives were being investigated for their involvement in a string of political dirty tricks in connection with the 1972 presidential campaign. Bob Woodward and Carl Bernstein of The Washington Post were leading the charge.

Like many young, idealistic students of that time, I was bitten by "the bug." While still in high school, I applied for a job writing for a weekly advertising tabloid called The Community Observer. Material for my Orono News column included wedding announcements, casts of school plays, local social events, and the like. The column paid by the word, so I was rewarded for being long-winded. Pretty soon, I started branching out into feature articles.

In the spring semester of my senior year in high school, I traveled from my home in Maine to Washington DC to visit my father, Edmund Urbanski, then nearing retirement from his career teaching Spanish at Howard University. Aware of my Observer column, Daddy suggested that I interview my senator, Edmund Muskie, who just two years earlier had been the front-runner for the Democratic presidential nomination.

Muskie's own campaign had been derailed by a letter planted by a Nixon henchman in New Hampshire's Manchester Union-Leader attributing to him an ethnic slur about Americans of French-Canadian descent. (For a Polish-American statesman who had represented a sizable French-Canadian population in Maine for decades, such a remark was not only improbable, but downright ludicrous.) Nonetheless, the letter ran, the mud stuck, and it — along with the press spin following Muskie's emotional denial — managed to bring down his campaign. For Senator Muskie, the corruption of the Nixon White House was not only a matter of grave national concern but of intense personal interest.

That I would receive an audience with the legendary senator seemed far-fetched, but being the dutiful daughter, I made the call to the senator's press secretary. To my amazement, I was granted an interview. Senator Muskie was gracious and eloquent as he discussed the prospect of impeaching President Nixon. When our discussion ended, he extended his hand. "I hope this isn't going to be easy for you to write about. It isn't an easy subject."

When I returned home with my interview in hand, I wrote an article. I knew The Community Observer would run it, but I wondered if I could push the envelope. Why not try to place it in a larger publication? So I worked up my nerve, rolled the dice, and walked into the newsroom of Maine's largest daily, the Bangor Daily News. There I found myself face to face with City Editor Kent Ward. I told him I'd just returned from Washington where I had interviewed Senator Muskie.

"We have a man in Washington," he said.

I asked him if he'd take a look at my story. The city editor read a few lines, then picked up his pencil and started marking the copy.

A few days later, March 29, 1974, my bylined story appeared on page one of the Bangor Daily News, with the headline "Sen. Muskie Feels Country Can Survive Impeachment." I have never felt a greater sense of accomplishment or exhilaration than I did on that day. At 18, and not yet a high school graduate, I knew without a doubt what I was meant to do.

That pride of ownership in my work has never left. Whether writing for print, my blog, or conducting interviews on camera, I continue to feel a sense of wonder every time I go to work. I cannot imagine anything more satisfying than meeting people, covering issues and stories, gaining a window on the human experience. When things are clicking and my engagement is complete, I enter into what celebrated psychologist and author Mihaly Csikszentmihalyi calls that optimal state of "flow." That is, I'm so mentally engaged in my work, nothing else matters: not my compensation, my growling stomach, or whether the rain is starting to fall on my clothes hanging on the line. The only thing that matters is the work at hand.

One of the things that I've noticed when I'm working well is that I'm in the moment. I'm not fretting over yesterday's mistakes or worrying about tomorrow's problems. During a telephone interview, a reporter once asked me the connection between simplicity and our time famine. "Living in the present," I told her without hesitation, "has become a thing of the past." I'm convinced that "living in the present" in our work and in our lives should be one of the primary goals of the simple life.

I know that I am fortunate to have found the work that I love so early in life, along with the opportunity to develop my skill. When you find your lifework — or right livelihood as it has been called — you know you have arrived. If, on the other hand, you are doing something you don't love — or maybe don't even like — you are missing out on one of the key elements of a life worth living.

Redefining Success

So why are so many of us discontented with our work? What stops us from finding our lifework, from engaging in honest employment that leaves us happy and satisfied?

Allow me to put on my sociologist's hat. The problem starts with not knowing ourselves. As Americans, we fancy ourselves to be a nation of rugged individualists out on the range, each of us calling it as we see it, shooting from the hip. A more accurate portrait, however, reveals us to be a nation of conforming consumers, looking around for cues and moving in lock step with what the marketers from Madison Avenue and dream makers from Hollywood dictate. To be *more*, these master manipulators tell us, buy more, buy bigger, keep up with the Joneses. In order to purchase that version of "the good life," most of us have to engage in highly demanding (and, if we're fortunate, highly compensated) labor: work that insists on being the center of our lives, consuming an ever-greater number of hours, eating up our downtime at night and on the weekends and even cutting into, if not eliminating, that once-sacrosanct family vacation.

"If you don't come in on Sunday," the workaholic working papers decree, "don't bother coming in on Monday." Whosoever climbs the ladder to success most rapidly is celebrated, sought-after, even idolized. Those with the biggest homes, the fanciest vehicles, and largest portfolios win. Such has been the prevailing picture of "success" in America, where we have become not so much the land of the free and the home of the brave, but the land of the frenzied consumer, the managed heart, and the stressed, overloaded worker.

The Puritan work ethic has taken hold to the extent that our society sees virtue in overwork. The person who is "crazy busy" represents the new norm, while the one who paces herself, refuses to multi-task, and carefully considers what to put on the plate of life is often dismissed, or even worse, written off as a loser. Work has become, in the words of time-life balance advocate and author Joe Robinson in his book, "Work to Live" (Perigee: 2003), "the most sacred of all cows, permitted to park its ubiquitous rear end in front of you just about anywhere you are." Hard-wired into our identities and self-worth, our work demands have led to "record levels of burnout, stress-related absences and depression," he writes. The question most working Americans ask themselves at the end of the day, he told me recently, is "do I have enough gas in the tank to get through tomorrow?"

Indeed, Americans are running pitifully low on fuel, with virtually no reserves in our "tanks" and no margin in our lives to help bring us over the daily finish line. Because greater workloads are heaped on fewer shoulders, our work burdens have become increasingly heavy. We drag through work and life, often so mired in the trenches of overwork that we put our health, heart and happiness in peril. Not only are we working longer hours than we did just a generation ago and more than workers in any other industrialized nation in the world (including Japan), but we're taking fewer vacations and less time off. What's more, cell phones, laptops, BlackBerries® and other electronic devices have put us on an electronic leash so that even when we *are* at home, or sitting on the bleachers at our child's soccer game, or out to dinner with family, mentally, we're still at the office. For many, the pursuit of wealth, material comfort, and status has simply become our source of meaning at work and sadly in life.

Up until recently, though, it seemed that there virtually was no way out of this restrictive treadmill. No way to question our American prescription of overwork and overspending. No way to call a halt to doing too much and spending too much on things we don't need and can't afford — things that further tie us to dependency on our jobs (i.e.: we need the paycheck to pay for the stuff that we buy to try to reward ourselves for working too much).

Reining in Overwork

The economic downturn of 2008 and 2009, however, has called this materially abundant, work-dependent formula for success into question, and provoked a national reckoning. It has begun to dawn on many of us that defining ourselves by our compensation levels and consumption patterns — our so-called "standard of living" — carries a steep psychic price tag, not to mention exacting its pound of flesh from our fragile eco-system. Juliet Schor, author of "The Overworked American," calls the professional trap into which so many of us have fallen, "the-work-and-spend cycle." "You've got to work the long hours to keep the job, and you need the job to maintain the lifestyle," she told me several years ago while taping an interview segment for "Simple Living." "It becomes a kind of self-reinforcing cycle."

In order to break out of this cycle, we must determine what really matters to us as individuals and as a nation. Does owning a closet full of dress-for-success garments cut it in the end? Is it worth it to buy the big house and the luxury vehicle if you have no time with your family? In order to redefine success, you must reconnect with your core values, identity, inner longings and higher calling. In many cases, after years or decades of chronic overwork, of pursuing work that doesn't suit us, the unfulfilled parts of ourselves are ripe for rebellion, for the chance for liberation from the golden handcuffs of high-paying jobs and high-consumption lifestyles.

Work-life balance describes a happier, more healthful state of mind and life. So how do you get there? No doubt about it, measurable steps can be taken to achieve it. Because the danger of burnout in our overworked society is so great, the best time to try to combat a life out of balance is *before* you go on the fritz. Balance, according to Joe Robinson, is not some "exotic condition, but the state that science tells us our brains crave for the best cognitive performance."

Tracking Your Time

Fundamentally, work-life balance begins with time. The very first step on any path to reining in overwork is figuring out how much time you spend on the job. So I'm going to ask you to try a relatively simple exercise, one that may be extremely eye-opening. All it requires is a little bit of … you guessed it, time. Just as a primary exercise for those wanting to get a handle on financial reality is to track where their money is going, jotting down income and expenditures and tracking fixed expenses along with discretionary spending for a certain period of time, the same exercise can be applied to tracking your time.

What I'd like you to do is to pick up a small notebook — one you can carry in your purse or pocket — and diligently record exactly how you spend each waking hour for a one-week period. Write down how long it takes to exercise, shower, dress, eat breakfast, drive to work, work, drive home, buy groceries, fix dinner, how much time you spend answering work emails before you go to bed. Record how long you read in bed at night or watch TV before falling asleep, and how long you sleep.

After you've kept this record for a week, add up how much time you spend on each activity. Then subdivide total time expenditure for work — including time spent on work-related duties, such as dressing for work, commuting, out-of-town business travel, as well as after-work and weekend job-related duties, such as obligatory socializing, certification trainings, and the like — from time spent on the rest of your life. Add all of these items together to determine the amount of real time you devote to your work.

You may be surprised how much of your life is devoted to commuting, for instance. Or styling your hair. With this data in hand, you may decide to move closer to where you work, or to replace your long hair with a shorter, shower-and-go 'do. If you're like most Americans, this exercise will reveal that your time investment leans heavily toward the work column. This may be fine with you, or not. But the main point of this exercise is to bring consciousness to your life about the expenditure of what is arguably your most precious resource: your time.

Time-wise, the ideal work situation would include:

1. Working no more than 40 hours weekly, preferably fewer. Work-life balance advocates, such as John de Graaf, executive director of "Take Back Your Time," suggests that 40 work hours per week is pushing the limits on the optimal number of work hours in order to achieve balance. "I prefer to see people work five seven-hour days or even four eight- or nine-hour days," he says. During the Great Depression, the Kellogg Company elected to reduce work hours across the board rather than lay people off. "Kellogg gave its employees five six-hour days."

2. Creating cushions of time at work. You may feel panicked at work, just barely making your commitments and turning your reports in on time. So how can you build in "extra time" between meetings, phone calls and other duties? This mind-altering strategy of creating cushions of time — of slowing your pace — can actually work to your advantage by building a sense of calm and control that will further your aims. Instead of trying to scrounge extra minutes on a task, develop the habit of completing one job before moving onto the next. Never rush to meetings. Always work to be early for appointments and phone calls. This cushion of time will cushion your life and make you more productive.

3. Reducing your commute. If you can work from home one day a week or more, you're bringing greater work-life balance to your work and your life. And you're also reducing your carbon footprint. An option to consider is moving closer to where you work. You may also want to look at taking mass transit instead of driving. If you're lucky enough to live really close, walking and biking are two other great options.

4. Devoting time *every day* to recharge your batteries. This means when you come home from work, you leave your work at the office and carve out some "time for self." To aid the wind-down process, it helps to establish and observe at-home rituals that are both comforting and nurturing. For most people, this means preparing and enjoying a sit-down dinner, uninterrupted by telephone calls, beepers, or even television. It could mean taking a daily walk, reading, doing yoga, gardening, or simply hanging out with loved ones.

5. Pursuing restorative leisure time during the weekend. Spend generous amounts of time on pleasurable activities such as enjoying satisfying slow meals, long bike rides, or hikes in the country, get-togethers and visits with friends, neighbors, and family. Unhurried weekend time gives workers the opportunity to catch up on longer-form tasks, such as home maintenance and repair, and helping children with science fair projects and the like.

6. Taking two weeks — or more — of vacation time *every year*. If possible, vacation away from home at a place of natural beauty where recreational opportunities abound. The ideal vacation effectively disconnects you from work. Studies show that a full *two weeks* — not one week, not 10 days — are needed to recover from burnout. Research reveals that vacations increase job performance once workers return with their minds and spirits refreshed and renewed. Iowa State economist Wallace Huffman estimates a 60 percent increase in productivity in the first two months after a vacation. However, even more optimal than two weeks is more time: three or four weeks per year. If you don't get that much time off, check into whether your company would allow you to "buy" vacation time in the form of unpaid weeks off.

While it may not be possible to reduce your work hours to less than 40 (or even 50) hours per week, please bear in mind that working less — relaxing more — represents a solid investment in your health and well-being. Setting reduced work hours as a long-term goal is something you may want to shoot for.

For the short term, see what you can do to create more balance in the job you have now. Sit down with your supervisor or boss during your next job evaluation and introduce the subject of reduced or flexible work hours. You may be surprised to find that he or she is delighted to have you work one day a week from home. Or even, once every two weeks.

The mantra of my television series, "Nothing's too small to make a difference," applies here. If one day at home every two weeks seems negligible, don't forget, this small step may establish a precedent, allowing your boss to realize that you *can* work from home and fulfill your job duties as well if not better than before. And, it'll offer you multiple benefits, such as saving you time from dressing for work and commuting, not to mention saving wear and tear on your vehicle, and gas money.

If you're anxious about meeting with your supervisor to ask for a change, develop a plan before you go in. If working long hours — into the evening

— is a chronic problem for you, establish your own boundaries. You may decide that you will never work past 5:30 p.m. on Tuesdays, Thursdays and Fridays, for instance. When you do sit down with your boss, explain your rationale. Couch your decision to "take back your time" in positive terms; express the need for greater work-life balance as something that will make you a more productive employee. If you need to, tell him that your doctor (or therapist) has urged you to spend more time at home building relationships with your family. If your marriage is suffering, put it out there.

You know your boss, so you'll know which buttons to push — and which to avoid — when making your case. Try not to be sucked into overwork by an office culture that promotes a guilt-induced regimen of long hours. This "who-works-whom-under-the-table" competitive Olympics of the American workplace benefits no one, not even the company that promotes it. Make your case to do your work and go home. And also prepare yourself for an array of responses — from outrage to sympathy. If you have a progressive boss, he may be receptive to introducing the concepts of time-life balance throughout the workplace. You may be doing not only yourself but your entire office a favor.

"Remember, there's no present like the time."

Time Guardian: John De Graaf

I first met John de Graaf back in 1993, when he read "Simple Living: One Couple's Search for a Better Life," the book I co-wrote with my former spouse, Frank Levering. John was so taken with the book that he included us in his PBS prime-time special "Running Out of Time." In 1997, he invited me to host another PBS prime-time special, "Escape from Affluenza: Living Better on Less." Over the years, we've become dear friends. I've watched as John has evolved into America's No. 1 guardian of our time.

In May 2009 in Washington, DC, John and I joined forces to speak at a Congressional press conference in support of legislation mandating paid vacation leave. This legislation was sponsored by Congressman Alan Grayson, a freshman from Florida's eighth congressional district which includes Disney World. John has been actively working for this bill — the first paid vacation bill in United States history — with his organization and other leaders in the field, including Joe Robinson and William J. Doherty, Ph.D., director of the Citizen Professional Center at the University of Minnesota. The bill, "Paid Vacation Act of 2009," is a modest proposal that would give one week of paid vacation after one year of employment to workers in firms with at least 100 employees, with incremental increases over time.

The United States is the only advanced economy that does not guarantee its workers any paid vacation time, according to a report by the Center for Economic and Policy Research. "By contrast, all Europeans get at least four weeks off by law and many get six," says John Schmitt, senior economist at the Center, who also spoke at the press conference. "It's a national embarrassment that 28 million Americans don't get any paid vacation or paid holidays."

Studies show vacation time is essential for your health. "People who don't take regular vacations are far more likely to suffer from heart disease or depression," says John de Graaf. "It's also essential to family bonding and provides the strongest memories many adults have of their childhood and family."

Vacation-leave advocacy is just one of several time-related issues that John is addressing. Back in 2002, together with several colleagues, he founded the group "Take Back Your Time" *(www.timeday.org)*, which has been promoting such policy initiatives as paid parental leave, paid sick days, and other work hour-reduction options for workers that protect their jobs and health care benefits. "Such policies give real choice to people, allowing them to live more simply," he says. "The great naturalist John Muir once said that 'compulsory education is a good thing but compulsory recreation might be even better.' I think he had something there."

Forbes magazine recently ran a story about the world's happiest countries. The United States didn't even make the top 10. One thing that characterized all the countries that were selected as exemplars — including Denmark and other Scandinavian countries — was attention to work-life balance and a strong focus on leisure time. Not coincidentally, all of these countries also were doing well economically. I'm with John de Graaf when he says: "It's time to re-think our obsession with producing and consuming things and turn our attention to our need for time to be of service, connect with others, appreciate the beauty of nature and restore our health."

My friend, Pilar Gerasimo, editor-in-chief of Experience Life magazine, has been providing her readers with guidance on issues of work-life balance and healthy living for years. She argues that one's "right livelihood" is a matter of personal sustainability, and that it's up to each one of us to find the right balance and to do work that sustains us and by extension those close to us.

Personality Sustainability

In an era where many of us put in 10 or more hours at work each day, only to come home and watch several more hours of TV trying to escape and unwind from stress, I suggest that the whole notion of personal sustainability deserves more attention than it has been getting. If current rates of illness, depression, divorce, addiction and bankruptcy are any indication, our lack of attention to personal sustainability is costing us dearly.

Gradually, grudgingly, in the realms of the environment and the economy, we've been waking up to the fact that approaches initially conceived as pragmatic and beneficial (namely, maximizing material consumption while emphasizing short-term profits and growth) have turned out to be extraordinarily destructive.

We've been slower, I believe, to apply the same kind of long-term cost-benefit analysis to our own lives and careers. Just as we've long resisted taking into account the massive carbon footprint of our fossil-fuel dependence, we've also vastly underestimated the destructive influences that chronic overwork and overstress have on our lives.

One of the key principles of sustainability involves considering the complete life cycle, paying attention to "upstream" resources and relationships as well as "downstream" byproducts and repercussions.

In the context of our lives and work, this sort of systems-thinking reflects the fact that, as individuals, we require not just material inputs like food, water, shelter and clothing, but also reliable reserves of physical and mental energy as well as a variety of emotional, social and spiritual resources that keep us healthy, happy, inspired and strong. In reality, we draw from these resources every hour of the day, and we impose very real impacts or "footprints" on these systems in the process. That's something the current world of work rarely acknowledges.

Within most workplaces, our performance is evaluated (and our pay determined) on the basis of our demonstrated commitment to a narrowly defined job. Employers typically define success in terms of quarterly performance goals — almost none of which take into consideration our personal health and happiness or the quality of the relationships we maintain with our families, friends and communities.

Yet, ironically, the quality of energy and attention we bring to work has everything to do with the quality and stability of our personal lives. When we are depleted, everything in our lives — our work performance included — suffers. To cope, we suck up even more resources. We overeat and overspend to make ourselves feel better, we numb out by drinking, smoking or doing drugs, and we watch television or go shopping to escape. We ask others to tolerate us at our worst, and we find we have less and less to offer. Our creativity, clarity and enthusiasm all dim. Our professional capacity plummets and enthusiasm fizzles. Far from giving our best gifts, we become obsessed with getting our share — or just getting by.

The downstream effects of this toxic ooze show up everywhere: Individual problems lead to professional and family problems, which lead to community and social problems, which lead to environmental and economic problems, and so on. It's the antithesis of sustainability.

So how do we turn this around? Gandhi wisely counseled us to "be the change we want to see in the world" and in my mind, that starts with creating a healthier, more sustainable sense of abundance in our own lives. The ultimate personal sustainability question is this: *Am I personally living in a way that is making me stronger and happier day by day — that amplifies my ability to create and offer things of value — or am I living in a way that's undermining my resources, depleting my capacity, and putting undue stress on the people and systems around me?*

Answers to questions like these can yield meaningful opportunities for change — the kind that only we, with the support of others who share our values, can successfully implement. So it's worth asking: Are you expending your time and energy in ways that give you satisfaction now and hold

(continued)

promise for the future, or are you squandering and depleting what matters most in exchange for status, stuff and a steady paycheck?

If your work life isn't trending in a sustainable direction, it's not something you can wait for a coalition or a task force to fix. It's up to you to seek out better models of living that reflect your values, priorities and ideals. If your own work pursuits are leaving destructive "footprints" in other areas of your life, the first step is to simply acknowledge that. From there, you can begin shifting your daily choices in more sustainable directions.

Nature teaches us that everything is connected. It also teaches us that sustainability is not something that's engineered "out there" but that's pre-programmed from within, inspired by the intelligence of a larger whole. That's why true sustainability must begin with each of us — with choices that balance productivity and purpose, with daily practices that create bodies, hearts and minds empowered enough to tackle the many big challenges we must ultimately face together.

— *Pilar Gerasimo, editor-in-chief, Experience Life magazine*

"I'm willing to work but I want work I can put my heart into, and feel that it does me good, no matter how hard it is. ... Even if I only do what my dear mother did, earn my living honestly and happily, and leave a beautiful example behind me ... I shall be satisfied."

— *Louisa May Alcott*

"Career Discovery": Finding Work You Love

As you begin to make choices and changes that help to bring balance to your life, at work and at home (namely, obtaining more time for your self, reclaiming your *life* as distinct from your *work*), the next major consideration is what you do for a living. That is, the content of your work. Is your work something you can put your heart into? Is it mentally challenging and emotionally satisfying? What are its intrinsic rewards? Do you believe that what you do for a living contributes to making the world a better place? Are you attached to your workplace? Your co-workers? The fruits of your labor? Or are you just hanging in there for the greenbacks? Are you counting down the months and years until retirement sets you free?

Having interviewed countless people around the country for books, articles, and my television series through the years, it strikes me that those who seem most joyfully engaged with their work share a certain trait. It's not necessarily having the highest IQ, the best education, or the largest portfolio. What they have in common is an infectious enthusiasm for what they do for a living. Often, they have created their work, started a new business, or put their own stamp on an existing job. Some are able to derive satisfaction in the greater scheme by helping others find their paths. They give their all to what they do.

Years ago, when I gained admittance to Harvard University, I'll never forget my father's reaction upon hearing the news. I remember it so vividly because it seemed so peculiar at the time. I was expecting something on the order of, "Halleluiah, my big little girl (as he used to call me for the fact that at 5' 10", I towered over him) has gained entrée to one of America's top colleges." Not bad for an immigrant's daughter! But no. Perhaps Daddy feared that my ego might swell, and he saw it as his duty to bring me down to earth. What he said was: "It doesn't matter what a person does for a living, as long as he gives it everything he has. If you sweep sidewalks or carry people's bags for a living, do it with dignity and gusto."

Of course, in hindsight, I see he was sharing the wisdom of age — and of the ages — with me. While gaining admittance into Harvard was no doubt a coup that would open many doors for me, the most fundamental reality is that no matter what your station in life, you need to find work that makes your heart soar, work you do with dignity and gusto.

If you suspect that you're not in the right field, or are actively seeking your life work — whatever your age — take heart. It's never too early, or too late to find your life calling. Or you may have enjoyed a successful career, but find it's time to re-career. Or perhaps you just want to put the work you do to the test and find out if you truly belong. If you're feeling called to change jobs, or just want to explore, following are some exercises to help you on your path to self-discovery.

Getting Started: Commit Your Thoughts to Paper

I'm a writer, so naturally I would recommend this. Start by doing some writing. Find a journal. (I like the unlined variety in which you can take notes and even doodle if you're visually inclined.) Call it your "career discovery book," then ask yourself some basic but probing questions. Make a note of your answers, jotting down the date beside each answer you give. (If you'd rather work on a computer, that's okay, too.)

Remember, you are seeking something intangible — insight into your true calling — something that once found will both enrich and energize your life. Don't expect to snap your fingers to uncover the truth with a capital T. Discovery and change are processes — not products that can be brought home and plugged in.

1. Write a short description of yourself as a child; be sure to include your temperament (i.e., shy, outgoing, bossy), as well as what activities you most enjoyed doing.

2. Think about what you wanted to be when you grew up. (I remember as a child wanting to teach third grade like my favorite teacher, Mrs. Dorothy Jones. I suppose as a writer and simplicity advocate, the work I do now qualifies as a form of teaching.)

3. As you move the picture of your life forward in time, what are your most cherished memories as they relate to your life and work experience? Can you name the five moments in your working life of which you are most proud?

4. If you are one of those people who can remember vivid images from your dreams when you wake up the morning, count yourself

lucky. Starting today, write them down the minute you wake up. Then devote some time and attention to reflect on what you believe these images may be telling you.

5. Make a list of your talents, even if they don't seem extraordinary. Be specific. For example, if you enjoy organizing the kitchen, or doing laundry, or making sales calls, put it down. Don't censor yourself. If you're a good listener or have leadership ability, make a note of it.

6. Now I'm going to ask you to think hypothetically. If compensation didn't matter to you, what would you do for a living? How would you choose to spend your time? If you need help here, think of how you like to spend your free time.

7. If you're still having trouble getting in touch with your ideal work self, go through a stack of old magazines and clip out pictures that appeal to you, ones you'd like to see yourself in. It could be an image of someone sailing the ocean, or pulling hot baguettes from the oven. This collage of your "ideal life" may help you think from a new perspective and hone in on what you really want to do.

8. Now I want you to write a short script for the professional life you'd like to pursue. It doesn't have to be long; a meaty paragraph will do. The next step is planning how to get from point A to point B. The final step, and doubtless the most challenging, is to devise a strategy for achieving your dream.

Planning to Soar

Once you settle on the work you want to pursue, you will need to create a plan of action. It may take months, or even years, to get started, let alone arrive at your destination. But mapping out a strategy is the essential first step. "Your life will not go according to plan," says Florida-based goal-setting guru Gary Ryan Blair, "if you do not *have* a plan." According to Blair, the vast majority of Americans live in the short-term, so the person who decides to create a future for himself has a leg up on most others.

Think of it this way: while certain events will occur that are beyond your control, why not take steps to shape your future to your liking? Put another way, if you do *not* plan for the future and take action steps based on those plans, it's almost certain that things will not go your way and you will *not* realize your dreams.

Steering the course of your professional life is not unlike planning a trip. For example, if you daydream about visiting India, the trip will never materialize until you develop a plan. You need to decide where you're going and when, and how long you plan to stay. You'll have to apply for your passport, book a flight, buy the ticket, and get your immunizations. Likewise, in life, the rubber of planning meets the road to results when you determine your goals, identify action steps, and pinpoint a deadline for achieving them.

Visualizing Success

Once you state a goal or desire, it's wise to visualize how you will *feel* once you get what you want. Tallahassee, Florida life coach Elizabeth Barbour mirrors her clients' goals back to them in the form of questions: "How would it *feel* to have that ideal job?" "What about finding your perfect life partner?" "Having a million dollars in the bank?" This "feeling" step, Barbour explains, helps transport clients into that place of acting as if they are where they want to be. That, in turn, sets the stage for actually arriving. *Feeling* their goals enables people to "try on" their dream in the shop before taking it home. You may fantasize about having a slim, muscular body, for instance, but experience guilt over being so much more attractive than your co-workers, siblings or (most especially) your mate.

Once people get comfortable imagining themselves in their future roles, the next step is for clients to take what Barbour calls "inspired action" to achieve results. Once you've determined that you want to move to Italy to study to be a chef, develop a timeline and a financial plan to get there. Write up a list of action steps and attach a timeline, such as, "Save for tuition and living expenses: 12 months. Purchase special software to study Italian on your laptop: 6 months." Or if, for example, you want to look for a job in a new field, an inspired action step would be to invite a new contact out to lunch in the coming month. If you find that this step feels right and proves effective, it will help lead to the next step. You make a mistake when assuming that steps taken in pursuit of a goal must be monumental. In fact, baby steps are probably best, as these small steps are more likely to be doable and point us in the right direction.

Once you've identified your plan of action, watch what you say to yourself and others to be sure that your thoughts and comments support your decision. Never undermine your own plan. Work to replace negative patterns and self-talk with self-reinforcing habits. Tap into the potent powers of your mind to move yourself closer to your goal.

To Achieve Results: Get Started

For many of us, the biggest barrier to forward motion is procrastination. Don't wait until every item has been checked off the to-do list of your life. Many of us know what we want to do, but put our lives on hold for a variety of reasons. (Some would call these delay tactics "excuses.") You know the routine: "I can't try anything new till my child finishes college; until my mortgage is retired; until I've lost 15 pounds." But the fact is, there's no time like the present, as the cliché goes. To achieve results, you need to get moving. As former president Calvin Coolidge once said: "You cannot do everything at once, but you can do something at once."

Getting results comes down to two words: *Everything counts*. This includes what you think; what you say; those things you do; and those things you don't get around to doing. Everything you do serves as an advance toward or retreat from the pursuit of your goals. When seen this way, you *should* sweat the small stuff. Once you learn to make these baby steps in the direction of your professional goals and dreams on a regular basis, bringing attention to detail, you are well on your way down the path of achieving results.

Put Time on Your Side: Take Your Dream Sabbatical

An outstanding tool for determining what you want in life comes from academia. It is the time-honored sabbatical. But no longer are these periods of "time out" from your normal job confined to the college campus. "The smart companies, the ones that have figured out that job satisfaction has a direct bearing on job performance," write Hope Dlugozima, James Scott, and David Sharp in their book, "Six Months Off: The Sabbatical Book" (Henry Holt: 1996) "view sabbaticals as an investment in their most important resource: their employees."

Sabbaticals can serve many purposes. You can use them to re-energize your present career, jump-start a new one, explore new professional or personal dimensions, or simply recharge your batteries. You may be an accomplished accountant who uses your time off to explore an artistic craft, such as weaving or glass-blowing. Or maybe you're a recovering politician, like former Tennessee governor Lamar Alexander, who took time off after a grueling term in office. "As governor," he said, "there was so much output. I was always saying things to people, giving instructions. ... And then for those six months away there was input. I was listening. I was sitting around, not running around. I was recharging. I was learning."

Those desiring to take extended personal time often meet with resistance from peers and others, including naysayers who suggest that once they get off track, they'll never be able to get back on. But, almost always, the experience from the person taking the extended leave is a feeling of joy and renewal — both during their sabbatical — and once they return home.

Leonard's Sabbatical

A week after his mother died in 1996, Leonard Kniffel had a heart attack. Losing a parent is always a huge blow, but because Kniffel had no wife, no children, and no siblings, his sense of aloneness was especially acute. Lying in a hospital bed, reflecting on the big picture of his life, he thought: " 'What have I accomplished?' 'What am I leaving behind?' "

Career-wise, he had accomplished a lot. At 49, Kniffel was at the top of his field as editor-in-chief of American Libraries magazine, the official publication of the American Library Association. But something churned deep inside him — the desire to stage a "second act" in life — to tap into a long-buried dream and make it real. In his case, he wanted to write a book. Kniffel had always written professionally, but, he says, "it takes having something you want to write about badly, something you feel passionately about," to produce a book.

Something he felt passionately about was his grandmother: Helena Bryszkiewska, a clever, enigmatic woman who, along with his mother, had raised him on a small farm north of Detroit. He wanted to understand her better by tracing his own roots to the country from which she had migrated in 1913: Poland. To that end, Kniffel devised a three-year plan that enabled him to take an eight-month sabbatical and not just visit the old country, but actually *live* there. He brushed up on the Polish he had learned in childhood and did "double time" at work for almost a year.

In 2000, Kniffel arrived in Sugajno, a pinprick of a Polish town northwest of Warsaw, near where his grandmother was born. There he was able to walk in her footsteps, absorb the rhythms of village life and unlock some keys to his grandmother's spirit and soul. The result of his quest is a poignant, affecting memoir, "A Polish Son in the Motherland:

An American's Journey Home" (Texas A&M Press: 2005). Kniffel's "second act" has launched a new phase of life, a phase of deepened intensity and meaning. "When you connect with people through books, you're connecting with people you'll never know. It's a very magical, mysterious thing for me," he says. "I wonder what took me so long." When Leonard returned to his post at American Libraries, he was refreshed, emotionally revitalized, and eager to write more books in the future.

Personal Pointers for Professional Discovery and Success

While not everyone can swing a sabbatical to determine if she is on the right work path or needs to head in another direction, there are things each of us can do in our present jobs to explore new options and at the same time enhance our work experience and performance.

More than once, I've observed that the difference between people who are genuinely contented with their work and find it fulfilling, and those who aren't and don't, is often less a matter of aptitude, but of attitude and approach. The difference lies in their willingness to determine their talents, their goals, and push themselves to reach them.

Following are some ideas to try that can help you find and forge a connection with the worker within and put you on the path to work you love.

1. Listen to your inner voice. Do not stifle that still small voice within, even if it's unpopular or rejected. If you feel a creative idea coming on, let it out. When that voice of your own conscience rears its head, take heed. If you and your co-workers are out on the town and you find yourself over-charging the company expense account, and that voice speaks, listen up. If your friends shoot down your unorthodox ideas, find new friends. Staying true to yourself is more important than keeping friends who don't share your values.

2. Choose the unorthodox. Margaret Fuller, the 19th century women's rights advocate, was widely ridiculed for saying that women could be "ship captains if they will." Maybe you'll come up with what seems like a wild dream — studying the healing properties of music — stick with your dream, despite the skepticism of your critics.

3. Stay "young" in your work. Remember my friend and CPA Hattie Brintle (Chapter 1) who saves every coin that passes through her hands? I have a similar fixation on saving aluminum cans, and even carry a plastic box in the back of my car to stow them from my rambles around town. Find some little pet projects that you can call your own. According to Frank Lloyd Wright: "Youth is a quality, and if you have it, you never lose it." Work to keep that youthful side alive.

4. When you achieve a victory, relish the moment. Do take time out to celebrate accomplishments large and small. "Make a special dinner, cut a bouquet of flowers, post a photo on Facebook."

5. When you make a mistake, admit it and move on. Learn from your mistakes, but don't dwell on them. Remember, time marches forward not backward. You can never undo what has been done, but you can deconstruct past occurrences and integrate them into your memory bank. Let past experiences — both mishaps and triumphs — offer guidance as you move forward.

6. Don't blame others for your failures. As I tell my son, Henry, always look for your part in any trouble that you experience — even if you're only 10 percent responsible for what went wrong, own that 10 percent. Don't try to distract yourself from your part in a thing by assigning blame to someone else.

7. Pick the hard job, including grunt work. No matter what your field or endeavor, strenuous work is always part of it. Remember how college students and new graduates are always moving from one apartment to the next? Think about your crowd. How many of your friends offered to help you move? And when they did show up to help, how many did the heavy lifting? Be the person who offers to move the couch rather than the one who makes a bee-line for the lamps. Heavy lifting helps build your character.

8. Remember always to compete against yourself — not others — in life. The winner is rarely "racing" another human being but rather trying to beat his or her best time. Remember your greatest foe is actually yourself. Likewise, your greatest ally and cheerleader. Harness the powers within you to succeed.

9. Make a decision. It's wonderful to plan and think things out, but a time always comes to take action. As the late Maynard Beamer, long-time mayor of Mount Airy, North Carolina once said, "There is no such thing as a right decision or a wrong decision — only indecision."

10. Connect with co-workers. Take an interest in their lives and work journeys by observing their special moments, such as their children's graduations and weddings, their personal triumphs and tragedies. The surest way to build community on the job is by lending your ear and extending genuine interest. You'll find out that once you start to follow the stories of your co-workers, TV soap operas and best-selling novels will take a back seat. Tune into those around you. It's time well spent. It's building community on the job.

Benchmarking Success: Your Golden Moment

If you incorporate the ideas presented above, you may realize that the job you have may be exactly the right one for you. Sometimes, the only element missing is the conviction that you are where you need to be.

In the case of Rob Sinton, a 62-year-old retired teacher from New Jersey, when he recognized the impact of his work on the world, he realized that his special gift was making a difference in the lives of students with learning disabilities. Rob taught special education in the Hopatcong, New Jersey public school system for 26 years, after having served in the United States Army for three years, including one year of combat service in Vietnam. Today Rob lives in Mount Airy, North Carolina where he devotes himself to his daily fitness routine, maintaining his sizable vegetable garden and performing volunteer construction work for Habitat for Humanity®.

When Rob started teaching emotionally disturbed youngsters, he wasn't sure if the commitment would be life-long. (In fact, in his low moments during the school year, he used to fantasize about leaving teaching altogether for better paying work as a mason or carpenter, skills he'd mastered during summers in college. At least at the end of the work day, he reasoned, he would have the satisfaction of seeing a framed wall or solid progress on a foundation.)

His performance in the classroom was never that straightforward. "On an average day, the academic subjects took a back seat to discussions of proper behavior, honor, respecting the rights of others and values clarification," Rob recalls. "Often as I watched my charges going to their respective busses at day's end, one would make a detour to get a final slap, punch or kick in on his fellow classmate. I would wonder if I had made any effect on the kids at all."

Yet, despite daily struggles with his hyperactive students, Rob hung in there. When his kids gave him fits, Rob reminded himself of his own difficulties with Latin in high school. "I could not see any benefit of learning a 'dead' language and had no end of trouble with verb conjugations," he recalls. "My students were of at least average intelligence, some with learning disabilities, most with the attitude that I had toward Latin, but in their case it applied to all academic subjects."

One afternoon after school, while thoughts like these were spinning in his head, Rob Sinton was summoned to the main office. A former student, whom we'll call Kevin, had dropped by for a visit. Rob recognized him immediately. Kevin had been one of his most "challenging" students ever; he was unable to sit still in class and was constantly fighting with his classmates. Now in his 30s, Kevin had come back on that day to thank his former teacher. He wanted Mr. Sinton to know that he'd followed his advice and gone to Sussex County Technical High School to study electronics, where he had blossomed.

"He came by to thank me for my patience and help in getting him into Tech," Rob says, recalling that golden moment between teacher and former student; it was a simple statement of recognition, telling someone that he had been instrumental in changing his life for the better. Kevin had gone on to become a licensed electrician and volunteer fireman and was married with two children. Ironically, while Rob had helped send his former student on the path to success, little did Kevin know that *his* expression of gratitude would prove to be a turning point in his former teacher's life.

"At that moment, my thoughts of a career change evaporated," Rob recalls. That one simple thank you changed everything.

All professions have benchmarks for measuring progress, such as promotions and raises, yearly evaluations, and letters of commendation or rebuke. Kevin's visit proved to be Rob's personal benchmark for professional accomplishment. Perhaps it was not as tangible — or impressive to others — as a plaque on a wall, but to Rob the visit was "infinitely more rewarding" than any "Teacher of the Year" award. It made him realize that working as a special education teacher in Hopatcong, New Jersey was exactly what he was destined to do. It was changing lives. It was building society. It was Rob Sinton's life work.

"Ecopreneuring": Cobbling Together an Income With Idealism and Flair

One way to pursue meaningful work that challenges different parts of yourself is to pull together an income from a variety of sources. The beauty of this entrepreneurial approach is that you're constantly exercising new parts of yourself; you're never bored; you're always stretching. In doing many different things, you may even uncover some wonderful synergies, or invent something new and exciting.

This is precisely what happened to Lisa Kivirist and John Ivanko, when the wife-husband team gave up their fast-paced jobs in Chicago to move to rural Wisconsin. Today their income is diversified and comes from their award-winning bed and breakfast, the Inn Serendipity, *www.innserendipity.com*, their creative services consulting company, and from their books, articles, photographs and workshops. They also sell organic vegetables, fruit and herbs they grow direct from the farm. They add a bit more to the income stream from the generation of wind and solar energy on their property (some of which they sell back to their utility) as well as from transforming fryer oil into biodiesel. They regularly contribute success stories about farmers and rural entrepreneurs to the Minnesota non-profit organization, Renewing the Countryside. Lisa also runs the Rural Women's Project, a venture of the Midwest Organic and Sustainable Education Service, to network and support rural women ecopreneurs in food-related businesses. Among the many benefits of working for themselves is the ability to creatively feed off each other, dream up ideas and decide whether or not to try them out.

"There's diversity in what we do," says Lisa, who is coauthor with John of "Rural Renaissance" (New Society: 2004) and "Edible Earth" (Paradigm: 2007). "A lot of little slices of income come in, which give us more control and freedom." When their son, Liam, was born in 2001, the couple was able to close down their bed and breakfast for several months as they welcomed their new addition into the world.

Before they began their careers as "ecopreneurs," Lisa, 43, recalls with a chuckle, "John and I both had cookie-cutter normal career paths." Both worked for the same Chicago company where they met and, on the surface, were doing all that was expected of them. They had jobs with regular pay-checks, apartments, credit cards, and what Lisa calls, "the normal accompani-ments of an urban yuppie lifestyle." Those accompaniments included eating a lot of "takeout food, out of Styrofoam boxes," never being home to cook, much less grow their own food. They lived for their leisure time — "to forget about the cubicle," she recalls. It was on their time off when they headed up to Wisconsin to bike, camp and detox from city life that they felt most alive; that feeling of vitality, in turn, led them to their new calling.

"We were draining ourselves living on someone else's clock. It was not nine to five but eight to seven. We were at someone else's beck and call." Though Lisa says that little in their background prepared them to be "en-trepreneurial," when the couple moved to Browntown, Wisconsin (a tiny rural community two and a half hours northwest of Chicago, and one hour south of Madison, Wis.), they hung out a shingle and went to work.

"Instead of having one job, one paycheck, we planted a lot of seeds," she says. That was in 1996. They have never looked back. In fact, their latest, award-winning book, "ECOpreneuring" (New Society: 2008), shares how you can make a life and livelihood filled with meaning, purpose, and enough profits to pay off the mortgage by your early 40s. In the almost 15 years since, Lisa and John have come to identify with farmers of yore, being conscious not to keep "all their eggs in one basket." One of the joys of their rural operation is connecting to flowers in bloom, produce in season, and their 10kW wind turbine powering their five-and-a-half-acre property.

I'll never forget the vivid colors of the eggs — blues, browns, burnt oranges — produced by a flock of chickens the couple kept when my "Simple Living" crew visited the family several years back. Picking up a hen and holding her like a cat made an indelible impression on my son, Henry. I was equally impressed to learn that their operation is a "carbon-negative" business, meaning that it sequesters more carbon dioxide annually than it emits. (Their business operation and lifestyle is powered by 100-percent renewable energy, which they calculated through the energy they over-produce as well as their participation in carbon-offset programs.) They set out to go fossil-fuel free from the get go.

Lisa notes that their lifestyles are "more seasonal" than before, both physically and mentally. "Summer is a busy time for us, between gardens and the Inn Serendipity." When they head into fall and winter — the dormant time of year — they are able to catch up on house and writing projects. The balance, she finds, "keeps us more balanced as people."

The two are now earning less than $20,000 between them. But they've found that the less they need financially, the greater their quality of life. "We were tracked to believe the opposite," Lisa says. "Our society says I should have a better quality of life if I can pay someone to clean my house for me, care for my kid and mow my lawn." But if you can raise your own food, cook it yourself, create a livelihood doing what you love, pay off the mortgage, and raise your own child, as they are doing with 8-year-old Liam, you have arrived. That's my definition of the good life — the simple life.

When you meet a person who is genuinely passionate about her work, engaged to her fingertips, there's no mistaking it. You know the real McCoy when you see her. People like Lisa Kivirist and John Ivanko are life's winners. They may not draw the largest paycheck or garner the most prestige in our world, but they're onto something that eludes so many of the rest of us. They exude a connectedness with their lives, a confidence, vitality and a sense of purpose, challenge, and excitement that draws others in. Sometimes they attract a flock.

Builders of Hope: Rescue Homes, Create Communities

As in the case of John and Lisa, finding work you love sometimes calls for an abrupt turn in one's professional path. It may ask you to create something from scratch. Nancy Murray, a charismatic, 42-year-old wife and mother of four, had climbed high up the corporate ladder as an advertising account executive at Leo Burnett Worldwide in Chicago; then, in mid-life, she decided to break new ground. Literally.

An idealist with a large interest in construction, Nancy spotted a niche, dreamed big, and decided to create an organization that could have maximum impact on making the world a better place. When Nancy realized that Americans demolish, on average, some 250,000 houses annually, according to the Environmental Protection Agency, many of them more solidly built than the new structures replacing them, she thought: Why not try to recycle these homes and turn them into affordable housing? To do that, in October 2006, Nancy founded Builders of Hope, a non-profit organization based in Raleigh, North Carolina that saves tear-down houses from the wrecking ball, performs green rehabs and sells them to low- to moderate-income workers who have been priced out of the market. Builders of Hope accepts the donation of these "rescue houses" and either moves them into new clustered communities or leaves them as anchors to help revitalize existing ones.

In order to get the ball rolling, Nancy tapped a substantial portion of the money she had saved during her high-flying years in advertising — an amount well into the six figures — to found the non-profit. "What I realized is that all of this money I was saving and working so hard to amass, I didn't need." It's the American way to always want more, she says. But after spending more than a year with her husband and children in Australia, living with only a fraction of their possessions, she had an insight — call it an epiphany. Nancy Murray realized that she actually wanted less. Fewer possessions, less money. "I thought, 'I have all this money in my bank account. Why not use it to make a difference and leave the world a better place?'"

Barrington Village, Builders of Hope's debut project, is a community of 24 densely clustered, rehabbed homes on a six-acre tract in Southeast Raleigh. Not only are the homes recycled, but each is "greenovated" with new, energy-efficient HVAC systems, plumbing, wiring, insulation and siding. Low-e, double-paned windows, conforming to Energy Star® standards, are installed, along with new roofs. The homes — which sell for between $89,000 to $175,000 — are rehabbed to the point you can call them "new" for insurance purposes.

For community-building purposes — not to mention safety — at Barrington Village and the newer project, State Street Village, currently under construction in downtown Raleigh, the relocated, rehabbed houses are positioned in cul de sacs and outfitted with spacious front porches to encourage neighborliness and porch-sitting.

"The community is peaceful and serene," says first-time homeowner Dawana Stanley, 33, who moved with her husband and five children from a three-bedroom, two-bath rental in nearby Cary, North Carolina into Barrington Village in August 2008. "There's space for a yard," she says. "I'm going to plant plants." When she first entered the 2,900 square foot house, built in 1965, she was taken with the hardwood floors — for their looks and because of her allergies — and the expanse of space. (Most of the rescue homes are much smaller than Stanley's.) Now president of the neighborhood homeowners' association, Stanley says the community is a far cry from the dicey public housing project in which she grew up in New York City. The fact that recycled homes form the basis of Barrington is an added bonus: "I was overjoyed someone was thinking about the planet."

The benefits of recycling houses are many. In 2008, Builders of Hope saved an estimated two million pounds of building material from the landfill, Murray says. The approach allows perfectly decent, stout and sturdy homes — most of them constructed in the 1930s through the 1960s — many containing pricey custom features such as wood flooring, solid countertops, moldings and built-ins to be salvaged. Nancy and the Builders of Hope team has developed a financial model whereby homeowners who wish to build on a property containing an existing home, can choose to donate the old house instead of tearing it down; they pay Builders of Hope $5,000 to help offset the cost of moving the home in exchange for a federal tax credit that can amount to as much as 80 percent of the home's appraised value.

The Builders of Hope model is rapidly gaining traction and national attention. The Wall Street Journal got wind of it and wrote a story, saying that Barrington Village might be "the most politically correct housing development on the planet." Nancy's business head continues to spin out new ideas. With the recent housing collapse, why not expand the mission of Builders of Hope and use government subsidies to take foreclosed properties off the banks' hands, perform green rehabs, and transform them into affordable housing stock?

"The first knee-jerk response to blighted housing is to tear it down," Nancy says. "But every home we save becomes someone's dream home all over again." As the Builders of Hope model seeks to go national, Nancy Murray is right there at the helm. "I'm an all-or-nothing person," she says.

As an all or nothing person, Nancy Murray can teach each of us by her example. She identified a need, took the plunge and created a new niche — not only for herself, but for America. You can bet that Nancy is not getting rich on what she's doing, but you can also be sure that boredom and mental fatigue are not part of her workplace vocabulary.

I've talked a lot about ways for you to find a new professional path and spotlighted individuals who have dreamed big, made plans, taken steps and created new roles for themselves. Those people, like Nancy Murray and Rob Sinton, who work for a higher purpose, to help improve the lives of others, walk on higher ground. By working to make the world a better place, they infuse their own lives with meaning and purpose.

For too many of us today, the pursuit of material comfort, wealth, and status has simply become our source of meaning at work and sadly in life. By allowing images of "the good life" presented by commercial interests — and often by those closest to us (or both in combination) — determine what we do for a living, we end up selling ourselves short, and in many cases, turning our backs on that special gift we have for the world.

My aim is to inspire you to tap into your own special gift. If you haven't yet done so, it's high time you step out and claim the work you were meant to do. Or maybe it's just a matter of your taking a few nips and tucks to make the job you already have more meaningful — things like reducing your work hours and increasing your connection with your co-workers. In either case, only you can determine your best course of action. So take some time out for reflection, develop a plan of action, and get going!

Chapter Three

The Path to
Housing Happiness

*Rethink the American way of housing,
and focus on small, green, and paid-for.*

Americans have been biggie-sizing their housing choices for decades now, with residential size increasing as family size has decreased. The path to reclaiming the good life with housing has many components, including infusing your living space with your values, personality and objects of meaning. As you reclaim the good life at home, the three most fundamental principles to bear in mind are: think small; think green; and think paid-for. These three principles will foster better financial, emotional, and residential health for you, your family and the planet.

My Evolving "Dream" Home

As a child, I could imagine no better version of the good life than living in an impressive house with a swimming pool. The fantasy of rolling out of bed in the morning and diving into my own backyard pool seemed indescribably delicious. I could just picture summer vacations poolside, engaging in endless rounds of swimming, diving, and cavorting in the water, letting the sun bronze my skin and bleach my already blond hair. Friends, family, and bottomless supplies of fresh fruit and chocolate-chip ice cream completed my ideal of happiness.

Through the years, I have devoted a great deal of mental energy to creating some version of my dream home: that ideal place that would provide shelter, comfort and nurture. As a girl, I frequently found myself sketching out floor plans for houses and apartments (and even on occasion layouts for summer camps and boarding schools), clearly seeking my place in the world.

My dream home has undergone numerous metamorphoses through the years. The latest incarnation — shaped by my concern for the planet's welfare as well as the practical impulses of middle age — is radically different from my childhood fantasy. *It's small, green and paid-for.* And though I now reside in a lovely renovated mid-century brick ranch home in North Carolina, I realize that I still haven't gotten it right. Though my Sunflower House has much to recommend it — mature plantings, abundant green features, a one-level floor plan and more — at 2,200 square feet, I've come to think that it's quite simply too large for me and my son, not to mention expensive for my long-term needs. Like many Americans, I need to downsize.

So my "dream home" is not the place where I live now, but exists somewhere out there in the future; it lives in my sketch book and imagination. In this new version, out has gone my childhood image of "living large" and in has come the ideal of living with enough, or *"lagom"* as the

Swedes call it, meaning exactly the right amount. My dream home today is the "right-sized" version of that girlhood vision of luxury living, but "luxury" for me today isn't defined by excess — a big piece of land holding a sprawling home, filled with the "finer things in life," those things that others can't afford. Rather, luxury to me is defined by sufficiency, manageability, and comfort.

The home I desire features an inviting, open layout; it buffers noise, streams light, and has enough quirky features to visually delight. It's constructed of quality, eco-friendly materials and carries a low carbon footprint. My fantasy home is not new, and, in the words of my friend and colleague Sarah Susanka, "not-so-big." And who knows? It might not be a *house* at all. As a single mother, I find myself increasingly drawn to denser developments, such as multi-family units and co-housing, enclaves that promote community and interaction. I am a people person and my brief experiment with suburban living has proved rather isolating. As my father used to say, "Who knows what the future will bring?"

Though my passion for swimming remains — in fact, age has only deepened the commitment — today, I wouldn't want to own a home with a pool any more than I'd wish for a bowling alley in the basement or a helicopter pad on the roof. I still swim almost every day, but my idea of nirvana is paying my yearly membership dues to the local community center and letting its staff handle the pool's pH levels, chlorine mix, and hairballs in the drain. In fact, once you get past the concept of your home as your fairy godmother — providing for your every need — you're well on your way to reclaiming residential sanity.

"We have gone beyond shelter and comfort. A home is now a lifestyle. ... Americans might want to reassess whether their passion for ever-bigger homes is good for them and the nation. Do we need to go from SUVs to Hummers? Maybe we should revert to sedans."

— *Robert J. Samuelson, The Washington Post*

Housing Size: Taking the Long View

Housing size in this country has been steadily increasing since the 1950s. According to Census Bureau data, the average home grew from 1,400 square feet in 1960 to 2,080 square feet in 1990, to nearly 2,500 square feet in 2006. Only recently have indicators begun pointing to a contraction in new home size. Not only have houses ballooned in size, but they're so cluttered with the objects of our shopping expeditions that they can be downright "stuffocating". Some homes have become so big that family members can coexist for days without having significant interaction. I'll never forget my dear friend, Linda Fuller, co-founder with her husband, Millard, of Habitat for Humanity, describing mega-houses in which some parents quite literally have to summon their children to dinner via intercom. Such grandiose configurations are almost as disruptive to family harmony, she said, as being under-housed.

When speaking on the topic of sustainable living, I often give my audience what I call my "simple-living readiness" quiz. "How many of you have ever bought something you already own because you don't know where it is and don't have the time to look for it?" I ask. Invariably, almost every hand in the room goes up.

This is a telling snapshot of America in 2010. The vast majority of us simply have too much stuff — more than we can possibly keep track of, much less thoughtfully possess. Our oversized McMansions, complete with their grand atriums, triple and quadruple garages, and even (dare I say it?) king-size beds match our biggie-size dreams. Most of our homes are not only "so-big" but "so-crammed," bulging with clothing, toys, CDs, and sporting equipment which spring forth from cabinets, attics, garages, basements and store rooms. Unless we employ conscious strategies to streamline and slim our living spaces — and put clutter-control mechanisms in place — our homes have become virtual sinkholes of stuff, clogging the flow of energy and movement in our lives.

But nothing lasts forever; often epochal shifts happen rapidly, as Malcolm Gladwell suggests, in a "blink". Witness the once-mighty SUV. The recent sacred status symbol of our high-carbon, devil-may-care lifestyle is now shunned on the used-car circuit. The hot new wheels of the moment are the Prius hybrid and Mini Cooper, which themselves will be displaced by even leaner, greener future modes of transport: Smart Cars, plug-in hybrids; and motion-activated, upright Segways.

The same goes for housing. Early signs indicate that McMansions will quickly become the white elephants of the real estate market. And new home construction trends are pointing toward smaller, greener homes. According to the American Institute of Architects' Home Design Trends Survey, as early as the first quarter of 2007, more residential architects reported home size to be declining (26 percent) than increasing (21 percent). The trend appears to be accelerating. According to Gopal Ahluwalia, vice president of research for the National Association for Home Builders, in the July-September quarter of 2008, the average size of new home starts dropped fully 7.3 *percent* to 2,438 from 2,629 square feet the previous quarter. "This is the first time we have seen such a significant decline," Ahluwalia told me. The trend continued into the fourth quarter of 2008 and first quarter of 2009. Going forward, Ahluwalia projects future homes to stabilize between 2,300 to 2,500 square feet over the next five to 10 years.

As we right-size our personal living spaces and move toward smaller and greener homes, a concomitant shift waits in the wings: reconfiguring the way of life inside these homes. Job No. 1 for most of us is paring down what we have to a set of possessions we can thoughtfully own. (Part of responsible stewardship of our possessions involves redirecting what we no longer need to worthy recipients.) Once we've purged our systems of the excess, the focus will be on creating lives that are dynamic and streamlined, where the carbon cost of a thing is weighed alongside its dollar price tag, where the focus is on usability rather than ownership, where we seek to reduce our personal waste streams.

Last year, after giving the keynote speech at a sustainability forum in Raleigh, North Carolina, I met Louise Griffin, a local realtor who promotes the principles of sustainability with her clients and colleagues. She first got into the real estate business in 2005 at the height of the housing bubble. Back then, she recalls, many of her clients bought more house than they needed. "The idea was that you were supposed to want it all and have it all," she says. These "wants" included home theaters, exercise rooms, bedrooms for children (sometimes not yet born), a guest bedroom, and another bedroom for a home office. Pretty soon, you're up to four or more bedrooms. "It was not questioned whether wanting it all and having it all was a fulfilling experience," she says. "Unfortunately, they did get it all, and now they can't pay for it all."

So how does Griffin, who serves as president of the Women's Council of Realtors in Raleigh, manage to steer clients toward more sensibly sized homes? "My job is to advise people to think about aspects of home ownership that they may not have considered," she says. She has developed a "Home Buying Lifestyle Analysis" (see page 92), in which she sits down with clients to pose a series of questions about how they live and work, and how their future home would fit into that picture.

"I remind people of the time and money they're going to spend in this home. If owning this home is their highest value in life, and their joy comes from maintaining the large yard, it might be a good fit for them," she says. "However, the reality is that most people feel both time pressure and money pressure acutely. The idea of being financial slaves to their homes and slaves to home maintenance is not generally the dream."

In the past couple of years, Griffin has started to see a mind-set shift on the part of some clients. "People are coming and asking for smaller homes," she says. "They're willing to consider 2,500 square feet instead of 3,500. They say, 'I'm open to not having the giant home I once thought I wanted.' And what they're telling architects is, 'As long as it has the kind of finishes we've been picturing, we're okay with it.' " They're also starting to think about trade-offs. If they want to live closer to their jobs and reduce their commute, they may not have as large a kitchen, as many bedrooms or bathrooms, or as spacious a lawn.

Another change that Griffin has observed is clients taking the long view of potential properties, looking at comfort and future functionality rather than seeing their homes as short-term investments to be lived in a few years, and then flipped for handsome sums. The portion of the population that is downsizing is also looking to a time when they will not be working anymore, she says. The house has to be sustainable size-wise and from an economics perspective. Even clients in their 40s are asking questions like, "What if we're no longer able to walk to the second floor?"

Your Home-Buying Lifestyle Analysis

If you're in the market to purchase a home (or even if you wish to build or rent), you may want to ask yourself the following questions, developed by REALTOR® Louise Griffin. These questions may shed light on vital information regarding size, location, and other critical factors that may help maximize your enjoyment of your home and your life.

AREA

How often do you go to the grocery store? (If daily, having one close by may be an important factor.)

What types of shops/restaurants do you enjoy patronizing? How often do you go?

Is walking to shops/restaurants important to you?

How long is your commute, portal to portal?

What activities do you perform daily/weekly that affect your commute?

Would you use public transportation if it were convenient to you?

How often would you use a park/ball field/local dog park?

Do you prefer architectural homogeneity, or diversity in age or character?

How much interaction do you desire with neighbors and community?

HOME

Do you have time/desire to maintain a large lot? Gardens?

Do you plan to clean/maintain your own home, or will you hire out these services?

Do you have time/money to upgrade the energy efficiency of a home?

What size home do you have in mind (number of rooms, bedrooms, garage stalls, and total square footage)?

Do you anticipate purchasing additional furnishings for this home? If so, how much will this cost?

What space do you not have in your current home that you would like in this home? Or, are there currently portions of your home that you do not use and do not need?

Do you like to have private areas at home? If so, for what activities (i.e., workshop, reading area, game room, private spa-bath)?

How much storage room do you anticipate needing? Are items you store used regularly or infrequently?

YOUR LIFESTYLE

Do you have pets, and what features do you need to accommodate them?

Do you have an interest in a "green built" home or ways in which the home/ location might minimize use of resources?

Do you anticipate a need for storage inside or outside the home?

What features would you be willing to pass up if you found the home that was "perfect" in every other way?

Housing's "Big Three"

Whether you're buying a new home, building from scratch, refurbishing or renovating an existing property, or are joyfully content in your current residence, reclaiming the good life around housing revolves around three fundamental principles:

● *Small* — that your home be *manageable in size*, no larger than you need; perhaps smaller than you want.

● *Green* — that it be created with eco-friendly building materials, systems, fixtures, and finishes that provide a healthful, healing environment for you and the environment; and that it be as energy-efficient as possible, possibly *energy self-sufficient.*

● *Paid-for* — that your home be affordable, not holding the Damocles' sword of debt over your head. If you do not yet fully own your home, this principle asks you to *designate the retirement of your mortgage as one of your top financial priorities.*

Each of these three paths offers multiple and overlapping benefits. For example, if your home is small, it's inherently green, given that smaller homes invariably consume less energy to heat, cool, and power than larger spaces. Unless you've gilded the walls with gold leaf and studded the trim with rubies, it's more likely to be worth less than a larger home. If your smaller home is not yet paid-for, generally its mortgage can be more quickly retired than one written for a larger, costlier property. And consider that in a smaller home, you need less furniture, so you'll be spending less money here, while at the same time, you'll have a smaller space to clean and maintain. With less storage space at your disposal, you'll be forced to be more selective in your consumption choices. I call this a triple hitter.

Rethink Housing Choices

Rather than being swept up by the American dream of housing, as I was as a day-dreaming youngster, it's time for you to rethink your housing choices. Because it's been drummed into our heads for so long that bigger is better, it can sometimes be difficult to envision alternate scenarios. What's more, we've been told that we should all *own* our homes, and that these homes should be *free-standing, single-family* units. However, the principles already outlined in the book — of frugality, of sensible money management, of finding that thing that sparks you — can point you in new and original directions about housing choices. I urge you to do some serious thinking about where you really want to live and in so doing make your own decisions, and co-create your dream home. Once you're figured out what you want, get started making it a reality.

To do this, put every imaginable consideration or possibility on the table as you go forward. In addition to answering the questions in the Home-Buying Lifestyle Analysis exercise, ask a few more. Do you even want to *own* a home? If so, do you wish to live in a single-family home or would you consider a town house, condominium or co-housing development? How important is having a lawn and garden to you? Is joining a thriving community something you desire?

Rental remains a viable — even desirable — option for many. My own father never wished to own a home, and he never did, even when he was in a position to do so. His rationale was simple: He was a scholar with neither time nor inclination for home maintenance. If his commode leaked, he simply wanted to call his landlord to have it fixed. Daddy always lived modestly. After retiring from teaching at Howard University in Washington DC, he moved into a modest, two-bedroom, one-bath apartment in Silver Spring, Maryland where he lived out his retirement years with my stepmother in tranquility, peace, and with a minimum of clutter. When Daddy died at the ripe old age of 87, he had no home equity to pass on, but he nonetheless managed to amass considerable savings from his frugal lifestyle to assure his widow's comfort in her final years.

> *"It might be time to reconsider the single-family house: either we content ourselves with smaller houses, or we will be obliged to look at alternatives like patio houses and row houses, and to resurrect such earlier housing types as the California bungalow court and the Georgian housing terrace."*
> — Witold Rybczynski in "Looking Around: A Journey Through Architecture"

Small is Beautiful

When considering archetypes involving housing size, the Grimm brothers' fairy tale, "Snow White and the Seven Dwarfs," comes to mind. The greed of the evil stepmother — who sought to have "the fairest of them all," her stepdaughter, killed — is personified by the forbidding coldness of the royal castle, whereas the warmth of the unusual but caring family of dwarves is all bound up in its cozy, thatched-roof cottage. Beautiful and virtuous Snow White finds salvation and shelter (not to mention an honest day's work) in close quarters. Small is not only beautiful for Snow White, but life-saving.

Ask yourself: Would you rather your home be your castle or your cottage? While your first response may be to choose the castle, fortified against the slings and arrows of outrageous fortune, think again. Do you really want your home to be large and forbidding — a fortress that walls you off from others, a structure standing to impress and intimidate, and into which you sink a king's ransom — or would you rather live in a place that's small, modest and sufficient, like a bird's nest that offers sanctuary as well as the ideal launching pad from which to take flight? Do you want your home to be a place that drains resources and energy or one that replenishes your supply of energy and supports your engagement in the world?

Another fundamental question worth asking is: How does your home fit into the overall picture of your life? Does it contribute to a sense of work-life balance? Often people invest in material comforts — such as luxurious bathing areas, upscale kitchens and sybaritic bedroom suites — to compensate for overwork. Then, they're forced into a vicious cycle of overwork to pay for these pricey extras. A better option is to scale back on material comforts, which will in turn reduce the amount of time you're forced to work to pay for your home.

It almost goes without saying that the smaller home is the more economical choice. If you're building a smaller home, it takes fewer materials, thus consuming fewer resources. If you're a new convert to small-home size thinking and were planning to build a larger property, consider this: You can earmark some of the savings for energy-efficiency upgrades and high-performance, green features.

Smaller houses can be placed on smaller lots, which will save on the cost of land, not to mention the *use* of land. "A modest one-story tract house typically needs a 60-foot-wide lot — that is, every house requires 60 feet of sidewalk, roadway, sewer and water line, and storm sewer," writes the celebrated architect and writer Witold Rybczynski in "Looking Around: A Journey Through Architecture" (Viking: 1992). "A narrower two-story cottage can be built on a 40-foot-wide lot, immediately reducing the costs by a third." He goes on to demonstrate additional economies of scale as housing size contracts further.

If you're not building new, but looking to buy a smaller home, once again, money enters the picture. In most cases smaller homes carry lower price tags at listing and purchase, but you also need to consider ongoing costs, such as powering and maintaining your home. Even taxes and insurance will be slimmer, saving you buckets of money in the short-term and over a lifetime.

"The best workers ... have loved themselves well enough to love the world and ... give themselves a home base that nourishes their own physical, mental, and spiritual vitality. Taking care of yourself is not selfish; it is a gift to all of life."

— Carol Venolia, *Healing Environments*

Serving the Soul

Of course, by now you know my platform. I'm here to advocate for the small home, which may be less than you want but as much as you need. In addition to saving money and reducing your carbon footprint, there is another, less obvious benefit to scaling back: *Smaller places are good for the soul.* Smaller homes tend to be cozier and homier, putting you in closer relationship with your furnishings, possessions, nature, and, most importantly, the people and animals with whom you live. One of the most tragic developments of our era has been the growing isolation of people, one from another, even inside the family.

This isolation has been caused by many things — the advent of technology, the breakdown of the family, and the transience and competitiveness of our culture — but the scale and configuration of our houses has played a significant though little noticed role. As housing size has escalated, so many American residences have lost their human scale. Simply put, large, alienating homes do not foster togetherness; quite the opposite.

No one has zeroed in on this issue as effectively as renowned architect and small-home advocate Sarah Susanka, who has intuited the qualities people crave in their homes. Susanka describes a 1990s visit to a Minnesota home of gargantuan proportions in "The Not So Big House" (Taunton: 1998), a home in which the residents were unhappy but couldn't put their finger on exactly why. "(Their house) had the required arched window topping off a soaring front entrance scaled more for an office building than a home," she writes. Like many of its vintage and design, the home was impersonal, oversized, and alienating; it had effectively shut down family life. The key to creating a house that fosters a nurturing home environment lies "in spending money on the quality of the space and less on the sheer quantity of it," Susanka writes. "(A) house is so much more than its size and volume, neither of which has anything to do with comfort."

When I speak to groups about their experiences of the simple life, people often begin to reflect on their college days. While most assume that this nostalgia is a yearning for their lost youth — that period of limitless possibility and new discovery — a factor not often mentioned is the compact size of their living quarters. One thing you quickly learn in a dorm room (or Army boot camp, or a New York City studio apartment, for that matter) is that you don't need all that much space to feel delightfully alive. I often hear residents of big, fancy homes say that they're happiest in their modest vacation homes. I submit to you that the modest proportions of second homes are at least partially responsible for blissful states of mind.

Exploding the Myth of the "Starter" Home

I'll never forget when my friend, Bonni Brodnick, and her husband, Andrew, purchased their first home in Westchester County, New York, back in 1991. It was a well-maintained Cape built in 1949 with three bedrooms, two baths, and a den on two sprawling acres shaded by sugar maples. Long on charm, but at 1,800 square feet, the house was small in comparison to others in their affluent community. Bonni fell in love with the slanted Dutch roof over a 16-pane window in the room that would become her daughter's. With two children under the age of 3, the Brodnicks found the house to be everything they needed (though perhaps not all they wanted). Initially they considered this to be their "starter home"; she and Andrew assumed — and family and friends contributed to the impression — that as two successful professionals (Andrew is an attorney; Bonni is in public relations and marketing), they would eventually "trade up" to something grander.

Though they have considered a larger home, at the end of the day, they realize that their manageable mortgage payments make the numbers work, especially while putting their two children through Cornell University. What's more, they're excited to think that soon their home will be paid off, allowing them early retirement and the opportunity to pursue passions and travel the world. Bonni would also like to spend time in her beloved France ... and Andrew, the bookworm, might even take time to learn French.

But financial benefits aren't the only reason they're sticking to the house. Their home has become a part of them, a hallowed ground holding sacred family memories. "When I see pictures of my son in his room at 2 years old and now in the same spot at 20 years old, there's something wonderfully special about this," says Bonni. It would be wrenching to walk away from the home her family has created with love and devotion. "Within these walls, my family has grown and come to fruition. You can't buy that. Even though we could afford more, after living here for 20 years, our home is just the way we want it. The colors are right and the pictures are hung just so. I would hate to start over again. I feel incredibly blessed to truly have a home-sweet-home."

The financial reality for many families like the Brodnicks is that they arrive at the position to "trade up" to larger homes just a few years before their children are poised to fly the coop. If they move when their kids are in middle school or high school, the window of time in which the space is fully utilized is surprisingly narrow. It's not long before the parents become empty nesters, saddled with more house than they really need along with a sizable mortgage to go with it. The Brodnicks were wise enough to resist the social pressure to buy a bigger, more prestigious home. Take a page out of their book and let your "starter home" become your "forever home."

Harvesting Space in Your Own Home

So maybe you did buy a bigger home when your kids were still at home and now find yourself swimming in space. What to do if you're attached to your property and neighborhood and don't want to move? My Seattle friends, Cecile and Paul Andrews, who found themselves in this boat, simply divided their house in three. Perched high on a hill overlooking Green Lake in the Phinney neighborhood, the 1927 wood-frame Tudor home that the couple bought in 1988 had four bedrooms, two baths, and a delightful, secluded garden stretching around the side and back of the house.

When they bought the house, both were working full-time outside the home, Paul as a technology reporter for the Seattle Times and Cecile as a community college administrator. Their children were already on their own, but Paul and Cecile had managed to fill every bit of space in the 4,000 square feet home. The upstairs became their home office; the basement filled with bric-a-brac.

In the mid-1990s, when Cecile resigned from her job to devote herself to writing full-time, she and Paul were casting about for additional sources of income and decided to rent out the top floor, which had once been an apartment. That worked out so well that Cecile, author of "Small is Beautiful" (New Society: 2006) and "A Circle of Simplicity" (HarperCollins: 1997), seized upon the idea of harvesting space in their underutilized basement for the same purpose. They hired a contractor, who carved out an apartment from the front half of the basement. (The rear part of the unfinished basement remains a common laundry and storage area for all three household units.) Adding a kitchen and a bathroom, they transformed the space into an attractive and livable apartment with a great view of the lake.

The two units bring in a reliable $1,600 per month. Cecile says that they could probably charge more in Seattle, but they consciously chose to keep their rents below market rates to promote tenant longevity. Keeping the rents low also gives them their pick of prospects when the units do turn over. When space becomes available, they advertise "eco-friendly apartments" on Craigslist™, inviting prospective tenants to submit essays about why they want to live there. Usually they get about 30 responses, giving them a wide selection as well as insight into their applicants' character. The technique has worked like a charm. Not only has every tenant become a friend, but the landlords have never once had to contend with deadbeat tenants, bounced checks, trashed apartments, or any of the perceived problems associated with rental.

Paul and Cecile now occupy 1,400 square feet of space on the main level, which includes two bedrooms, one bathroom, a large living room, dining room, and kitchen with pantry. One of the bedrooms serves as Paul's office, and Cecile has set up shop in the dining room, the walls of which are lined with books. To find space for her storage needs, Cecile had to be resourceful. "I used the coat closet at the front door to house my filing cabinets," she says. She sees all kinds of bonuses in their downsized arrangement. As a clutter bug, having her office in a public room forces her to clean up frequently, every time guests are coming — something she scrupulously avoided when her office was upstairs, out of sight. "It forces me to get rid of clutter on a regular basis, as opposed to letting it build up."

Turning their home into an income generator has enabled Paul to follow his wife's suit and quit his job as well, joining the ranks of the self-employed. This lifestyle affords them tremendous freedom; most years, the Andrews arrange house swaps with like-minded folks in the Bay Area, where they spend several months with their beloved bichon, Maggie. When they're home in Seattle, they have plenty of time to devote to causes about which they're passionate, including developing the Eco-Phinney Neighborhood Association. They consider transforming their single-family house into a multi-family residence to be an act of ecological stewardship. The house now accommodates six residents, instead of two, thus dramatically reducing the house's per-person carbon footprint.

Both cite additional benefits that add dimension to their quality of life. Before they had renters, when Paul traveled, Cecile felt uncomfortable staying home alone. "Now, there's always someone there. And if Paul and I travel together, there's someone to water the plants. It's been a totally positive experience," Cecile says.

"Americans tend to like their privacy while not realizing the drawbacks of isolation," Paul says. "Most people think in terms of negatives regarding this kind of arrangement rather than the positives. It takes a flexible approach and some accommodation, but the payoffs in community, friendship and safety/reassurance are many times worth it. If you manage it correctly, the positives far outweigh any negatives. In fact, the negatives disappear."

The Andrews' positive experience offers a lesson to us all. Instead of fearing the hassle of tenants, potential conflicts and loss of privacy, think of what you have to gain: community, friendship and cooperation, not to mention additional income and the potential for tool-, service- and knowledge-sharing.

Sarah's Solution: Re-Configure Existing Space

While describing my remodeling plans for the Sunflower House to my friend and colleague, renowned architect Sarah Susanka, at a green building show in California in September 2007, she excitedly grabbed a paper napkin and began sketching an alternate configuration for my laundry nook. I had made the decision to bring my washer and dryer upstairs from the basement and incorporate them into the sunroom, thus placing them within easy reach of the kitchen, my study and the outdoor clothesline I was planning for the yard. Sarah suggested removing the wall separating the sunroom and study and capturing space for the appliances from inside my study rather than placing them along the existing wall in the sunroom (which would partially block a window).

"People need to think creatively about reconfiguring existing spaces," she said. With Sarah's tacit blessing, I continued applying this same principle throughout my home. In my bedroom, which was "not so big" to begin with, I did the unorthodox and captured existing space to add a closet. That allowed me to wall off the existing closet, which I opened up into Henry's adjoining room. The cut-out also provided a nifty entry alcove into the bedroom, allowing me to set up a welcoming table with lamp and books.

(continued)

When Sarah traveled to Mount Airy some months later to check out the results, she affirmed my decision to capture and re-purpose existing space. "I love what you've done," she said, snapping photos of my bedroom closet as well as the Sarah-inspired laundry nook setup.

As you develop plans to remodel your home — before you even consider adding on — try reconfiguring your existing space. The footprint of your home will remain the same, and you'll feel incredibly creative for how you've made it all work, like fitting together pieces of a giant puzzle. Taking space from my study turned out to be a brilliant move. It not only incorporated the laundry room more gracefully into the sunroom, but it shortened my long study, adding definition while making it cozier. That one move improved two rooms. I often think of Sarah's spur-of-the-moment contribution to my home. With her remarkable instincts for spatial definition and clarity, it's easy to see how this visionary woman has spawned the much-needed "not-so-big" movement in America.

Mama's Roomer

While you may not have space enough to carve out apartments in your home — nor Seattle's enlightened zoning ordinances permitting such construction — you may have an extra bedroom, or bedroom-bathroom combination that could be rented out for income. Try it for a summer and see if it works for you.

When I moved from the East Coast to California years ago, I felt badly about leaving my mother, then an English professor at the University of Maine, alone in her home in Orono. At the time, I suggested she take in a roomer (for companionship as well as some extra spending money). Initially, Mama resisted my idea (after all, her home had only one bathroom), but then she decided to give it a try. Her roomer was an English teacher at Orono High School, who lived with his wife in Blue Hill, some 50 miles from where he taught. Though he could make the hour-long commute each way every day, he preferred staying in town three nights a week, especially when there were night-time school functions to attend, a stack of papers or tests to grade, or the roads home were slick with snow and ice.

Mother's friendship with her part-time roomer blossomed. They enjoyed eating together at least once a week and discussing literature and experience. He became a friend and confidant, almost like the son Mama never had. Though she left Maine more than 15 years ago to move South near me, Mother still receives birthday cards and calls from her one-time roomer. She has come to regard the experience as one of her life's most unexpected and meaningful friendships.

There are lessons to be learned from the stories of Mama and her roomer, of Cecile and Paul carving up their home, of the Brodnicks staying with their "starter" home, in spite of social pressure to seek more spacious quarters. The lesson boils down to this: Happiness in one's home is more closely connected to the people who live there and the harmony and connection within than with a large, imposing space. And although you might not want to live with your entire family in a Motel 6 room indefinitely, if you spread your family out too thinly, family members stand to lose that vital connection — that glue — that makes you whole. If you have so many bathrooms in your home that your child never has to wait for toilet privileges, how is she going to fare when she goes out into the real world where she has to learn to wait her turn? Not only for toilets but for a job, for the right relationship, for the many experiences that come your way in life? Small is beautiful. Small doesn't have to be about sacrifice, but rather about learning to live with humanity — learning to live on a human scale.

Green, Energy-Efficient Homes

Waste Not, Want Not: Residential Adaptive Reuse. For a number of years early in this decade, I lived in the Renfro Lofts Condominium complex in downtown Mount Airy. Once a hosiery manufacturing plant for the Renfro Hosiery Corporation, the building sat vacant for a while until 2000, when two enterprising local developers saw potential there for an upscale residential community. Working with the National Historic Trust for Preservation, they converted the old factory into 39 high-end condominiums with a cutting-edge feel. The units are spacious, open and inviting, featuring brick walls, high ceilings with open ductwork and vintage oak flooring. It's the kind of development you might expect to see in San Francisco, Chicago, or even Asheville, North Carolina, but not in Andy Griffith's hometown.

The Renfro Lofts project surprised many naysayers not only by selling out quickly but becoming a recognized statewide model for urban redevelopment, in part because of a sophisticated formula in which state tax credits flowed back into the pockets of the original residential buyers (rather than staying with the developers).

When I purchased my unit in 2001 — one of the smallest at 1,250 square feet — I was consciously placing my faith in, and directing my dollars toward, eco-friendly living. With so many units so densely packed, I knew my energy costs would be low. From an aesthetic viewpoint, something about the refinished oak floors and brick walls softened with age, spoke to me in a way that new flooring and walls never do. Outside my bedroom window on the brick wall was a stone insert carved with the year 1930.

When I read about a similar New Urbanism project in Asheville, North Carolina — the Lofts at Mica Village — I had to pay a visit. This 10-unit project, completed in 2008, was built on the grounds of the former Asheville Schoonmaker Mica Company. As the processing facility, built in 1892, gradually phased out of business, the factory became a dumping ground for old tires, broken bottles and miscellaneous debris. It was purchased in 2006 by developer Regina Trantham and a partner, who saw potential in the old building with its great bones and walkable proximity to both historic Biltmore Village and downtown Asheville. Adding to its appeal was the fact that the property occupied a brownfield site for which EPA redevelopment money was available. Trantham brought in engineer David

Smith, who tested the building and determined that its structural integrity exceeded modern building standards by 27 percent. (David Smith was so taken with the project that he later bought a unit and moved in.)

Passionately committed to reducing, reusing and recycling, Trantham set about rehabbing the property, reclaiming more than 60 percent of existing materials — everything from old concrete to steel window frames to cast-off piping. Old glass windows were broken down and added decoratively into concrete countertops. Smashed concrete was used in the landscaping, the old window frames set off interior vanity mirrors, and the old plumbing lines were re-purposed as handrails for staircases in the common areas. The walls in the entry lobby and common areas were finished in mica-clay. Local contractors and artisans were given work whenever possible.

When Memphis residents Reb and Mary Haizlip were looking for a *pied a terre* in Asheville, they happened onto Mica Village and immediately fell in love with the spare lines and open feel of their 850-square-feet unit. (The only doors in their condo connect to the bathroom and closets.) Their Memphis home is four times this size, but here, they need less. "Everything is in its place," says Mary. Reduced space and a minimum of personal items lend a feeling of freedom and lightness to their life in town.

The Haizlips have woven the eco-restoration story at the heart of Mica Village into the narrative of their new home and proudly point out to a visitor the recycled materials in their lair. One-hundred-year-old cedar planks, sourced in nearby Charlotte, North Carolina, were used to make their bar top, which is itself propped up by re-purposed sprinkler pipes. Their kitchen backsplashes were cut from old windows. "This really is an example of cradle-to-cradle rehab," Reb says.

Each unit is different, but they all incorporate salvaged and recycled materials: wood floors, brick walls, and exposed hemlock posts and beams that are overt markers of the building's industrial past. The units were all retrofitted with Energy Star® lighting, energy-saving windows and

Green Guard®-certified insulation. Ceiling fans were installed throughout to promote good indoor air circulation and reduce heating and cooling costs. Trantham is proud to mention the *total* cost for utilities — heating, cooling, electricity, and water — averages an amazing $60 per month per 1,000 square foot unit. Powering the complex are 14-Seer HVAC systems — exceeding Energy Star® standards — which help to keep operating costs down, along with keeping ductwork inside the rooms rather than tucked out of sight.

Even the grounds were restored in an environmentally friendly fashion. Trantham recalls winning battles with city inspectors who wanted her to cut trees on the property and replant. (She refused.) She also fought city hall on the installation of storm drainage on the property, which abuts the Swanannoa River. "I just thought that was ridiculous. If the river swells, we'd like for the water to perk back down into the groundwater." Pervious pavers were installed to direct rainwater into the ground. And Trantham proudly mentions that the first "successful" green roof in Asheville, composed of sedum, makes its home at the Lofts. Even with the downturn in housing, the complex sold out within seven months of completion in 2008. Six of the 10 residences are now occupied by residents who have cut their commutes from up to 45 minutes each way to less than five minutes, saving precious time, money and carbon emissions. Now that's green living!

"I sought to reform the environment, not the humans."
— R. Buckminster Fuller

Toward a Smaller Footprint

Although modest housing size is a crucial component of better living, it is by no means the only measure of a green home. On your path to the good life through housing, reducing the carbon footprint of your home through efficiencies of energy- and resource-use is a bar to which we all must aspire. Some leading thinkers say that homes of the future will have the capability of producing as much energy as they consume. Why, you might ask, is this so important?

Buildings represent the largest single source of greenhouse-gas emissions contributing to global warming. According to The Washington Post, houses in America account for fully half of building-related carbon emissions. What's more, as energy costs continue to soar while supplies of fossil fuels diminish, energy efficiencies become more important than ever. When you remodel your home or build new, be sure to check around for tax credits that may be available for upgrading energy efficiencies. Additional tax incentives can help pay for groundwater geothermal heat pump systems and other emerging advanced systems. Be sure to check out the Department of Energy (DOE)'s Weatherization Assistance programs for rebates and incentives for upgrades.

Indeed, author and consultant David Johnston, who developed the first green remodeling program in America, is now promoting the concept of "zero-energy homes," which he defines as homes employing established green building principles and super-insulation techniques while drawing on a variety of renewable energy sources. "Two-way utility metering," Johnston writes, "allows homeowners to sell power to a local utility when the house produces more than it needs, and on an annual basis means net zero-energy consumption."

Green Upgrades: What I Did to My Sunflower House

Precious few homes in America today can claim the "zero-energy" rubric, but a number of measures now exist that anyone can take to upgrade existing homes, regardless of size. In the fall of 2007 and spring 2008, in consultation with David Johnston and Natural Home magazine editor-in-chief, Robyn Griggs Lawrence, I oversaw the "greenovation" of my Sunflower House in Mount Airy. The renovation was documented on two episodes of the "Simple Living With Wanda Urbanska" series and re-ported extensively on my Web site blog. The following list of suggestions — based on green upgrades throughout my home — may give you ideas as you seek to retrofit your home or look for elements to incorporate into new construction.

1. Upgrade insulation.

In order to improve my home's comfort level, along with lower-ing the carbon and dollar cost of heating and cooling, we added what David Johnston calls "the greenest of the green" — closed-cell polyurethane spray foam insulation — onto the rafters and sheathing of my attic. We also sprayed foam — fabricated locally by NCFI Polyurethanes — into the wall cavities in my bathroom, thus greatly augmenting its comfort level. Formaldehyde-free Johns Manville® rolled insulation was installed on the ceiling in the unfinished portion of my basement, directly underneath my main floor. The overall conditioned space remains comfortable regardless of the season, while energy costs have been reduced dramatically.

2. Improve windows.

We removed my energy-inefficient, double-glazed windows and replaced them throughout the house and basement with double-paned, low-e windows fabricated in North Carolina by Noran-dex. Low-emissivity windows increase the insulation value of your windows, reflecting summer heat out and absorbing heat into your home during the chilly winter months. As much as I can during the year, I aim for a "floating" environment, in which I use neither heat nor air conditioning, but instead rely on natural ventilation from open windows and ceiling fans.

3. Upgrade appliances to Energy Star®.

All the major appliances in my home were upgraded to Energy Star® appliances by KitchenAid® and Whirlpool®. Though the initial investment in these appliances is high, when you consider the return on investment, or their life-cycle cost, the cost goes down. The washing machine and dishwasher both save water. As a bonus to the overall quality of life inside my home, all my new appliances are quiet. You can enjoy dinner party conversation in the dining room — or retain your concentration while writing in my adjacent study — while the dishwasher is running in the kitchen.

4. Use low-VOC (volatile organic compound) paints.

When you move into a new home or remodel, the first order of remodeling business generally involves paint. With the exception of Henry's bathroom, the entire main floor of my home was painted in soothing tones of gold, sage, and aqua with low-VOC paints from Ace Hardware®. All major paint lines now offer low- or no-VOC products — manufactured without lead pigments, cadmium, or mercury — which improve air quality inside the home. Conventional paints off-gas volatile organic compounds into your interior long after the paint dries in the form of airborne "micro-flakes." Because no- and low-VOC paints either don't off-gas at all or do so only slightly, you can sleep comfortably in a room the same day you paint.

5. Add ceiling fans.

I admit it. I'm a ceiling-fan freak. I love them and would happily outfit every room in my house with one. I find circulating air to be soothing, and, at night, the low-level whir from my overhead fan provides white noise that helps promote sound sleep. It turns out that ceiling fans represent a smart way to cut energy costs, as well.

Some calculations demonstrate that ceiling fans have the potential to reduce utility bills as much as 40 percent in the summertime. According to the Winston-Salem Journal, it costs approximately 43 cents an hour to run the average central air conditioning system, 16 cents per hour to power a room air conditioner, but just *a penny an hour to operate a ceiling fan.* (In the winter months, you can run the fan in reverse to redistribute the heat that's risen to the ceiling.) In the Sunflower House, I installed ceiling fans in all three bedrooms, the living room and the sun room. My only regret is not putting one in the kitchen.

6. Use local materials.

I was fortunate to be able to obtain a number of local materials and products for my remodel. When you use materials that have traveled long distances to your home, you are responsible for the embodied energy involved in transporting them, thus raising your carbon cost, and in many cases your dollar cost. What is more, when you opt for local materials, each item contributes a special charm to the overall mix, and you can feel positive about contributing to your local economy. In the Sunflower House, I proudly point to:

a. *"Local granite."* My salt-and-pepper granite countertops and backsplashes from the North Carolina Granite Corporation — two miles from my kitchen as the crow flies — provide a beauty and practicality that I've never before enjoyed. I love not only the look of the granite, but the ability to place hot pans directly onto my counters.

b. These *gorgeous countertops* were fabricated by Acme Stone Company here in town. My friend, Cathy Stevens, assisted with measurements (while dispensing savvy decorating wisdom on color choice and many other matters throughout the home), while her son Kenny oversaw installation.

c. Forms & Fixtures of nearby Greensboro, North Carolina constructed by hand a lovely, *all-hardwood bathroom cabinet called Provence.* The piece shows a lightly distressed finish and sets the tone for the entire bathroom.

d. My study *mantelpiece* was made by Mill Creek Arts in Grayson County, Virginia, fabricated by using wormy chestnut planks removed from an old abandoned barn. Due to the chestnut blight, this wood has to be at least 100 years old, probably much older. Adding character and depth to my work space, my mantel's presence stands as a continuing reminder of my commitment to reuse and recycling.

e. The *limestone marker* placed in my front yard near the entrance was fabricated by Rock Solid Dimensional Stone in Mount Airy. The idea of naming your home, providing it a sense of identity, has always been appealing. The yellow-and-brown sunflower carved into the stone signals the home's bird-friendliness and love of the sun. The front door was painted a welcoming yellow to match the stone sunflower.

7. Water-saving upgrades.

a. The first time I laid eyes on *dual-flush commodes* was back in 2004 during a "Simple Living" production trip to Poland, Sweden and Denmark. At the time, I thought this water-saving winner — which allows users to choose the appropriate water load depending on whether the waste is liquid or solid — would easily translate to our country. But except for the one in Ed Begley Jr.'s Studio City home, I never saw any others in use or heard much about them in the U.S. until I ran into Glenn Sheargold at a Caroma booth at a green building show in California. I promptly installed two Caravelles — the one-piece, easy-height model — in the Sunflower House. My Caravelles average one gallon per flush, a no-brainer in the Southeast with our droughts. Each flush packs a powerful punch, and the industry-leading three and one-half inch waste trap is said to be virtually impossible to clog. I can attest to it; neither of mine has clogged yet.

   b. All *faucets and shower heads* in my home were upgraded to high-performance models that save water. According to David Johnston, an ideal shower head uses one to one and one-half gallons per minute — up to 60 percent less water than a traditional head. These fixtures will pay for themselves in water and energy savings within a matter of months.

   8. Connect with nature.
One of the reasons I decided to leave my condominium at Renfro Lofts and move into a house with a yard was my own personal "nature deficit" — simply put, I was missing the outdoors. I was longing to garden and spend more time outside. I wanted to grow tomatoes, zucchini and peppers, and yes, sunflowers, and enjoy a greater connection to nature. When David Johnston assessed my new house, he suggested removing one of the railings on my deck in order to improve access to the garden. He also pointed out a major inadequacy on the short stairway running from my deck to the concrete sidewalk skirting the backside of my house; it was not built to code. We made those improvements along with several others, and as a result, more time is spent outside. (See Chapter 5 for more about the garden.)

Think "Paid-for"

   By now, you've heard my case for smaller housing choices, and I've laid out environmentally friendly options for you that can help reduce the consumption of valuable resources in your home. Now we're going to explore another vital dimension to achieving the simple life around your home: that is, paying it off. My CPA friend, Hattie Brintle, puts it this way, "Until you pay off your home, it doesn't really belong to you."

It's simple stuff, but the truth is you'll rest more easily when the title to the home is in your safe-deposit bank, not held by the bank or mortgage company. I know because I've lived in homes that were paid off (back in my days at the orchard, and later, at my condo in town) and ones that weren't. (I still hold a substantial mortgage on the Sunflower House. And I'm here to tell you that you don't rest as well at night, owing significant sums on your home.) Yes, I know what I'm asking involves fiscal discipline, but I want you to make paying off your home a major financial priority.

So, yes, I'm going to be a hard-nose about this: If you come into a windfall, like an inheritance or you hit the proverbial jackpot, *pay off your house*. Another way to go is to try paying it off as quickly as you can, incrementally. For instance, if you get a pay raise, continue to live on your original income and earmark the extra money directly for mortgage retirement. If you get a tax refund, instead of buying a flat screen TV, pay down your mortgage. Make a goal of paying off your home as soon as you can, but most especially before you retire. (Please note that before you put everything against paying off your home, it's wise to have at least six months of liquid assets available in case an emergency, such as illness, job loss or some other emergency arises.)

Depending on the rate of interest of your home loan, making just one extra mortgage payment a year could reduce the life of your loan by a number of years. For example, according to calculations in The Washington Post, if you have a $118,500 loan at seven percent, with monthly payments of $788, just one extra payment of $788 annually reduces your 30-year loan term to 24 years. That's *six years of mortgage-free living* for biting the bullet and making one more payment each year. Cutting back today will help you breathe easier tomorrow.

So *do* sweat the small stuff. Remember how I preached frugality in Chapter 1? Instead of buying that new vacuum cleaner, repair the one you have. Instead of springing for that riding lawn mower, make do with your push model another season. And another. Put your so-called "discretionary spending" money on something really important: your home mortgage. Read on to see how just this choice made a difference in the life of my friend, Hattie Brintle.

Hattie Speaks: Mortgage Retirement or Tax Deduction?

"In my practice as a certified public accountant, I've heard this more times than I can count: *"I can't pay off my house; I need the tax deduction."* My response: The tax savings on mortgage interest expense is just a small percentage of what you actually pay in interest. Clients tend to forget that their money is, well … *their money.* Regardless of whether you pay it to the bank in the form of mortgage interest, or if they pay it to the IRS as income tax, it's the same pool of money: yours!

Here's how it works: I'll use my tax return as an example. I had a $307 mortgage interest deduction on my 2008 income tax return. My partner Luke and I paid off our house on July 1, 2008, after 48 payments. We originally bought our house on May 4, 2004; our first payment was due July 1, 2004. And, even with a 48-month payoff, we paid $14,480.93 (aarrrggghhh) in interest on the $96,800 we borrowed. Remember, we paid 20 percent down when we purchased the house and had a 15-year mortgage at 5.25 percent interest. Our interest expense for 2008 would have been $4,100.73 if we had paid no more than our regular monthly payments. Remarkably, this may not seem like that much given that some pay two and three times that much home mortgage interest. I have seen tax returns with 10 times that amount.

If I had deducted $4,100.73 in mortgage interest on my 2008 tax return, my taxes (both federal and state) would have been reduced by $1,221. Let me help you with the math. I would have paid $3,793.73 more in interest to have saved $1,221 on my taxes. This results in a net cash *outflow* from *my pool* of money in the amount of $2,572.73.

People try to fool themselves into believing that debt is good, especially mortgage debt. It actually is the only debt that isn't classified as "bad" because you have the ability to deduct it on your income tax return but, that isn't a reason *not* to pay if off as quickly as you possibly can.

If you can pay more per month on your mortgage and you are not because your "reasoning" is "for the tax deduction," you are fooling yourself. And, remember, you do not own your house until it is paid for. I know that not everyone has the financial ability (even if they have the desire and or stamina) to pay off their home as quickly as we did. However, before you spend on all of the "wants" of life … a vacation home, boat, costly vacations, designer clothing, and so on, develop a plan to get your mortgage paid as quickly as feasibly possible. Develop the plan and stick to it. Numerous financial calculators are available online to help in developing a plan of action.

FYI: If we had paid our normal monthly payment on our mortgage, after 15 years, we would have paid $43,268.80 in interest. Had we opted for a lower monthly payment and asked for a 30-year mortgage, our payment would have been $534.53 per month and after 30 years we would have paid $95,630.80 in interest on our $96,800 loan!

Just for fun, I calculated what we would owe today if we had paid our regular monthly payment on our 15-year loan. Today we would still owe $72,986.03! Whew, it makes it all worthwhile!

I have other clients say: *"I shouldn't pay off my house, especially since I have a low interest rate. I plan to make the regular monthly payment and invest the rest."* Oh yeah, I can see where that would have gotten me today. Even in a nice safe CD, I would not have saved anywhere close to the mortgage interest expense we would have paid. And, if we had invested it in the stock market well … it might be worth 60 percent of our original investment, that is … if we were lucky! Instead, our home is paid off. Now I can turn my attention to drawing up plans for future home projects, such as the screen porch we plan to add once we've saved enough money to pay for it in advance."

— *Hattie Brintle, CPA, Mount Airy, North Carolina*

If you're inspired to follow Hattie and Luke's example in aggressively paying off your home, good for you! If you can't swing something as dramatic as a four-year repayment plan, then try sending off an extra full mortgage payment each year, and cut your mortgage down extensively. But if this is too much to handle, even slipping an extra $50 or $100 against your principle payment each month will be doing yourself a huge favor in the long run.

Smart Mortgage Financing and Refinancing

While the recent economic downturn has certainly slowed the increase in home ownership in America, no one is suggesting that investing in your own home is not a wise investment for many, even most, of us. However, when you do buy, shop smart. Many prospective homeowners spend months (sometimes years) shopping for a new home, yet devote almost no time to researching mortgages. Considering the amount of money involved for the biggest purchase of your lifetime — most Americans spend at least a third of their income on housing — you should spend a commensurate amount of time learning about your mortgage. It's important to understand how to save money on a mortgage, whether you're buying a new home or refinancing your existing home. The first thing you need to do to avoid being overcharged is to educate yourself on the terminology and process.

New Purchase Tips

Educate Yourself

• Buy a book that explains the home-buying and mortgage process, such as "Homeownership for Dummies." Or go online to learn the terms, choices in mortgages, and the factors used to determine mortgage terms for borrowers. Following are some reputable Web sites:

1. Www.mtgprofessor.com
2. Www.freddiemac.com/corporate/buying_and_owning.html
3. Www.hud.gov/buying
4. Www.finance.yahoo.com/how-to-guide/real-estate/12819

• Obtain a credit report for yourself and any other borrowers. Examine the report(s) in detail, making sure that there are no errors. Pay to find out the credit (FICO) score for all borrowers, since this will greatly affect the terms of a mortgage you can get. Your credit report(s) and FICO scores can be obtained from *www.myfico.com/Default.aspx* as well as through the credit reporting agencies, Experian, Equifax and Transunion.

• Decide how much you are able to put down for your mortgage. Most consumers need to be able to put between five to 20 percent down out of savings since "nothing-down" loans have become very difficult to obtain. It is advisable to put down more rather than less. Twenty percent is a good sum.

Do Your Calculations

• Determine approximately how much you can pay on a monthly basis. Make sure you are including taxes and insurance in your calculation. Include about a five to 10 percent allowance for home maintenance and furnishings per year. (A study of federal statistics recently published by the National Association of Home Builders shows that buyers of new detached houses spend an average of $4,900 during the first year in their home for such items as appliances, window treatments and furnishings.)

• Look in the newspaper or online at *www.freddiemac.com* for what the typical rates are for a home mortgage. A 30-year fixed rate loan — called a "vanilla or conventional loan" — is generally the best and most economical choice for most borrowers.

• Using a calculator at one of the Web sites, determine the total amount of a mortgage you can afford. For example, if you can afford to pay $2,000 per month for a 30-year fixed rate mortgage using a typical rate, the calculator can tell you how much you can borrow. Aim to be conservative in your estimation. What if you or your spouse loses a job, one of you dies, or you are divorced? Be sure to build in a cushion, and try not to max out this figure.

• Taking into consideration your down payment and the amount you can comfortably borrow, determine the price range of homes you want to visit. If you visit homes before performing these steps, you may be tempted to fall in love with homes that you simply can't afford.

• Next, check with three to five local banks and/or credit unions to see what their rates and fees are. Include both nationally based as well as community banks. (Note: They may not be able to give you final specifics until you actually have located a property to buy, but they should be able to give you information about rates and fees.)

• Note that you may go to a mortgage broker to check for rates; however, be aware that the broker will be getting the loan funds from a bank, so this will add another layer of compensation to your product. However, using a mortgage broker may be appropriate if you have unusual circumstances, as such brokers generally work with multiple lenders.

• Make sure you are comparing apples to apples, so ask for a 30-year fixed conventional loan and get the annual percentage rate (APR) and typical fees charged for the size of loan you are considering. Tell them the credit scores of all borrowers. Ask for a Good Faith Estimate from each bank and compare them.

• Get pre-qualified from one or more of the banks that you checked with. See if the bank agrees with your previous calculation on how much you can afford. If they state that they can loan you more than you are comfortable borrowing, stick with the lower figure.

Finally, Shop for a Home and a Mortgage

• With the price range in hand, shop for homes in your price range.

• When writing up a contract for purchase, bring your pre-approval letter with you, as it will make you a more desirable buyer.

• When you've chosen the home you would like to buy, go back to the banks whom you contacted originally. Carefully compare rates and fees among them.

• Tell all banks that although you understand that they will charge for their services, you do not want to pay junk fees. Examples of junk fees are those that are not third-party fees, such as documentation, underwriting and any other sort of miscellaneous fee. Third-party fees such as for the appraisal, title insurance, and credit report are normally required, so can't be negotiated.

• Negotiate with the banks, for example, asking one to match the fees and rates offered by another. Choose the bank that has the lowest rates and fees.

• If the bank you've chosen materially changes the fees charged on the Good Faith Estimate at closing, object to the change. They may back down if you are confident enough.

Refinance Tips

1. If it's been years since you purchased your home, you may want to review the "Educate Yourself" tips on pages 118 to 119.

2. Calculate similarly as shown on pages 119 to 120, reducing your needs by any equity you have in the home.

3. Determine how long it will take to recoup the amount that you are spending on the refinance. If it's longer than you plan to stay in the home, refinancing is not a good idea.

4. If you have paid down the mortgage so that you owe — for example — for 25 more years (from the original 30), even if your monthly payments will be lower after the refinance, it may not be worth it to extend out the loan back to 30 years.

5. Check to see if you would be able to manage the monthly payment for a shorter-term mortgage, since rates for 15-year fixed rate loans are lower than for 30-year fixed rate loans, saving you thousands of dollars over the life of the loan.

6. When purchasing title insurance, check to see if you can obtain a renewal policy, which is normally cheaper.

7. Similar to following the steps above, tell the bank that you do not want to pay junk fees. Choose the bank that has the lowest rates and fees. Ask for a Good Faith Estimate from each bank and compare them.

8. If the bank you've chosen materially changes the fees charged on the Good Faith Estimate at closing, object to the change. Since you are doing a refinance, you have more power than for a first-purchase loan, since you can walk away from the deal more easily.

9. If the rates aren't low enough to make it worthwhile to refinance at this time, continue checking rates, since they can change daily.

Make smart financial choices around purchasing your home. Refinance your home if you're committed to it for the long-haul and if it makes sense for you. Depending on your situation, make paying off your home a No. 1 financial goal. When you do pay it off, make a celebration of it, complete with a party and a cake that looks like your house. It's a major milestone, like graduating from college or getting married, or having your first child. Savor the moment.

Moving to a Small Town

One way to afford a home of your own — that might be out of reach in a major metropolitan area — is to consider moving to a small town where housing prices tend to be cheaper — significantly cheaper. When I co-wrote the book, "Moving to a Small Town: A Guidebook for Moving from Urban to Rural America," published by Simon & Schuster back in 1996, I interviewed dozens of Americans who sought out the good life — including a slower pace, greater community involvement and a lower cost of living — in small town America. Bear in mind that there are 35,320 small towns from which to choose.

If you decide you are a good candidate for a small town, this is an option for you to consider. But before moving, you need to determine if you're right for small-town life. For example, ask yourself whether community or anonymity is more important to you. If anonymity wins out, you may prefer city life. Once you've identified a town, pay an extended visit there and do some research into the town's health-care system and educational and recreational options; you'll also want to determine how many businesses are locally owned as opposed to chain stores. (The more local businesses, the better.)

If you chose the right town for you, real estate can be a real bargain. Who knows? You might even be able to sell your own home in the city and buy a less expensive place in a small town outright — with no mortgage at all!

Reclaim the Good Life With Housing

As a child I looked to large, impressive homes for security, stability and status. As a girl, having a house with a swimming pool was my image of having arrived in the world. No longer would I want one. A pool of one's own is a metaphor for the high life to which Americans have grown accustomed in our homes. Media rooms. Large screen TVs. Spa baths. Saunas. Untold automated luxuries and conveniences. Bathrooms and closets the size of bedrooms of the past; storage spaces large enough to hold a general store from yesteryear. The list goes on. But for each of those "extras" there's a price to be paid. In energy costs. In maintenance. In upkeep. In insurance. In life energy — the blood, sweat and tears it takes to pay for these goodies, not to mention the environmental cost.

Reclaim the good life with your housing. *Think small; think green; think paid-for.* Think about what you really need in your living space. These concepts will provide you with the basis for the security and peace of mind for which we all yearn. At the end of the day, I've come to see that serenity and stability come through having a home that is just enough — no more — and provides a healthful environment for you, your family, and the planet. As for status, remember your sense of worth comes not from your home, but from within. Once you get your home right, it will become your cottage of nurture, your nest from which your soul can take flight.

Chapter Four

Reclaim Homemaking

*Streamline, personalize and authenticate
your decorating choices; adopt non-toxic
cleaning methods; and simplify your wardrobe.*

Bring yourself — and your family members — "into your home" by personalizing your decorating choices. Make lifetime commitments to your furniture and fixtures, which will encourage you to buy quality and buy consciously. Incorporate systems into your home and regimen to reduce your personal waste stream. Adopt non-toxic cleaning methods to create a healthful environment and save money. The path to freedom with your apparel involves reducing the size of your wardrobe, taking care of the items you do own, and making thoughtful choices when purchasing.

My Abode, Myself

Forget the therapist. To get a true read of someone's emotional state, all you need do is walk into her home and take a look. On some fundamental level, your home is a reflection of your state of mind. If you can spot dust bunnies lurking, catch a whiff of the cat's litter box in dire need of attention, if the dishes have piled up in the sink and towels are strewn carelessly around the laundry room, more than likely, the home's resident is not at her best.

Conversely, when you're feeling balanced and whole, your home reflects that positive energy. I know it's true for me. When I take time to clean up promptly after each meal, make my bed every morning, and hang my clothes neatly, I feel happy at home. When I make subtle changes to the décor to reflect the changing seasons, such as scattering bud vases throughout the house with wildflowers in the spring and summer, or making displays of pumpkins, gourds and dried grasses in October, it shows I'm truly present in time and space. The order and condition of my home seems to invite the world in.

> *"The entire process of creating and inhabiting a place is as important to our well-being as the place itself."*
> — Carol Venolia, Healing Environments

A major thoroughfare to the good life at home involves reclaiming the domestic arts. Of course, cooking and at-home meal preparation rank near the top of any list of domestic arts (and I will address those in Chapter 5). But other significant domestic arts that have fallen by the wayside in our time-pressed, 24-7 world include interior decoration, cleaning skills, and wardrobe maintenance.

With regard to interior décor, putting your singular stamp on your home requires a fair measure of self-knowledge and often soul-searching. But the first step is to streamline your current holdings. For the vast majority of us, this streamlining takes the form of de-cluttering. Once that occurs, you have set the stage for transforming your home into a lovely, nurturing abode. When it comes to cleaning, in order to create a truly healthful home — with superior indoor air quality, absent of noxious inputs — you'll need to cut your dependence on toxic, store-bought cleaning products and re-learn the art of whipping up our own concoctions (or else identify quality commercial organic cleaning products).

As for wardrobe, isn't it obvious that the vast majority of us simply have too many items to thoughtfully possess? In this chapter, I'll present a plan to help transform what you have into something manageable — a wardrobe with distinction, personality and limits.

Your Décor: An Extension of You

Anytime I visit a home that I love, I always mentally move myself right in. I imagine how I'd rearrange the furniture, which pictures I'd reposition or replace, what colors I'd paint the walls, the geraniums I would put out in a window box, how I'd make the place mine.

What's striking these days is that not many houses I visit inspire these fantasies. So many homes totally lack character, distinctiveness — anything that reflects the owner's unique personality. It's not that they're not furnished or finished handsomely, they often contain expensive things. But when I visit such places, they seem soulless, as if no specific person lives there. Rather than peeking into someone's inner life when I visit, these places give the feeling of walking into the pages of a shelter magazine.

To take center stage in your own space, to let your home become an extension of you, I'm going to invite you to create your own home — your own look — using timeless pieces and personal items that will bring *you* back into the picture. The furnishings and appointments that reflect and reinforce your dreams, yearnings and passions have the potential of changing the nature of your home — and life.

But first, before you start introducing new elements into your home, if you're like most Americans, you'll need to deal with all that stuff. You need to unclog the arteries of your home to let the blood of your home flow, to provide some breathing space. Then and only then can you reclaim the good life in your home.

> *"It is only framed in space that beauty blooms. ... A tree has significance if one sees it against the empty face of sky. ... Even small and casual things take on significance if they are washed in space."*
> — Anne Morrow Lindbergh, "A Gift from the Sea"

Clear Your Clutter; Start Anew

Unless you're hard-wired as a minimalist, you've probably been on an acquisition phase for years, if not decades, now. Walk into a typical American home these days and what do you see? A family room cum entertainment center, overflowing with DVDs, video games, toys, catalogs and recreational equipment; a kitchen teaming with a cappuccino maker, margarita blender, cookbooks, grill. Check out the bedrooms, basement and garage, and you're also likely to be confronted by clutter — clothing, jewelry, tools, you name it — either in your face or bulging out from inside drawers, closets and storage compartments. In America today, we live with an unprecedented number of possessions — so many things that they're migrating from our ever-larger homes into storage units. And still we don't have enough space for it all.

To be sure, keeping up with clutter is an overwhelming, never-ending undertaking; all that stuff is taking a toll on our psyches, standing between us and peace of mind. "There's a strong connection between physical clutter and mental clutter," says Cindy Glovinsky, a psychotherapist and author of "Making Peace with the Things in Your Life" (St. Martin's: 2002). "For most people, the more clutter you have, the less energy you have, the less focus you have. The clutter on the outside makes you feel more mentally disorganized."

How can something as inert as clutter have such power over our mental state? The way it works is this: The moment you walk into a room, the contents of that space start to interact with you. It's all subconscious; your eyes scan the room. When you see things in your space, they reflect back at you. Your eyes pick up on the stack of travel brochures on the shelf in the corner for the trip never taken; the parts for that toy that your child received but you've not found the time to assemble. They will take in that defective toaster-oven in the box that needs to be returned, but it's been — how many months already?

"Your things are saying things to you," says Menomonie, Wisconsin-based de-cluttering consultant Andrea Gerasimo. "You have to ask yourself: 'Do you like what they're saying?' " For the vast majority of people who live in a cluttered place, messages sent evoke what Gerasimo calls "a whole host of negative feelings." These feelings range from self-judgment, defeat, and failure for being perpetually behind or for being unable to engage those with whom they live on a de-cluttering regimen.

The choice is yours. You can live with the status quo, or you can assess the "cost" of your clutter — namely, the degree to which it's bogging you down, mentally, spiritually and emotionally. Until you realize what it's costing you, you may not be able to do the hard work of slogging through and letting go. Gerasimo says that one way to get her clients motivated into action is by challenging them to identify some higher purpose — or meaningful goal — which de-cluttering can help them reach. What do you want to see in your life that is currently absent: Achievement? Spontaneity? Joy?

There are several methods for de-cluttering: the *major attack mode* that involves full-day or full-weekend sessions, or the *gradual, chipping-away-at-it process*. As a paid professional, Gerasimo works with clients for six hours in a concerted, distraction-free marathon ("I ask that we turn off phones and have our lunch be pre-made," she says). Working together with a client, they tackle one area at a time. You can hire a professional, too, or do it on the cheap, by arranging a de-cluttering barter with a buddy (one Saturday session at her place, another at yours). Another option is to do it yourself by committing to short, daily or weekly de-cluttering sessions. As little as 10 to 15 minutes a day — or an hour a week — will add up over time.

Eight De-Cluttering Avenues

1. Superhouse Sweep. Does anyone remember that old 1960s show, "Supermarket Sweep?" It's the one where contestants ran through the grocery store with a timer going, grabbing groceries from the shelves and tossing them into their carts. The winners were the ones who correctly guessed the prices of items and grabbed the greatest dollar amount. Try setting up a *Superhouse Sweep* in your home — a fast-action game where you give yourself a fixed amount of time to rush through your home and deep six everything that doesn't need to be there. Do it in rounds. For round No. 1, take a trash bag and throw in things that should be tossed. Set the timer for five minutes. Then do the same for donations. Ditto for consignment items. Don't deliberate over anything; just toss and dash. (Don't forget; the camera's not rolling; if you have second thoughts, you can always retrieve an item later.) At the end of your time, you've likely accomplished a lot.

2. Baby-step approach. If you're not the "Supermarket Sweep" type, try the baby-step method. Go through your house and jot down a list of your de-cluttering goals. For instance, write down: de-clutter basement tools and paints; kitchen drawers; holiday decorations; baby clothes. Include everything that needs attention. Then tackle them, one at a time. Once again, use three containers: trash, donation and consignment. Once you complete a project, pat yourself on the back. Each session should lend you energy for the next. Remember, baby steps add up to miles; it just takes a little longer.

3. Assign a home for like items. We've all heard the expression, "A place for everything and everything in its place." One reason so much clutter accumulates is that we either haven't assigned a home for that item, or haven't taken the time to put it where it belongs. The cardinal rule of efficient storage is to put things near where they're used. For instance, when I made the changeover from paper to cloth napkins some years ago, I designated the

(continued)

top two drawers of a chest of drawers in my dining area for their home. (The lower drawers are filled with tablecloths and cloth place mats.) As a result of this assignment, there is never a clutter problem with the napkins, and I never have trouble locating them. As soon as they're washed, they're folded and put away. The same goes for hats. I'm a hat nut, so my hat rack was wall-mounted in the sunroom near where I exit the house each day. When I return, the hat goes right back up on the wall.

4. *Streamline your foyer.* When you walk into your home, encountering an entry that is welcoming, uncluttered and open to the widest part of the room sets the stage for future harmony, happiness and prosperity. According to *feng shui* theory, a resident or visitor's first impression of a home is crucial for the quality of life inside the house. If space permits, position an entry table on which you place a plant, bouquet of flowers, or lovely piece of art. A mirror may increase the flow of energy. If space allows, position a bench or coat rack in which to stow shoes, boots, umbrellas, and whatever accessories may march into the front door.

5. *Make a binder for your instruction manuals and warranties.* As soon as you purchase an appliance, piece of furniture, or any major item, tuck the receipt in an envelope and staple it to the front cover of the manual, then pair it with the warranty in this special binder. When your refrigerator conks out, you can go straight to the instruction manual, diagnose the problem, and quickly determine if the warranty is in force.

6. *Container de-cluttering.* Capture unharvested space under your bed and other nooks and crannies by storing out-of-season blankets and sheets in opaque plastic boxes. For items sensitive to moisture, such as heirloom photographs or memorabilia for scrapbooking, select airtight boxes. Use opaque plastic boxes to store Christmas wrap and decorations, seasonal clothing, stuffed animal collections — the works. If you plan to stow boxes on the floor, you can opt for big and bulky ones; for things that you plan to place on a high shelf, select boxes that are more compact in size.

7. *Watch what you bring in.* Once you've de-cluttered your home, your next challenge will be keeping future clutter at bay. You'll need to promise yourself you won't let this happen again. Become a conscious consumer by casting a critical eye on every potential new purchase or item you might bring into your home. Be vigilant about yard sale finds and freebies because

they are still stuff and accumulate. Ask yourself if you really need something and if you have a place to keep it. If you do buy a new iron, and the old one's still working, donate it to charity.

8. *Slow down.* A key to de-cluttering is slowing down. The root cause of most clutter is lack of time. When people get rushed, they stop putting things away because they're attempting to save little bits of time. Lack of time drives them to buy extra stuff. For instance, they may go out and buy another Phillips-head screwdriver because they don't know where the one they own is and don't want to take the time to look for it. You may save a few seconds by not filing your bill stub in your paid bills folder. But then you may spend 20 minutes three weeks later trying to retrieve that same piece of paper.

Home-Office Clutter Cutters

Clutter central for me has always been my home office. I rarely meet a book, magazine or news clip that I don't see value in keeping — often for years. The same holds true for old files, letters, stationery, envelopes — even old mailing pouches. They can be reused, after all. Personal papers — such as bills, medical reports, Henry's school work and camp applications — enter into the mix, as well. Since moving into the Sunflower House in 2007, I've worked hard to keep my office space well-organized. I've made tremendous progress here by simply being more hard-nosed about recycling papers I'm not likely to use again and filing the rest.

A winning organizational idea I recently adopted was assigning an old Smead® accordion file folder to greeting cards. (I like to buy cards in advance, on sale, and at yard sales and thrift shops.) As a result, I now have an eclectic selection of cards (including some golden oldies!) divided into such categories as: birthday, get-well, congratulations, graduation, anniversary and sympathy. Another file folder slot holds myriad miscellaneous ones, including Easter, Thanksgiving, Halloween, Happy Retirement cards and the like. I keep stamps in assorted denominations on the top shelf of my left-hand office drawer. I'm well-supplied with one-cent, two-cent, and three-cent varieties, as my usual stash is invariably out of date and needs boosting. I enjoy matching stamps to the message in the missive. Butterfly stamps go to Aunt Ruth whose late daughter loved butterflies; pollinating bees to my friend, Mary Woltz, who keeps bees on Long Island. Having cards and stamps at hand helps me stay on top of birthdays and unplanned celebrations.

When I'm engaged in a major project, such as writing this book, it can be easy to lose sight of the importance of staying organized. (The excuse is: I'm too busy to file that document. I'll set it aside for later. The reality is: *When you're busy, you need to be more organized than at any other time.*) Before I started work on this chapter, I played organizational catch up in my office space — removing all the file folders that lay spread beneath my wormy chestnut mantel. I sorted and discarded several inches worth of clippings. Now that everything is tucked away in a proper file, the energy in the room has mysteriously — even mystically — improved. The words seem to be springing off my fingertips. Even business decisions — unrelated to my book project — have been easier to make.

Following are some ideas that can help you cut the clutter in your office:

• *Try staunching the flow of papers by separating them when they first come into your hands.* Immediately chuck throwaways into a recycling box (I keep mine on the floor adjacent to my desk); separate non-urgent items from those needing immediate attention and place in appropriate stacks.

• Often people can't find the right file because they can't read the words on the folder. *Use colored file folders to sort your papers; mark the tabs in black felt-tip pen with a few key words, such as Bills — House Repair.* I always keep my hot files on a graduated organizer in plain sight so I don't even have to open a file drawer.

• Hattie Brintle, my certified public accountant, makes a point to *remove all files from her office once they become inactive.* "If there's nothing to be done with them, they must be out of the office," she says. "Otherwise they cloud the horizon."

• *Cover your desktop with glass.* I am able to stash important phone numbers, business cards and a calendar under a glass top. Fun family photos and Henry's baby pictures are included. This layer of protection lets you place a hot coffee mug or sweating iced beverage on your desk and not mar the wood.

• *Clean off your desktop every night* when you shut down the office. Because your office is at home, resist the temptation to work day and night. Set "office hours" for yourself and stick with them.

Bedroom Bliss

Home offices are clutter magnets, but so too are our bedrooms. People often tuck their "homeless" possessions out of sight in a bedroom because it's not a "public" room. While one's bedroom often ranks low on the list of home-improvement wish-lists — below the more conspicuous rooms where you host family and friends — the reality is, putting your bedroom in order may well be the smartest investment of time and money you can make. Andrea Gerasimo calls your bedroom your sanctuary. "Studies show that what you're thinking when you nod off affects the quality of your sleep as well as your mood when you wake up." And if your last mental image is of chaos and clutter, that's not setting the right stage for restorative, quality sleep.

To create an atmosphere of bedroom bliss, you need to start by pulling everything out and creating a clean slate. Certainly the piles of unfolded clothing, boxes, shoes and assorted chotchkes will have to go, along with the stacks of DVDs. The good news is that you don't *have* to remodel to make a huge impact on streamlining and transforming your bedroom. You can do a lot by taking simple steps, such as rearranging furniture (even better, *removing* a few major items), de-cluttering, and adopting a resolute mind-set that will keep your space harmonious and clutter-free in the future.

Following are action steps to help transform your bedroom from cluttered chaos into a serene retreat.

1. Remove Furniture

• *Trouble spot*: One of the most common problems in bedrooms is too much furniture. Too many dressers, tables and chairs jammed into a space — no matter how large — make it feel smaller. And stuff invites more stuff. As we add more pieces, we tend to fill them, inside and out.

• *Solution*: Invite a friend with a fresh set of eyes over for a Saturday streamlining session and move everything out. Look at the room empty and open your mind to new arrangements. If you're top-heavy with furniture, think about what you can let go of, use elsewhere in your home, sell or donate. Candidates for the chopping block may include exercise equipment, a recliner, even your television. Family manager coach Beth Dargis of Holland, Michigan, recommends replacing the long low dresser with a highboy which will hold roughly the same amount of articles but with a smaller footprint. (If you don't want to buy one, try arranging a swap.)

When all your things are out of the room, consider spiffing up your walls with a fresh coat of paint, using the no- or low-VOC variety to minimize off-gassing. If you want to change your window treatments (adding organic hemp, bamboo or cotton fabric), this is an ideal time. At the very least, give your bedroom a good, thorough cleaning before moving your furniture back in.

2. Streamline Your Bedding

• *Trouble spot*: Sometimes the bed itself — including the attendant bedding and show pillows — can create visual clutter, even a bottleneck in your boudoir.

• *Solution:* Now you may be attached to your king-size bed, but have you ever missed the coziness of a smaller bed? Bed size — just like everything else in America these days — has ballooned. But just because everyone else is buying king and queen beds, doesn't mean you have to. I, for one, am content with my old-fashioned, four-poster double bed that I've had since high school. So when you're shopping for your next bed, why not scale back and opt for a smaller model. As America moves back into smaller homes, smaller furniture fits better.

While you're at it, consider streamlining your bedding. Instead of feathering your nest with colored, matched bedding sets, why not go for basic whites? If you spill red wine on your birds-in-flight pillowcases — or if your zebra-print bottom sheet fades more quickly than the flat upper — you may feel you'll have to discard the entire set to achieve harmony. But if you go with white, these pieces are interchangeable; you can simply make up any loss with a generic replacement. You also can pick up spare white linens at thrift shops and consignment stores. Using all-white bedding simplifies your life and always looks right. If possible, purchase linens made with organic fabric.

Instead of piling on the pillows, why not pare down to just two? It makes for a Zen-like bed and you don't have to juggle all the extra show pillows when you get into bed at night.

3. No Place for Your (Home) Office

• *Trouble spot:* Your home office is in your bedroom, allowing you no mental escape from the busy-ness of the world where you do business, pay bills, haggle and hassle.

• *Solution:* If you're one of the many people who has put your home office in your bedroom, try your hardest to issue an eviction notice. *Any* place in the house is better than your bedroom — including the kitchen, dining room or guest room. Even the basement.

A friend of mine in Los Angeles was able to convert a garden shed into a home office, giving her physical separation from her house and a designated space to do her work as a freelance writer. Another enterprising Los Angeles friend (also a writer) managed to barter five hours a month of her writing/PR services in exchange for free space in a lawyers' office. They even threw in use of their copier!

If, however, you see no other solution than putting your office in the bedroom, choose a place where you can shut the doors at night, such as a closet or computer armoire. Being able to physically close off your home office will help promote peace of mind and better sleep, which, in turn, will make you more productive with your work.

4. Daily Rituals

• *Trouble spot:* Jumping out of bed at the last minute can throw your morning routine out of whack.

• *Solution:* Establish daily rituals in your bedroom (and the rest of your house, as well). Follow them religiously and you're sure to improve your bedroom's serenity quotient. Following are three of my daily rituals:

a. *Open your draperies or blinds to let the sun shine in.* This will connect you with nature and the greater world outside. I always love the moment of pulling up my shades and seeing what the world has to offer.

b. *Make your bed every day.* I do it before I get dressed or start on my juice, vitamins and coffee routine.

c. When you come home at the end of each day, avoid the temptation of tossing clothes on a chair; *immediately hang your clothes* in the closet or place directly into the laundry basket.

My Singular Retreat

When I went to work remodeling my 1956 brick rancher in Mount Airy, North Carolina, my fantasies revolved around creating a guest-friendly chef's kitchen and a soothing bathroom retreat. But, soon after the job was complete, it dawned on me that the change that has had the greatest impact on my quality of life was the transformation of my bedroom.

Measuring 12 feet by 11 feet, the size is just right: neither too large nor too small, but ideal for one. My idea was to streamline and beautify, to focus the space on nurturing my inner spirit, while de-emphasizing externals like personal appearance. As host and producer of the nationally syndicated public television series, "Simple Living With Wanda Urbanska," I've been forced for years to concern myself inordinately with pleasing the camera — minimizing wrinkles, matching accessories, and keeping coffee and wine stains off my teeth — not always easy for one who came of age in the 1970s. As an escape, I decided to banish all mirrors from the bedroom. No television need apply, either.

With some sage advice from my friends, a lot of elbow grease, and a few sound investments, my bedroom has become my singular retreat. We started by removing, then walling over, a dated sliding-door closet (which allowed for the expansion of my son's closet next door) and reclaiming some space for a deep built-in for stowing jewelry, scarves, and tucking a dirty clothes basket out of sight. A new, deeper closet was added on the north side of the room.

We installed energy-saving, low-e windows with screens and a ceiling fan to keep the air circulating while providing lulling white noise. The dull beige walls disappeared under a coat of soothing, sage green, low-VOC paint. The dirty wool, wall-to-wall carpet was replaced with regionally sourced oak flooring stained cherry to complement the traditional, dark case goods. Crown molding made of finger-jointed scrap wood completed the look.

We streamlined the furnishings by removing a hefty antique pie safe and creating a corner reading nook with a 1930s overstuffed chair and footstool. I added a low-slung, woven, water-hyacinth basket table at the foot of my bed and bought an antique mahogany side table with cabriole legs, which serves as the "foyer" to the bedroom. Sparingly adorned with a few books

(continued)

and framed family photographs, it's topped by a lovely original watercolor by Rosemary Lindan, the mother of my first best friend, Krysia. Clutter is banished from the room, with only a few carefully selected items on display. I topped the surfaces of my bedside table, side table and highboy with glass tops that are easy to clean and prevent surprise stains.

Magical, majestic Roman shades in beige, basket-weave hemp by Kathleen Redmond of Magnolia Lane complete the retreat effect while enhancing in-door air quality. A matching duvet cover in hemp, topped by a re-purposed, 1940s tablecloth decorated with hand-embroidered wheat sheaves, and a silk crepe bed-skirt on my not-so-big bed make it into an inviting, soporific retreat. In this appealing, healing environment, I sleep through the night and wake up rested, refreshed and ready to enter the fray.

Less is More

A critical aspect of my decorating style — indeed *any* decorating path that leads you to reclaim the good life — is simple: *less is more*. A spare, uncluttered look will do more to create a feeling of serenity and peace in your home than you can imagine. If this weren't so, why would every realtor in America recommend de-cluttering a home before putting it on the market? The fact is, clients like the streamlined look when they see a home. It is what we all wish for, but find so hard to achieve and maintain. Achieving a clutter-free home is not only aesthetically pleasing, but lifts your mood, clears your mind, and gives you the clarity to focus on what matters most in life. Once you've accomplished this, you can go about the business of establishing a look that expresses who you are.

"Home is still the place where we spend most of our time, and the environment over which we have the greatest control. Home becomes an extension of the self and a metaphor for the body."
— Carol Venolia, "Healing Environments"

Home Décor

Back in the 1990s, I encountered a book that was nothing short of life-changing. Carol Venolia's book, "Healing Environments" (Celestial Arts: 1988) examines all aspects of home-making and creation: making one's roost healthful, healing and personal. Long before green building and remodeling became the rage with its own orthodoxy and terminology, Venolia pioneered discussion about such issues as sourcing eco-friendly materials, finishes and furnishings, as well as the role of light, sound, temperature, and orientation in a home. But she also examined that intangible quality that a home can provide — being a cauldron for the integration for mind, body and spirit.

Not surprisingly, during a "Simple Living" production trip, we hauled our cameras to Northern California to interview Carol for one of our programs. Her book and that seminal interview crystallized my thinking about the ideal home environment I wished to create for myself and my son. It almost goes without saying that my ideal home is an environmentally friendly, "green" home, but just as important, it's a place embedded with personal meaning. Having surroundings that remind me (and my son) of our highest values, and reinforce our preferences and achievements, provides a continuous, positive feedback loop.

The Venerable Owl

Though I resist the idea of collections or themes — too much of anything can easily become cloying and cutesy — I must admit to a fascination with owls. With their large, fixed eyes and upright bearing, they represent wisdom, prophecy, and flight. Owls strike me as creatures that see clearly the foolishness of humanity and understand that the passage of time and the inevitability of change will have the last word. A plastic life-size owl — a casual gift from an employee at Riverside Building Supply in Mount Airy — perches prominently atop the mantel in my living room, and sets the tone for my public spaces. But I treasure most three little hand-carved owls that I picked up at a shop near the Old Town in Warsaw, Poland, during my 2006

(continued)

trip there. Hand-carved and painted with striking, searing eyes, I bought them for around six American dollars each. These iconic treasures, which sit on a table behind me in the cover shot, rest atop Henry's piano, encouraging him to keep his own counsel and to some day take flight.

Residential Transformation: Bringing "You" into Your Home

In order to create a home that moves with the seasons, that has personal resonance, that uniquely belongs to you and your family, you'll need to bring your "self" — along with the "selves" of your family members — into your home. In the Sunflower House, I have come closer than in any of my previous homes to achieving my domestic ideal. My personal stamp in home furnishing and style involves incorporating reclaimed materials, items from the past, from my own past, along with original works of art and handcrafted items.

In my case, I am deeply connected to my family, so I have ornamented my home with artifacts from my parents' past — especially those from my colorful father's life.

Let's take a look at how this plays out in my study — the place where I spend most of my waking hours. Directly above my computer monitor is a framed copy of my mother's Ph.D. diploma from the University of Kentucky dated December 21, 1973. Above that is a certificate presented to my father from the National University of Mexico in August 1941. To its left is a framed head-shot of former president Jimmy Carter, inscribed in silver ink to Henry. And below this is a photograph taken in November 2002 of Jimmy and Rosalynn Carter, my then 5-year-old son, Henry, me, and my dear friend, Linda Fuller, on the grounds of Maranatha Baptist Church in Plains, Georgia, directly after President Carter's Sunday school class.

What does the presence of these framed items on the wall mean to me? On those occasions when I'm down, touchstones of my family history and the best moments of my own professional narrative buoy my spirits.

When I see the oval, black-and-white photo of my 32-year-old father, so handsome, so young and stoical, I am reminded of his dramatic escape from Europe, where he faced death at the hands of the Nazi and Soviet occupiers in his native Poland. I am reminded of how Daddy started his life over in Mexico before moving to the States and eventually marrying my American mother. When I see him up on the wall, my own problems seem pretty small by comparison.

When I take in Mother's diploma, I recall her years of arduous work — against a background of institutional sexism and ageism — in earning her Ph.D., with her pioneering dissertation on Margaret Fuller's writing. The photograph of Jimmy Carter, taken during his presidency, brightens my day each time I see his famous smile and those searing blue eyes, which beam out "integrity" and "courage." I am reminded of President Carter's improbable journey from peanut farmer in Plains to Georgia governor to president of the United States. I flash on the privilege of interviewing him back in 2005 for our "Simple Living" television series. His mantra — "Why not the best?" — calls me to aim high. Even if I don't consciously think each of these thoughts when I look at the wall, all of them, taken collectively, are at the ready, within easy reach at all times. These objects lend strength, courage and continuity, and I know Carol Venolia would approve their placement on the wall.

"Within our home," she writes, "our environment expresses our relationship with ourselves. If we feel weak or inconsequential, we may be passive, accepting the place as it is, or leaving its creation to others; we put up with inconvenience, shut down the un-encouraged parts of ourselves, and do all the molding and adapting inside. ... Consciously and unconsciously, expressing ourselves in our environment lets us see who we are and helps us shape who we become."

I've shown you how I put myself into my home — how I'm working to shape the person I am becoming — most especially with examples from my bedroom and study. Now let me invite you to tap into your inner self by posing some questions. Take a piece of paper or notepad, and jot down answers that spring to mind.

1. Inside your home, are there objects that have been handed down from parents, family members, or key people in your life?

2. If yes, can you tell a compelling narrative about these pieces: i.e., what they're made from; their age; how they were acquired. If you went on "Antiques Roadshow," would you have a good story to tell about the piece?

3. To which color or palette are you most drawn?

4. If nature moves you, as it does me and so many others, how do you incorporate plants, flowers or images of landscapes in your home?

5. How much light do you have/would you like in your home?

6. Are you a "quiet freak" as I am? If you prefer a quiet environment, what steps are you taking/would you like to take to buffer your home from noise?

7. What passions and causes are you drawn to and which important symbols represent them?

8. Are you a collector? If so, what do you collect and do you display your collection in your home?

9. Think back to your childhood memories of home. As you reflect on images, in which places in your home were you most at peace? Where are you having the most fun? Did you love sitting in a grape arbor in the

backyard? Was there a special nook under the stairs in which you enjoyed hiding during games of hide-and-go-seek?

10. With which ethnic, racial, cultural or religious group (or groups) do you identify? Are those affiliations reflected in your home?

Exploring what Venolia calls your "inner landscape" through questions like these may spark your own ideas about creating your home of the future. As you do so, consider letting go of items that aren't "you" and incorporating objects that reflect your personal taste, identity, heritage and strivings.

The "Wabi-Sabi" Look

As we seek to reclaim the good life at home, one direction in which to look is the past, the old, the weathered, the many things we have devoted so much time, money and energy to creating. I have always been more drawn to older objects than newer ones. This orientation stands me diametrically opposed to the cult of perfection that has defined so many American interiors for years. Every atom in me rebels against the idea of throwing out a perfectly decent piece of furniture, for example, due to a few cracks or frays, or a slight stain on the upholstery. When you add environmental imperatives along with economic ones into the equation, it's clear that the concept of "wabi sabi" design has come of age. For the uninitiated, what exactly is it?

My friend, colleague and editor-in-chief of Natural Home magazine, Robyn Griggs Lawrence — the woman who offered superb interior design recommendations for the green remodel of the Sunflower House — is a leading proponent of "wabi sabi" décor.

Wabi sabi is the ancient Japanese philosophy of finding beauty in imperfection, austerity, and the natural cycle of growth, decay, and death.

"It's simple, slow and uncluttered — and it reveres authenticity above all," writes Lawrence in "The Wabi-Sabi House" (Clarkson Potter: 2004). "Wabi-sabi is flea markets, not warehouse stores; aged wood, not Pergo; rice paper, not glass. It celebrates cracks and crevices and all the other marks that time, weather and loving use leave behind. It reminds us that we are all but transient beings on this planet — that our bodies as well as the material world around us are in the process of returning to the dust from which we came."

The wabi-sabi decorating style encourages us to admire the beauty in what is at hand. It recoils from furnishing a home with matched sets, giving a place the "Rooms to Go" look, in which every piece is perfectly coordinated with everything else. I'll always remember the gracious welcome the orchard community gave me and my ex-husband when baby Henry arrived on the scene. An outpouring of baby gifts along with the leading question: What theme had I chosen for his nursery? A Disney character? Spiderman? Winnie the Pooh? I tried to answer as graciously as I could that I wasn't choosing a theme. I had painted his small room yellow, outfitted it with a borrowed crib, and hung cream muslin curtains with blue ribbon trim on his single south-facing window. In all its simplicity, that was Henry's first room.

So what's the takeaway wisdom here? Instead of buying things new, give a fresh look at the things you have, including stuff tucked away in your attic or basement. You can do a lot by artfully rearranging your furniture, or updating it with fresh paint and fabric. You also can go treasure hunting in your grandmother's basement, at your sister's yard sale, or at auctions and flea markets. Look for used items that are inherently imperfect, marked, scratched, and worn with age. Consider handmade items. Then give your creativity a chance to bloom.

"Things That Refuse to Die"

Before I met Robyn and learned about "wabi-sabi" (which remarkably describes my own personal decorating proclivities), I had coined my own term for older items still in use. I called them "Things That Refused to Die" and created a recurring segment for the "Simple Living" television series. "Things That Refuse to Die" are items that people have taken care of past the date of planned obsolescence. So, for instance, on one segment, we featured Pat Woltz's woolen, skirt-and-sweater outfit from 1960 that she still wears (it still *fits!*); in another, a 1923 cash register still in use at the Palace Barber Shop in Mount Airy; in yet another show, we showed a 1960s Electrolux® vacuum cleaner in working order in New Orleans. You get the picture. Not surprisingly, this was my favorite recurring segment in the series as well as many viewers'.

My own house is full of such "Things." Probably my most memorable Thing is my father's Danish modern chair from around 1960, which I had refinished and for which new cushions were made. I also have a 1930s Jenny Lind spool bed of Mother's from the 1930s, bought new for her as a girl with some inheritance money my grandmother had received. This twin bed — its twisted spools lacking finish in many spots — resides in my guest room.

> *"When life is too easy for us, we must beware or we may not be ready to meet the blows which sooner or later come to everyone, rich or poor."*
> — *Eleanor Roosevelt*

Age Is the Thing

But aside from the aesthetic pluses of older things, the vast majority of older pieces have it all over most of their newer counterparts from a healthy-home, indoor-air quality perspective; many were constructed more sturdily, made of solid materials, as well. Unless it's extremely high-end stuff — custom-crafted pieces made of solid woods with all-natural, non-toxic finishes and sealants — most new furniture contains questionable materials that can pose dangers to your indoor air quality and, by extension, your health. Much mass-market furniture is made of plywood or pressed wood with urea-formaldehyde resins holding together layers of pressed wood and plywood. Formaldehyde is a known carcinogen which off-gases for a number of years after installation. From a healthy-home perspective, if you're lucky enough to have, say, outdated, solid wood kitchen cabinets in your kitchen, it's far better to update them by stripping, refinishing and adding new hardware than by tearing them out and replacing with mass-market cabinetry. If you own new or newish pieces made of pressed wood, be sure to seal off all exposed surfaces with a non-toxic sealant. Ironically, even older versions of inexpensive pressed wood pieces (read: used furniture) are superior to the newer ones, as they're more likely to have completed the off-gassing cycle. The takeaway here is when in doubt, *used is better than new.*

When we were doing the green remodel on my Sunflower House, I retrieved some handsome white sectional organizers from the closet in my bedroom. After removing them, I spotted the tell-tale pressed wood at the edges. I asked Robyn Griggs Lawrence whether they would have to be discarded. First determine the age of the pieces, she counseled. I emailed the previous owner and found out that they had been installed at least eight years previously. "Whew!" said Robyn. "Any off-gassing that they will do has already happened. You can keep them."

Commit First; Buy Later

My attraction to older things doesn't mean I'm opposed to buying new on occasion. Though I lean toward used items, in some cases, new is the best solution. I've been persuaded by building-science experts like David Johnston and others that this is the case for major household appliances so many chemicals. Even at low levels, exposure to a variety of chemicals over time is thought to be dangerous to our health. In the 1980s, a condition called "multiple chemical sensitivities" (MCS) was identified for those who respond adversely to exposure to so many chemicals. Indeed, whether or not we've come down with MCS, all of our bodies are carrying a heavy load, something that Jeffrey Hollender and Geoff Davis in their book, "Naturally Clean" (New Society: 2006) refer to as "body burden." Many synthetic chemicals made today, they write, "do not easily break down into harmless bits and pieces as natural materials do. ... Once they're introduced into our air, water and soil, they tend to remain there for long periods of time. ... A large number of these compounds are fat-soluble, that is, they are easily absorbed by fats and oils. The fats into which these chemicals readily dissolve include human fatty tissues. ... Once absorbed into our bodily tissues, these toxic compounds tend to remain there because they aren't easily broken down and excreted." According to a recent study by the EPA, every American carries at least 700 pollutants in his or her body.

While we think of toxic substances as being "out there," the fact is that our greatest exposure is likely to be inside our own homes. The average home today, writes Debra Lynn Dadd in "The Nontoxic Home" (Tarcher: 1986) contains more chemicals "than were found in a typical chemistry lab at the turn of the century." Most American homes are filled with cleaning products containing ingredients that can cause cancer, birth defects and weaken the immune system.

Making the change to natural, non-toxic cleaners carries multiple and overlapping benefits. Natural cleaners are good for you, the environment, and they save money. They smell better and improve indoor air quality; what's more, they'll do no harm to you, your children, your elders, guests, animal companions or the planet.

— like refrigerators, stoves, washers and dryers — which use significant amounts of energy. (When you're upgrading those, be sure to select appliances carrying the Energy Star® certification.) If you decide to purchase new furnishings, save your money and spend it on quality products made with Forest Stewardship Council (FSC)-certified woods or salvaged material. Instead of wall-to-wall carpeting, invest in natural-fiber area rugs made of wool, sisal, cotton and the like.

When you decide to buy a major item, do your homework first. Shop and compare. Scrutinize the materials used in the product; consider where it was made, and how it will be recycled or disposed of at the end of its life cycle. Factor in the warranty. Then, save the cash before you make the purchase. Instead of rushing to furnish your place, acquire pieces piecemeal, over time, savoring the introduction of each one. Once you have bought something, make a lifetime commitment to your new Thing, and keep it in working condition. This way, you do everything you can to transform your new thing into your own "Thing That Refused to Die."

Reduce Your Personal Waste Stream

The concept of maintaining possessions, large and small, is an important mind-set shift on the path to simple living. On average, every American discards *four and a half pounds of waste per day*. I find that statistic disturbing, not to mention shocking. How could we individually and collectively generate that much trash? We toss not only the obvious like paper towels, plastic bags, Styrofoam cups, lunch plates and packaging, but footwear, kids' toys, computers, even furniture. While recycling is a good and necessary measure, the ultimate objective in reclaiming the good life is making the move from disposability to durability. It calls for reducing your personal waste stream to a trickle.

The good news is that you *can* swim against the tide of disposability inside your own home by *organizing your possessions* so you know what you have and where it is; making conscious choices about what you bring into your space; and by creating systems to make recycling and reuse easy and close at hand.

Commit to Reusables

We've already addressed the so-called big-ticket items in your home, like furniture, so now let's direct our attention to the smaller stuff, such as napkins, paper towels, and the like. Take the plunge and *commit to reusables,* thus minimizing the use of throwaways in your home. They're ubiquitous and, to my way of thinking, insidious. I'm talking about things like disposable cups, plastic plates, paper napkins and towels. At my home, china dishes hold food for our sit-down dinners every night; when Henry and I go picnicking, we take reusable plastic dishes. Cloth napkins are used at all times, along with cloth towels to dry dishes and the counters; rags wipe up spills on the floors, walls and cabinets. When I go out to eat, I make a point to carry storage containers in which to bring home leftovers thus eliminating the dreaded foam doggie box.

Household batteries are major items in the throwaway column. The EPA estimates 350 million of them are used every year in America, and most end up in landfills leaching cadmium, alkaline, nickel and mercury into the ground; others are burned in incinerators contributing vile additives into our atmosphere. In addition to damaging the environment, these disposable batteries drain the pocketbook. Simple solution? Invest in a battery recharger. (They make great holiday, birthday, graduation or wedding gifts.)

You may be the recycler in your family. I am a dedicated recycler, which means that I recycle even though (at present) there's no curbside service here in Mount Airy. I would recycle even if it meant having to walk down the stairs to the basement to dispose of a single glass bottle. (Okay, I'm a fanatic; I'd do it for a plastic bottle top.) But many others aren't as

dedicated as I am. They will do it only if you make it as easy to toss something in a recycling bin as the trash can.

To bring these people onboard (and make it easier on yourself), position recycling receptacles close to where they will be used. For example, in my kitchen, I removed the two bottom pull-out drawers from my pantry so I could insert two large recycling tubs into which I toss co-mingled recyclables, i.e. plastic jars, milk jugs and cardboard cereal boxes. My box for recycling newsprint and magazines is in the sunroom close to where I read the morning newspaper. By applying systems thinking throughout your house, you can effectively reduce your personal waste stream. Lighten your load. You'll sleep better for it.

Green Cleaning

My mother has never been my role model when it comes to cleaning. The reason? She's sloppy. Her view about cleaning is and always was, the less you do, the better. Though I like her concept of minimizing time spent cleaning, I do enjoy a home that's neat and tidy. Still, I'll never forget a cleaning-day fantasy Mama expressed eons ago. "I wish I could clean my floors with a water hose," she once remarked. How cool is that! (Maybe someone somewhere now cleans her floors that way.)

Mother also engendered in me a healthy skepticism about common household cleaning products, which includes numerous untested and unregulated chemicals. Mother has never liked sprays of any kind — spray fragrances, oven-cleaning sprays or window cleaner. (In fact, she used to be the oddball at the beauty parlor for refusing hair spray after having her hair styled.)

"Body Burden"

Turns out, Mother was ahead of her time. Increasingly, Americans are becoming aware of the burden our bodies bear in ingesting and inhaling

Simple Solutions

The beauty of green cleaning solutions is that they're relatively simple. They rely on commonly available ingredients, like baking soda, lemon juice and vinegar. Think about it, these items we also can *eat* safely. Wouldn't you rather have your stove or the inside of your fridge cleaned with something that's safe to eat than something carrying cautionary warning labels? Let me lay out some formulas for you to whip up your own solutions around the house. If you are just too busy to do this, I'll steer you to some groups that sell products you should consider buying. Web sites abound which provide reliable information.

Kind to the Environment (Indoor and Out) Cleaning Solutions

• *All-purpose cleaner and disinfectant:* This recipe from Natural Home magazine works as well on kitchen and bathroom surfaces as popular antibacterial cleansers. Mix 2 cups (480ml) hot water; ¼ cup (60ml) white vinegar; ½ teaspoon (2.5g) washing soda (similar to, but more caustic than, baking soda); 15 drops tea tree essential oil; 15 drops lavender essential oil. Combine ingredients in a reusable spray bottle and shake well. Spray on countertops, cutting boards and toilets, then wipe with a dry cloth.

• *Mop the floor:* If your floor calls out for a serious cleaning, mix up a bucket of hot water with ¼ to ½ cup (60ml to 120ml) of vinegar and go at it. This works on all floors — vinyl, tile, stone, linoleum or wood. (Use water sparingly on wood as its finish can be damaged by allowing water to sit on the surface or seep in. The best idea is to use a spray bottle with the same solution and damp-mop.)

• *Tile scrubbing:* If your tile needs special attention, you may want to sweep or vacuum first to remove accumulated dirt in the grout, then use a borax and water paste to give it a hard scrub. Be sure to wipe off thoroughly afterwards. Although borax is all-natural, it can be toxic if ingested by children.

(continued)

● *Old-fashioned carpet sweeper:* Bring back your grandmother's carpet sweeper! For the uninitiated, Jill Potvin Schoff, author of "Green up Your Cleanup" (Creative Homeowner: 2008) calls it "a cross between a broom and a vacuum." It's human-powered, so uses no electricity and makes no noise.

● *Taming the toilet monster:* If you like to see a sparkling commode (and who doesn't?), sprinkle baking soda on a long-handled cleaning brush, then drizzle on vinegar and give the bowl some old elbow grease.

● *Window wonderland:* Whip up your own glass, mirror and window cleaner by pouring the following into a plastic spray bottle: equal parts water and white vinegar. If you like the scent of lavender, tea tree or peppermint, add in a few drops of essential oil. Spray away.

● *Dirty, dusty screens:* Try sweeping them first, or using the brush attachment on your vacuum cleaner. If they're especially dirty, remove and hose down.

● *Carpet freshening:* Sprinkle some borax (sodium borate) on your wall-to-wall carpet or area rugs to freshen them and discourage fleas. Borax is stronger than baking soda and can kill mold and mildew.

● *Furniture wax:* Try waxing your wooden furniture with all-natural beeswax. It works like a charm. For my reclaimed wormy chestnut mantel, I apply the stuff every six months. If you're in a bind, pull out some olive oil from your cabinet as a substitute for wood polish.

● *Dust-busting:* Studies show that household dust contains many microscopic pollutants, including pesticides, heavy metals, flame retardants and more. Keep up a regular sweeping and dusting regimen. Whenever possible, try to prevent dust from being circulated into the air as you may end up inhaling it. Use a damp cloth and wring out frequently as you dust window blinds and the like. If you're working in an especially dusty area, wear a sneeze guard over nose and mouth.

Minimizing Cleanup

Preventative measures — Just as it's better to prevent illness through healthy living, a primary solution for smart cleaning is preventing dirt and grime from accumulating in the first place. The first measure I took to this end was placing door mats at every entrance to my house — the front door and two doors that access the sunroom. Make a point to wipe your shoes or boots whenever you enter your home.

Shoes be gone — In my home, the sunroom is shoe central, the place where I like to leave my shoes and slip into my house slippers. A great rule to adopt in your home is making it a shoe-free zone. This keeps dirt, grime and potentially toxic pesticides and other matter from marching into your home.

Regular cleaning — By the same token, it's better to keep up with your cleaning on a regular basis than to let it "get away from you." So if you spill some milk, clean it up immediately. A broom and a long-handled dust pan are the tools of choice in my home; because our grey-haired cat, Whiskers, has run of the entire house except for the guest room, we're constantly gathering his fur. I am loathe to use the vacuum because I hate the noise and using electricity, but when company is coming, I do haul it out.

Carpets — When remodeling the Sunflower House, we removed wall-to-wall carpet on the main floor. All that remains are area rugs in the bedrooms, bathrooms and one made of recycled soda bottles from the Viva Terra catalog in the sunroom. When I go on a cleaning kick, my favorite recipe is to take the rugs out to the elm tree in the back and beat the dirt out of them. It's amazing how much dirt flies up in the process.

Your natural cleaning tool kit: tried-and-true ingredients. You'll be surprised by how few materials you really need to get started with natural cleaning. You'll want to use a plastic squirt bottle or two in which to concoct your cleaning solutions. The list of ingredients is small and includes: baking soda, borax, hydrogen peroxide, distilled white vinegar, lemon juice, club soda and essential oils if you want to add some delicious scents to your home. You can find myriad cleaning solutions using these simple ingredients in Casey Kellar's book, "Natural Alternatives for You and Your Home" (Krause Publications: 2009).

> *"If you feel depressed, clean your house."*
>
> — Ann Williams

Buying Commercial Products

The good news is that if you have neither time nor patience to mix up your own green cleaners, most supermarkets and even big-box stores are now carrying green cleaning lines. But be sure that you scrutinize the labels to be certain that you're not being sold a green bill of goods. You can order products over the Internet, but bear in mind that a carbon cost is associated with shipping these items long distances. It's better to try to persuade your local supermarket or health-foods store to consider carrying the lines.

Check out the following lines, which I've used and with which I've had good luck:

• Arm & Hammer® (makers of baking soda); *www.armhammer.com;* 800-524-1328.

• Begley's Best™ (all-natural cleaning line); *www.begleysbest.com*; fax orders to 818-766-6064.

• Bon Ami® (nontoxic cleansers); *www.bonami.com*; 816-842-1230.

• Dr. Bronner's Magic Soaps; (USDA certified organic bar and liquid soaps); *www.drbronner.com*; 760-743-2211.

• Restore Products (plant-based, biodegradable cleaning line); *www. restoreproducts.com*; 612-331-5979.

• Seventh Generation (nontoxic cleaners and products); *www.seventh-generation.com*; 800-456-1191.

• Naturally Yours (biodegradable, eco-cleaning product manufacturer); *www.naturallyyoursclean.com*; 888-801-7347.

Begley's Best Works Magic

I've met actor and environmentalist Ed Begley Jr. a number of times in my work to advance the field of simple living and sustainability. When he told me that he wanted to do for green cleaning products what Paul Newman did for upscale salad dressings (make a quality product and donate profits to charity), it got my attention. Ed introduced his Begley's Best green cleaning line several years back. I had the opportunity to try out several of his products, which work wonderfully well! Recently I learned that Begley's Best All Purpose Cleaner won a "Cradle to Cradle" Design certification from the sustainable product and process design consulting firm McDonough Braungart Design Chemistry. Made with extracts of pine, palm, de-acidified citrus, maize, fermented sugar cane and olive seeds, the product is non-toxic, non-caustic, non-fuming, non-flammable, non-irritating, non-allergenic and 99 percent biodegradable in seven days. If you're searching for one natural, all-purpose cleaner, give this one a try.

As Ann Williams says, if you're depressed, clean your home. Even better, to help further lift the fog and make your home smell like a summer meadow, try switching to green cleaning with non-toxic products made of ingredients derived from nature. It's a change that you'll never regret.

Green Your Wardrobe — and Closet

The summer of my sophomore year in college, as an intern at Newsweek magazine in New York City, I lived at a New York University dormitory in Greenwich Village. I was paired with a French student taking summer classes there. I brought with me the typical American college girl's wardrobe — a full complement of skirts, sweaters, tops and slacks — which took up most of my closet space. By contrast, she brought with her just two dresses. When one dress needed laundering, she hand-washed it in the sink and hung it out to dry in the bathroom. She took beautiful care of her two dresses and always looked better than any of the American girls on the hall. All these years later, I don't remember her name, but her sartorial approach left an indelible impression.

Another woman who has had a direct influence on the development of my philosophy of dressing is the designer Eileen Fisher. I met her quite by accident when her firm offered to wardrobe me for my "Simple Living" shoots. Over dinner at her home in New York, I learned that the genesis of her minimalist design philosophy came from her youth as a Catholic school girl in Chicago. Though she hated the restrictiveness of her school uniform at the time, once she entered the working world, she missed the ease of dressing the uniform had provided. Her eco-friendly line of clothing is meant to offer women easily interchangeable mix-and-match items in solid colors and lush textures. Today the French girl and Eileen Fisher serve as models for me as I strive to simplify my own wardrobe.

Toward a Manageable Wardrobe

If you have clothing closet clutter (and who doesn't!), instead of aspiring to a larger closet, reduce the number of clothes you own. Most people wear 20 percent of their wardrobes 80 percent of the time, according to Karen Kingston, author of "Clear Your Clutter with Feng Shui" (Broadway Books: 1998). Of the things you wear infrequently, go through them ruthlessly; if there is *anything* you don't like about them (fabric, fit, feel, style), consign or give them away. If you haven't worn something in two years, move it on down the pike. Try on any items about which you aren't sure. (In the process, I guarantee you'll discover at least one "treasure" that you'll want to reclaim!) Once you've eliminated the dead weight in your closet, you can gradually build a wardrobe that you can thoughtfully possess. And, finally, resolve *never to purchase anything again that isn't exactly what you want.* If you buy something and have *any* doubts about it, it's destined to wind up in the 80 percent pile, and you've wasted precious money, resources and closet space.

Closet Organization

Once you've reduced your holdings, you'll be surprised at the amount of space you've freed up in your closet. Take this moment to sort everything by category — place all the shirts, dresses, pantsuits, and tops together, positioning the shirts and blouses according to color, from light to dark. This helps you see what you have. (If you still have more clothing than your closet will bear, and if you have climate-controlled attic or basement space, you can rotate out-of-season items.) To further streamline your closet space, remove as much as possible from the closet floor. A door- or wall-mounted shoe rack gets the shoes off the floor and in sight. The same goes for ties, belts, scarves and hats. As you organize your wardrobe, it'll be easier — and more obvious — to see what you have and which items it's time to let go of. This will help you dress more creatively.

To keep your closet space streamlined, I recommend a practice I've been following for years. Position two containers in the back of your closet — one for donation and one for consignment. (I use paper grocery bags, marked in bold magic-marker letters!). As soon as I find something that no longer works for me, I place it directly into the bag. As soon as the bag fills, I drop it off at my charity or the resale shop.

Finally, once you pare down your holdings and fill your wardrobe with things you love, you'll want to keep them in pristine condition and good repair. Whip out the needle and thread if a button falls off or a seam rips.

Just as with home décor and furnishing, developing your own personal style with what you wear can bring your wardrobe to another level. Style is not something you pick up from a fashion magazine; it has more to do with being in tune with your own inner lights. My friend, Bonni Brodnick, has a wonderful sense of style, which comes from self-knowledge and self-respect. (Excellent posture completes the package.) When Bonni finds a style or design that suits her, she owns it, often buying multiples.

Bonni's signature is beautiful shoes, which she traces to her father's work as a shoe salesman. In warm weather, you rarely catch her out without a pair of Jack Rogers T-strap sandals on. "They are a great way to pull together an outfit and add a little pop," she says. What is your signature wardrobe item? Once you learn your own style, your wardrobe with limits — and pizzazz — will emerge.

Pilar's Sense of Style

"My mother tells me that as a child, I was something of a fashion plate — and a major pain as a result. I was particular about the kind of tights I wore at age 3. I begged for a tutu at age 4, and for chunky-heeled, white vinyl go-go boots at age 5. Every year brought a new clothing obsession.

My fashion predilections were soon curbed by one key factor, though: Our family didn't have much money. Plus, my parents were practical, down-to-earth types who could not fathom why any daughter of theirs would want to "express herself" through her wardrobe. So the deal was struck early: If I wanted to do any fancy dressing, I'd have to do it on my own dime.

In high school, as it turned out, all I really wanted to do was fit in. So I spent my meager part-time wages on basic jeans and tops from Ragstock (a then-trendy Twin Cities-based used-clothes chain). When the preppy look got hot, I dug through giant thrift bins to find three-dollar cashmere sweaters. When the Flashdance look came around, I snipped off-the-shoulder necklines into countless used sweatshirts.

In college, I went through an arty phase. I took to altering antique, paisley-print pajama bottoms into pants. I'd hip-sling one of my dad's brass-buckled leather belts around a washed-thin olive green T-shirt and call it a tunic. There was an elegant 1930s bathrobe I wore as a dress. And a white split-tail marching-band jacket with silver buttons I wore as a blazer.

Then, in my 20s and early 30s, I went through a long, hardcore vintage phase. It was all about 1940s and '50s dresses, pencil skirts, sequined sweaters and suits. Those clothes were so well made and so beautifully tailored. The fabrics hung like a dream and wore like iron — and still looked almost new 30 years into their useful lives.

Best of all, I really enjoyed shopping for these things — mostly at estate sales and thrift shops, sometimes at garage sales and consignment stores. I loved the hunt, the discovery, the "will it fit?" dressing-room anticipation. I loved the history and mystery, too, speculating about all the women who had originally purchased these clothes, imagining what their lives had been like.

And, I loved the bargains. Compared to most of the cheap, mass-produced clothes being manufactured today, these handmade articles were works of art — clothes I could never have afforded then had they been sold new. Back then, most of these items sold for less than $25, and many sold for under $10.

These days, vintage clothes carry bigger price tags. And I don't shop for them quite as often as I used to, in part because I shop less for clothes in general (my fashion passion has waned in recent years) and in part because the demands of my busy professional life mean that when I do shop, I often run in and out of a store in search of something utterly boring and basic, like a pair of black capris, and simply do not have time or inclination to go in search of a decent used pair.

Still, I sometimes miss those long afternoons spent prowling the vintage racks. And I haven't given up the hunt entirely. Every now and then, I still slip into a vintage store in search of treasures, and every rare once in a while, I find something wonderful.

Today, I'd estimate that pre-owned items make up about a third of my wardrobe. I mix them in with newer things, and when people compliment me on what I'm wearing, and I always seize upon these moments to share my tales of thrift and good fortune: "Thanks," I say, "I found it at Goodwill for five bucks!" Or, "I bought this at the garage sale of a lovely old woman who used to play for the St. Paul Chamber orchestra." Many of my previously owned clothes have marvelous stories, and some have narratives that I suspect will outlive me. But alas, even the best used couture doesn't last forever.

I finally wore one favorite 1951 Handmacher-label jacket a bit threadbare last year and reluctantly let it go — back to Goodwill, that is. But having paid $15 dollars for it in 1989 (less, amazingly, than the original 1950s retail

(continued)

price of $25) and having enjoyed wearing it for nearly 20 years myself, I can definitely say I got my money's worth. And, besides, I have another jacket much like it — an indestructible herringbone number I bought at the same estate sale — that I still wear on a regular basis.

My innate fashion-plate tendencies notwithstanding, I guess I must have inherited at least some small part of my parents' practicality. Whatever the reason, vintage clothes have always appealed to both my creative and down-to-earth instincts, and wearing them has always given me a deep sense of satisfaction.

Take the 1950s light aqua, silver-flecked cardigan with rhinestone buttons I bought at a thrift shop about 10 years back. This one-of-a-kind sweater cost me $12, which is probably less than I forced my mother to shell out for those awful vinyl go-go boots way back when. And unlike the boots, which are probably moldering away in some landfill, the sweater shows virtually no signs of wear. In fact, it just keeps getting better with time."

— *Pilar Gerasimo, editor-in-chief, Experience Life magazine*

New — or "New to You" — Clothing

Just as with furniture and about every other possession, I prefer used items to new ones, and this applies to clothing, too. I already have more clothes than I need, so I'm not in the market. Occasionally, on the spur of the moment, I may splurge on a seasonal novelty item. This spring, I picked up some floral print capris at the Snob (consignment) Shop in Winston-Salem. But my rule is to never spend more there (and hopefully less) than my pay-out check nets me.

Henry, however, is a growing boy — a *rapidly* growing "tweenager," so he actually *needs* new clothes. For all of his clothing and footwear needs, we always shop in this order: first, consignment stores or resale shops; second, thrift stores like Goodwill; thirdly, as a last resort, we go to a department store or specialty shop. (If I *have* to buy something new, I avoid big-box stores and try to buy locally, whenever possible.) The reason I shop in this order is that generally consignment or resale shops carry a better selection of higher quality merchandise; it's still cheaper than retail and has the benefits of buying used. If we strike out there, we next try Goodwill or Salvation Army, then head to retail.

As with all simple-living choices, buying used clothing offers multiple and overlapping benefits. Not only do you save money by buying second-hand, but you're being a good environmental steward. Precious resources were not expended producing a new garment, and, by extending the life of an existing one, you're actually preventing it from clogging the landfill. I prefer older pieces because they tend to have character. And, used clothing is softer and feels better on your skin. (This is especially important for my son who has sensitive skin.)

If I weren't already on board with used clothing, when I learned that many new garments are treated with formaldehyde to disinfect and prevent stains and wrinkles, my preference for used became hard-wired. If such a finish had been added to a used garment, by the point you buy it (as with used furniture), it's probably already off-gassed. But if you do buy a new piece of clothing (or a used one, for that matter), be sure to launder it before wearing. Then, hang it out on the line to let the sun and air work their magic, as well.

Lightening Your Laundry Load

Line-drying is so important in my homemaking cosmology, that I must confess that it was the one covenant restriction I checked into before purchasing the Sunflower House in the Burkewood development of Mount Airy. I asked my attorney, who happens to be a resident of this neighborhood, if old-fashioned clotheslines were permissible here. I'd read horror stories about upscale communities banning them because they seemed low-brow. To my thinking, any community that considers ecological stewardship beneath it, is a community in which I don't care to hang my hat. Luckily, no such covenant was on the books in my development, and I was able to purchase the home, install the clothesline and hang out my wash.

I will say that my house is the only one in this well-established neighborhood that has a laundry line.

As a kid growing up in Illinois and Kentucky, it was just expected that you hung clothes on the line to dry. When my family moved to Maine, I remember we had a hookup for a washing machine in the kitchen, but neither a place (nor the money) for a dryer. Naturally, we hung our clothes to dry outdoors; and in the cold Maine winters we hung lots of clothes in the bathroom and on an indoor drying rack. During college and my laundromat years in California, I fell into the habit of using clothes dryers. Today, when I hang my clothes out, I reconnect with my past. This job takes me outdoors, puts me in relationship with the items on the line, with the birds drawn to my garden, and the weather outside. I don't consider hanging the wash to be a chore or a burden, but rather a privilege, a meditative experience.

For my laundry room in the Sunflower House, I selected Whirlpool®'s Duet Steam washer-dryer combination, which carries Energy Star®'s seal of approval. (This pair saves significant amounts of energy, water and soap, and represents a good long-term investment.) This front-loading pair stands on pedestals, a desirable feature given my 5' 10" stature. I also set up a portable indoor drying rack from Ace® Hardware, for use in the winter and during rainy weather. There, I hang bathing suits and those unmentionables that don't need to be tumbled in a conventional dryer, no matter how delicate the cycle.

Following are some tips to make your laundry day ritual more eco-friendly:

1. *Wash full loads to save energy*, but don't overfill capacity.

2. *Select the cold-water option whenever possible*, thus saving an estimated 85 percent of the energy consumed by a hot water load, according to statistics cited in "Naturally Clean."

3. Avoid chlorine bleach and opt for hydrogen peroxide-based bleaches, commonly known as oxygen bleaches. These are kinder to your clothing and the environment when they break down.

4. Clean out your lint filter every time you use your dryer. This will improve air circulation in the dryer, thus making it more efficient.

5. Wash clothes only when dirty. Wean yourself from the habit of tossing clothes into the hamper after every wearing. I recommend giving garments the old sniff test. If it doesn't smell, hang or fold and wear it again.

6. Hand-wash delicates such as bras, panties, woolens, silks and other items in cold water with a dollop of liquid Castile soap. Rinse and gently wring out water, then hang-dry.

7. Check the ingredients in your laundry detergent and be sure they are phosphate- and bleach-free and contain no non-degrading optical brighteners. Vegetable oil-based detergents and soaps are optimal.

8. Avoid the use of dryer sheets and fabric softeners in your wash as they tend to build residue and cause an overall greying.

9. To brighten and remove residue build-up on clothes and linens, wash with a quarter cup of white vinegar per load to brighten — no detergent.

10. Use underarm sweat pads, which save you from frequent washings of work blouses and dressy apparel.

Once you adopt these pointers for more natural, non-toxic laundry, wash day promises to become a satisfying ritual. Laundry has always been at the top of my list of favorite household chores. Make it yours, too!

As with any journey, the changes I suggest making in your home, to your cleaning routine and with your wardrobe — streamlining your possessions, developing your look, incorporating items with age and meaning into your home and closet — are gradual and will take time. But remember, reclaiming the domestic arts is part of living well. Give yourself some brownie points for the changes you have already made. Then decide what's next on your list. Believe me, you will feel empowered and your family will thank you for creating a home that's comforting, welcoming, and well-tended: your true sanctuary.

Chapter Five

Back Into
the Kitchen

Cook healthful food at home; schedule sit-down meals
and relish the pleasures of the table.

Ritualize sit-down meals at home by staging them thoughtfully, slowing the pace, and removing annoying distractions — especially interference from electronics and media. Reclaim your kitchen and home cooking. Organize a working kitchen for efficiency, waste reduction and bulk cooking. Reconnect with your sustenance by sourcing food locally, whenever possible, learning its nutritional value and how it was grown. Make every effort to eat lower on the food chain. Then, plan your menus and cook up a storm. You'll be healthier and happier for the effort.

Reclaim the Pleasures of the Table

One of the greatest casualties of modern life is the demise of the sit-down meal. Too many families these days simply do not eat together. We have become a snack food nation. At the approach of that first hunger pang, we grab a snack to satisfy, then on with the task at hand. Often food travels from freezer to microwave to mouth (or from bag to hand to mouth) — never once stopping at a table, not to mention a plate or fork. Or it's fast food, eaten in the car, or on the run. These quick-fix meals are just that, "quick fixes," usually loaded with preservatives, over-refined carbohydrates such as white flour and rice, refined sugar and animal by-products. Not only are they nutritionally lacking, but they are wolfed down without the communal ceremony and reverence with which humans have traditionally taken their food.

The only time many of us sit down at an actual table to eat with others simultaneously is when dining at a restaurant or enjoying the occasional holiday meal. Sadly, the regular pleasures of the table — savoring our food in the company of others — have been all but lost and forgotten.

Yet, experts tell us that no ritual is as essential for family cohesion, mental health, nor predictive of a child's future success than participating in regular family-wide, sit-down meals. "The research is clear: There is no more important activity for the health and well-being of children than family meals. Nothing — not studying, not church-going, not even soccer-playing — is more important than eating and connecting at the family table," says William J. Doherty, Ph.D., professor of family social science at the University of Minnesota and author of "The Intentional Family: Simple Rituals to Strengthen Family Ties" (Harper: 1999). "Dinner is the only time in most days where we are all together in the same place at the same time with an opportunity to connect. Meals are where family culture is created and passed on."

Numerous studies indicate that regular dining together not only increases psychological well-being but buffers youngsters from risky behaviors such as smoking, drinking, and taking drugs. Evidence also suggests that regular family meals reduce the risk of eating disorders, childhood obesity, and can boost a child's grades in school. Not only are sit-down meals good for kids, but for us adults, our elders and friends, in short, for everyone. (My friend, Leonard Kniffel, reminds me that in days past, even a cluster of unrelated roomers *living in a boarding house* customarily sat down together for a common meal.)

When seeking the simple life, no other action ranks quite as high as resuscitating the old-fashioned, sit-down meal! The good news is that you don't need a degree in home economics to prepare and stage regular family meals, nor must you spend endless hours slaving over a hot stove to make it happen. You simply need to make meals a priority, get organized, and commit to following a regular schedule. Then, sit back and enjoy the results in increased family cohesiveness, life satisfaction, and improved physical, mental, and emotional health for you and your family.

Organize Your Kitchen

Once you've decided to bring back the family meal, more than likely, you'll need to learn your way around your kitchen. As with other areas of your home, de-cluttering is generally the first task at hand. Schedule a day — or a series of days — and divide your kitchen into three zones: kitchen drawers; kitchen cabinets; pantry and refrigerator/freezer. Starting with the kitchen drawers, for instance, take everything out of all the drawers and lay it all out on the counters and tables to assess what you have. As with clothes you haven't worn in a year or two, place kitchen gadgets you haven't used in a long time into a "donate" or "consign" receptacle. If you find that you have four kitchen spatulas, for instance, move two or three down the pike. If something's broken beyond repair, throw it away. Repeat the exercise with cabinets, fridge and freezer.

Then take a hard look at your kitchen. If it is not organized efficiently, with the most frequently used items closest at hand, move them. Regroup and reassign drawers and shelves, placing like items together. In my kitchen, a full lower cabinet is assigned to pans, skillets and lids. My steamer basket stays there as well. Another cabinet houses all my larger mixing bowls along with small, seldom-used appliances, such as my blender, manual vegetable chopper and juicer. My coffee and tea paraphernalia (see page 169 for my coffee-making method) reside in a drawer to the left of my stove: coffee-cone filter holder, paper filters, tea eggs, and an old tea-bag rest that dates to the kitchen of my late father.

My glasses and coffee mugs are stashed on the lowest shelf above the kitchen counter in one long cabinet, with lesser-used tea cups and saucers, wine glasses, novelty crystals and the like on the harder-to-reach shelf above these. Plates of varying sizes occupy another cabinet, while bowls reign supreme in another. (Rather than organizing by china patterns or sets, I choose to organize by function. This puts my plastic bowls, alongside my Japanese lacquer miso-soup bowls, alongside my ceramic cereal and soup bowls, alongside my fine-bone china bowls.) Similarly, in my pantry, one shelf holds canned sauces and soups; another pasta noodles, cereal, crackers and so forth.

As with your closet and other areas around your home, once you've de-cluttered and organized your kitchen, resolve to make it a clutter-free zone. That means saying "no thanks" to those freebies such as refrigerator magnets, stadium cups and foam aluminum can holders given out at ballgames and on special celebrations. The best way to prevent clutter from accumulating is stopping it at the source. My method is to keep donation and consignment boxes on hand at all times so that clutter goes in on a regular basis. If I have the thought, "I don't need this *thingamajiggy* in my life," it goes into the container immediately, if not sooner! Typically, once people lighten their load in the kitchen, they feel giddy. "A weight has been lifted from my shoulders," one woman told me after eliminating her kitchen clutter. Others report that streamlining their kitchens has opened the door to cooking once again.

Another discipline to maintain that goes hand in oven mitt with de-cluttering is keeping your kitchen clean and sparkling. This will go a long way to maintaining organization. When you make a habit of cleaning up after every meal, your kitchen will never "get away" from you. At night after dinner, I load the dishwasher, wipe down my beautiful granite counter as well as my stainless steel sink. At night before turning in, I fill the tea kettle with water, pour my coffee grounds mixture into my cone filter, and put it atop tomorrow's mug. Then, I set out the morning's vitamins in a small bowl at the ready for breakfast. These simple acts of preparation for the next day give me an automatic jump-start in the morning.

Rethink Food Storage — and Plastic Bottles

Because controversy remains about the impact of plastics — specifically what's lurking in plastics, such as phthalates that are known endocrine disruptors — on human health, my recommendation is to use glass or ceramic containers to store your food and leftovers whenever possible. (Never cook or reheat food in the microwave in plastic containers.) The Breast Cancer Fund's "Strong Voices Newsletter" (Winter 2005) suggests avoiding the following plastic types: No.3 Polyvinyl Chloride (PVC or V); No. 5 Polypropylene (PP); No. 6 Polystyrene (PS) and No. 7 Other.

If you're a bottled water drinker, get a glass or metal reusable water bottle for use. This will save money, reduce landfill waste, and remove the danger of chemicals such as bisphenol-A (BPA), a hormone disruptor.

"De-Convenience" Your Kitchen

After several automatic coffee makers conked out (and I couldn't stand to contribute one more to Goodwill or the landfill), I decided to return to a hands-on method of making coffee. My inner barista comes out each morning by boiling water for coffee and pouring it over grounds in a plastic

(continued)

cone atop my coffee mug. I can vary the amount of coffee grounds, adding a dash of cinnamon and brown sugar into the mix. My regular formula is half caffeinated grounds and half decaf, but if I need an extra pick-me-up, I might increase the proportion of caffeinated. I find this slow method of coffee preparation inherently satisfying: watching the boiling water slowly transform the receptive grounds into a kind of frothy brown soup that eventually yields to gravity and drips down into my cup. Or cups, I should say, as I generally drink two. I set the tea kettle back on the burner, watching a streamer of steam rise up from the kettle while biding my time till the cone needs another dousing of water.

This one small step toward "de-conveniencing" my kitchen allows me to reclaim the pleasure and connection of coffee preparation. Another parallel track is shunning a food processor in favor of a mortar and pestle to grind basil and pine nuts into pesto. I bet you can think up many more applications of this principle! Think of my mantra of how simple living choices yield multiple and overlapping benefits. By preparing your pesto by hand, you're reducing your carbon emissions, getting a little bit of exercise, and engaging more fully in the preparation of your food.

Reduce Your Personal Waste Stream

Setting up a system in your kitchen to reduce your personal waste stream is a fairly straightforward undertaking. All you have to do is designate a handy place for recycling receptacles in your kitchen. In mine, I removed the two bottom pull-out shelves in my wall pantry to make room for the two jumbo plastic bins that make up my center. Into these, I deposit plastic and glass jars and bottles, and cardboard. This way, tossing something in the recycling is no more bother than pitching it into the trash can under the sink.

For organic waste, I place an attractive, ceramic-lidded, compost pot on my counter. A charcoal filter in the lid neutralizes any smell and wards off drosophila and other pesky insects that tend to hover around decomposing fruit. When working in the kitchen, potato peels, fruit scraps, egg shells and coffee grounds swiftly move the short distance to the compost pot. Once it fills, Henry or I carry the pot to the backyard where we deposit its contents directly into the compost pit in the ground. This task generally happens every day or two; an increased frequency of trips to the compost pit is a good indication that we're eating well. Every couple of weeks, the base of the compost pot is washed and sterilized in the dishwasher.

Not surprisingly, I'm an advocate of reusable everything, starting with my travel mug. I take this mug when I'm going out carrying coffee. Same goes for a water bottle. I am also mastering the habit of carrying Tupperware containers whenever I go out to eat so I'm not stuck with taking leftovers home in a foam doggie box (destined to be pitched after its single use). Taken together, all of these measures mean that my trash can is never more than one-tenth filled when I roll it out to the street for the garbage truck each Wednesday.

Laptop Lunch

When I learned about a product called Laptop Lunch — a lunchbox system composed of washable components that allows your child (or you) to pack a zero-waste lunch — I wasted no time in ordering one. *Two*, actually: One for Henry to carry to school; the other for the dishwasher. What a great opportunity to prepare our own healthful lunches while reducing our contribution to the county landfill. Statistics cited in the accompanying "Laptop Lunch User's Guide" estimate that the average school-age child carrying a disposable lunch bag or container generates *fully 67 pounds of waste per school year* — through sandwiches sealed in disposable plastic bags; yogurts in single-use packaging; juice boxes and pouches; and paper napkins, etc.

This Laptop Lunch box is equipped with reusable tubs with lids to hold sandwiches, chips, veggies and fruit, along with a plastic beverage container and stainless-steel forks and spoons. (The User's Guide suggests that you pack a reusable cloth napkin for the child to bring home each day.) Interestingly, not only do we save the packaging, but anything Henry doesn't eat at lunch comes back home, too, so he can snack on lunch leftovers like peanuts, a cookie, or a sandwich — so less food is wasted. In addition to reducing our waste stream, this system enables us to save a ton of money in zip-lock bags and individually wrapped items such as raisins and other snack items.

Another great outcome of adopting this "pack our own lunch" program is that Henry has taken ownership of the job of lunch preparation. As a staging area for him, I designated a narrow counter between the fridge and pantry with an overhead cabinet in which to stow his selections.

Wanda's Diary - Friday, June 1, 2007

I've always had an aversion to unnecessary waste of any kind, but disposable coffee cups somehow stand at the top of the heap. Use 'em once and toss 'em. Out of sight and out of mind, right? Actually not. Whether foam or plastic, they live on for generations in the landfill, long past the time that you and I remain on this earth. Disposable cups — unlike say, disposable syringes, for instance — strike me as unnecessary, even frivolous, in all but the occasional situation.

Why? Because there's a simple alternative: a reusable container, like the ceramic variety or the travel mug. All it takes is a moment of consciousness before you leave your home or office. The thing is: We all can carry travel mugs, but most of us don't. For me, the disposable coffee mug, especially the foam variety, has become emblematic of our culture of disposability.

In fact, in the first episode of our "Simple Living" television series, we did the math. I calculated that in the 20 years I've been carrying a travel mug everywhere I go (including to church on Sunday), I've saved more than 7,000 disposable cups.

I was delighted, on a shoot for the series, to stumble upon a place that encourages waste reduction on the ground: The Tate Street Coffee House in Greensboro, a delightful locally owned and operated coffee shop that is the place to chug your Joe near the University of North Carolina at Greensboro campus. At the time we shot there, back in 2007, it struck me as one of the smartest practices I've seen anywhere in my travels around America. What Tate Street Coffee House owner Matt Russ has done is devise a system that, in effect, punishes customers for *not* bringing a travel mug. He has devised a "fast lane" — affectionately known as "MEL" ("morning express lane") — for customers carrying travel mugs. If you buy one of his house, green-colored mugs (which sells for $4), you pay $1 for a medium cup of coffee that would ordinarily sell for $1.35. (That $1 includes tax so you just show up with a buck, pour your own and move on with your day.) Not only will you save money, but you save time. Those who are not carrying a travel mug, in contrast, must stand in line to order their drink from an attendant, and are often out not only the extra 35 cents but five, eight or even 10 minutes of their precious morning time. (And if you have your own non-Tate Street Coffee House mug, you still get to use the MEL lane but you only get 10 cents off your order, so you pay $1.25.)

What the good folks at Tate Street Coffee House are doing strikes me as the kind of thinking America needs to engage in right now. During lunch a few weeks ago, a friend used the term "smart green" to describe the smart approach for business leaders and citizens to take in tackling the enormous environmental challenges we all face today. My hat's off to Matt Russ for his simple, low-tech solution to the disposable mug problem. In fact, I'm so excited about his approach that I think it should be instituted in every coffee shop in America. Starbucks™, take note!

Aesthetic Touches

When I step into my kitchen, I feel as if I'm entering some magical kingdom. Because I do so much cooking and baking here, generally some aromatic smell emanates into the rest of the house. Plus, my kitchen has great bones. You enter it one of two ways: through an inviting rounded arch from the dining room, or from an open doorway from the living room in the front of the house. The first thing you notice is a vast expanse of grey granite, setting off sturdy, solid wood cabinets painted off-white. If you live in Mount Airy — home of the world's largest open-faced granite quarry — how can you resist installing "local granite," the North Carolina Granite Corporation's signature "salt-and-pepper" granite countertops and backsplashes, which were quarried less than two miles as the crow flies from my kitchen?

Granite countertops or not, you can make your kitchen magical in myriad other ways. Though my kitchen is not huge by contemporary American standards (it's 12' 4" x 9' 6"), nonetheless, keeping it decluttered makes it seem larger. I have found room to install permanent objects of art to delight the eyes and senses. My wabi-sabi inspiration was in creating curtains from my mother's 1960s cotton novelty skirt featuring lively images of scarecrows. A hand-painted, antique wooden mouse that I found for a song at a thrift shop in New Zealand in 2007 holds court on my counter. And nearby, a lovely ceramic tray festooned with my signature sunflowers — a gift from my friend and assistant Ann Williams — presides atop a plate stand on the counter. Creating an environment in which you want to spend time in your kitchen will go a long way toward institutionalizing your new role as chief cook and bottle washer!

Source Your Food

One primary concept for reclaiming the good life around food is to eat as much local food as possible. It's not only fresher and more healthful and supports your local farmer and economy, but you minimize use of fossil fuels in transporting food from farm to table. Because it's fresher, the taste is superior. Because it's local, it may be less pricey, but no matter, buy it if there's any way you can swing it with your budget. If you can find local *organic* food, so much the better. The best way to learn about food is to meet the person who grows or prepares it. The next step is to develop an ongoing relationship with this person, which will establish a basis of trust.

An incipient local food advocacy movement — its proponents are called "locavores" — is organizing around our nation, with the mission of revitalizing local food sheds, while declaring food independence from major multinational agricultural corporations. Local food advocates maintain that big agri-businesses are on the wrong track, working against the long-term interests of the public — their customers — by seeking to push small- and medium-sized farms out of business. At the same time, these companies are advancing a host of self-serving but risky practices, including introducing genetically modified organisms (GMOs) into the food chain.

"We've seen the seeds of genetically modified plants spread out from the fields where they were planted to areas in which they are unwanted," write Sharon Astyk and Aaron Newton in "A Nation of Farmers: Defeating the Food Crisis on American Soil" (New Society: 2009). "More sinister genetic manipulation has led to the creation of terminator seeds, or genetic manipulation that renders a plant sterile after just one generation ... (preventing) farmers from engaging in the millennia-old tradition of saving seeds and slowly breeding plants for characteristics beneficial to certain situations and localities." While such genetic manipulation no doubt threatens the small farmer and the small-farm economy, as yet, the impact of genetically modified food on human health has failed to be given a clean bill of health. In fact, studies of animals who have eaten genetically modified foods raise significant red flags in many areas, among them interaction with their immune and reproductive systems. In some cases, according to the Institute for Responsible Technology, large numbers of animals died after ingesting GMO foods.

In order to do your part to counteract these disturbing — and potentially devastating — trends, throw your support behind small-scale food production whenever possible. Do everything you can to keep your local, small- and medium-size farmer in business; if you can, go one further and cultivate your own garden. (For more, see Chapter 6, Beating a Path to the Garden.) While few of us can find 100 percent of our food locally, following are some ideas that anyone can try to increase the amount of local food on your table:

1. Patronize farmers' markets. The good news is that farmers' markets are flourishing in America, so look for one in your community. (If one doesn't exist, try organizing one; if you pull together with a group of like-minded supporters, prepare a solid plan and get the word out; it's bound to be a hit.) When you do buy, get to know your farmer by name; ask questions about which produce is most flavorful; if sprays or chemical fertilizers were used on it; how to prepare a particular item. And try new things! You'll be amazed at how much better eggplant tastes when you're 45 than when you were 12.

2. Join a CSA. CSA is short for "Community Supported Agriculture" a system whereby you purchase a share of a farmer's crop and share the risk — and reward — once the crop comes through. This is a great way to get seasonal produce delivered to your door, generally on a weekly basis during the growing season. Most CSAs are organized so you pay extra to have your share delivered to your home, and less if you go to the farm or some other central point to pick up your bounty. Some CSAs allow you to assist with farm labor in exchange for some portion — or all — of your share, thus allowing you to enjoy the benefits of sunshine, camaraderie and agricultural knowledge-building.

3. Request that your supermarket carry local produce. Most supermarkets receive their produce just as they do their cereal, on a truck from central headquarters. While it may be more trouble for the produce buyers to carry local items, if enough consumers request (or demand) it, at least some stores will accommodate them. So talk to your store manager and share with him the benefits of local food.

4. Plant your own vegetable garden. This is the single best way to source local produce. Step into your garden and pick it! You know exactly what went into your soil and on your plants. What indescribable pleasure it is to stroll into your own backyard to harvest cucumbers, tomatoes and spinach for the evening's salad.

5. Swap/barter vegetables and fruits with neighbors and friends. This is a wonderful way of extending the depth of what you grow in your garden, while building community in the process.

6. Plan your meals around seasonally available produce. My friend, Lisa Kivirst, co-owner with John Ivanko of the Inn Serendipity in Browntown, Wisconsin, extols the pleasures of eating things in season. "We wait for the first strawberries and we gorge. We look forward to it." When you eat what's in season, it's a way of making what Lisa calls "the dailiness of your life" more special. The couple frequently has guests at their bed and breakfast who taste produce right out of the field — maybe even still warm from the summer's sun — who experience for the first time the taste of fully ripe produce.

7. If you have an enterprising child or teenager at home, invite him to sell extra produce. I haven't yet been able to persuade Henry to start up a door-to-door produce business in our neighborhood in the summertime, but I am convinced that it would fly if he were game. Our neighborhood is filled with older people who would be delighted to buy Henry's produce, and have the chance to interact with a child on a regular basis. Maybe he'll take it up next year. Or try it yourself!

8. Buy from local bakeries. Inquire about a product's ingredients, including whether certified organic ingredients are used in the baked goods, as well as which environmentally friendly practices are observed in the bakery generally. Also, be sure to ask about when the particular loaf of bread or pie you have your eye on was baked.

Start Cooking

As often as you can, prepare meals from scratch. There is something inordinately satisfying about having a hand in what you bring to the table. Believe me, your children, your spouse or significant other (and you!) will know if you've made something from scratch. What's more, when you prepare your own meals, you know better than anyone what is going into the recipe. Moreover, the aroma of cooking food will permeate your kitchen and waft into other rooms, thus whetting your appetite.

You also can take old standby recipes and with simple adjustments make them more healthful. For instance, with some baked items, you can substitute applesauce for butter or margarine. Pureed prunes work well in many dishes. Another heart-healthy tip is to substitute two-percent evaporated milk in recipes calling for heavy cream. In place of butter, you can dissolve cornstarch in water, whip it up and add it to pan sauces for depth and body.

Since most of us are busy, try to identify strategies for making the time in your life to cook from scratch, such as preparing a week's worth of meals on the weekend. Another sure way of being smart with your food is to eat your leftovers. Americans are said to waste about 30 percent of our food through spoilage. Make every effort to "clean your plate" metaphorically speaking. Eat what you put on your plate. Save your leftovers. Freeze what you can't eat immediately, and be creative with such things as wilted veggies. (Chop them and freeze them for use in omelets, stews and the like.)

Create Your "Signature" Recipe

Just as we wear certain garments over and over because they look and feel good, so too, most of us bring out the same proven recipes time and again because we feel confident of their success. Building on this concept, I suggest each of you develop at least one "signature recipe" — something that you love to make, which people can't resist and for which you're known.

My good friend, Twyla Sickmiller, businesswoman extraordinaire and proprietor of the Maxwell House Bed & Breakfast in Mount Airy, North Carolina is known for her famous chicken salad. She serves this recipe on sandwiches, beds of lettuce and spinach and as hors d'oeuvres in little phyllo shells. After a bit of friendly arm-twisting, Twyla allowed me to include her heretofore secret recipe in this book. She calls it "308 Bistro Chicken Salad," in honor of her new restaurant located in the old Belk's Department Store on Main Street in Mount Airy.

Twyla's chicken salad happens to be a favorite of mine and has been served at nearly every "Simple Living" event we've held in Mount Airy. It's not only delicious, but heart-healthy, due to its low-sodium and low-fat content. "This is a twist on my grandmother's recipe," she says, "and has become a signature dish for 308 Bistro."

308 Bistro Chicken Salad

4 large chicken breasts

½ cup (75g) chopped walnut meats (more if you like)

½ cup (75g) finely chopped onion (sweet Vidalia, if available)

½ cup (75g) tender chopped celery (inner stalks are best)

½ cup (116g) light or no-fat mayonnaise

½ cup (116g) fat-free ranch dressing (Kraft is preferable)

1 cup (92g) grapes (green and red seedless)

Cook chicken breasts by either steaming or baking; cover to hold in the moisture. (Twyla prefers steaming.) Look for smaller grapes and cut in half. Place all the ingredients together in a bowl and mix thoroughly. If not moist enough, add more fat-free mayo. "The salad tastes great the first day, but even better the second day because flavors blend more," Twyla explains. Serve on 12-grain or whole-grain bread or stuffed in a large fresh tomato.

Eat Lower on the Food Chain

For those items that can't be obtained locally, do your homework. Learn which foods are most important to buy organically. If you're not a vegetarian, work on reducing your consumption of meats — for your health, for your pocketbook, for the planet. When I interviewed Frances Moore Lappe for a "Simple Living" segment several years back, the author of the best-seller "Diet for a Small Planet" (Ballantine: 1971) made a compelling case for following a "plant-centered" rather than an "animal-centered" diet.

"When you sit down to a one-pound steak," she said, "you do not see the invisible waste that has gone into it ... (or) that it takes 16 pounds of grain and soy to produce that one-pound steak. You do not see the (enormous amount of) wasted water." But, as important as the huge environmental costs of beef production, Lappe said, is the health and mind-set transformation that comes from making this simple change. A whole-foods, plant-centered diet really meets a body's needs, and ushers in a whole host of benefits, including "dropping weight." "In the diet that Americans eat today, there is so much guilt and anxiety about the weight and the health consequences that eating is not the fun that it could be, as it should be," she said. "Once we choose that style that really meets our bodies' real needs, we let go of that compulsive thinking about (food) that wastes life energy and we can enjoy eating again."

If your family typically eats meat every night, *reduce your meat-based meals by one or two a week.* Increase your offerings of plant-centered meals. I've found lasagna and soup to be great vegetable catch-alls, wonderful avenues to induce my son to eat mushrooms, peppers, kale, onions and garlic — things he might refuse as stand-alone offerings.

One way to work more produce into your menus is by prepping your veggies in advance. If you can set aside some time on Sunday afternoon for food preparation, you can chop onions, bell peppers, celery and carrots for soups, stews and salads. This will make it at the ready on a week night, so you can toss your chopped matter into a stirfry, soup, or whatever you're preparing. (Because fresh fruits tend to discolor, cutting apples in advance is not recommended. However, you can prep and chop some fruits to freeze.)

Food sequencing is another great way to fill up on the "good stuff." The way it works is this: *Eat your fibrous items first — like lentils, bran, apples, celery, almonds —* in order to fill your stomach, thus robbing you of the desire to stuff yourself with heavy proteins, cheeses, desserts and the like. So instead of starting your meal with heavy appetizers, put out a plate of sliced apples, almonds, celery sticks and dried cranberries. Then move onto dinner.

Cooking Parties

Another great idea to produce a quantity of healthful food in a short amount of time is to host — or participate in — a cooking party. I've heard of church groups and social and cooking clubs organizing Sunday afternoon or evening cook-fests, for instance, where large batches are cooked so the participants can take the freshly prepared meals home and have dinners for a week. The rules vary, but in general, everyone contributes ingredients and has a hand in prep work, cooking and baking. Ideally these groups gather in a place with institutional kitchens — a restaurant or church kitchen — so more food can be prepared. People also bring along containers in which to cart home the fixings. Like so many simple-living ideas, this one carries multiple and overlapping benefits: you're building community, whipping up healthful fare and having fun at the same time!

Cook in Bulk

Probably the best strategy for busy people who want to cook from scratch is cooking in bulk. Whenever I stumble upon a recipe that my son and I love — that we don't mind eating again and again — I prepare it in large quantities. Cooking in bulk for my family of two usually amounts to doubling the recipe. The idea is to make enough to have meals to freeze for nights when I don't have time to cook — just time to reheat. When I do make a large batch, I make a point to share my bounty with my elderly mother, who's not likely to cook complicated meals from scratch. Often I'll invite her to eat at my home and then pack her a care package to take home and eat on her own for dinner the next night.

One great way to cook in bulk that's coming back into vogue is using a crockpot or slow cooker. The beauty of this method is that you can pull together a meal in the morning and have it cooking all day and walk into a home filled with good things in the making. Slow cooking is the ideal method for those of us living on a budget as inexpensive cuts of meat work best (they disintegrate), and beans perform beautifully. An added benefit: contributing the smell of slowly cooked foods to your home.

This past year, I started baking scratch biscuits in bulk. I tried several recipes and then concocted my own. I whip up the ingredients, roll them out on a wooden cutting board or on my granite countertop and cut out biscuits. What I don't bake just then, I store in a large flat reusable container in my refrigerator. (You also can freeze them, making sure the biscuits don't clump together when freezing.) When I'm in the "dough," I serve homemade biscuits every morning. All you do is pop them into the toaster oven and in 10 minutes, voila! Fresh biscuits: what could be better? (This is my not-so-subtle way of working flax, wheat germ, cinnamon and other goodies into Henry's system. He loves them so much, he never objects to the healthful additives!)

Wanda's Heart-Healthy Biscuits

Yield: 3 dozen medium-size biscuits or 2 dozen jumbo biscuits

1 cup (240g) softened butter or margarine

1 ½ cups (360ml) cold milk

2 cups (240g) self-rising flour

1 cup (120g) all-purpose unbleached flour

1 cup (120g) whole-wheat or buckwheat flour

$1/8$ cup (14g) wheat germ

$1/8$ cup (14g) finely ground flaxseed

1 teaspoon baking powder

½ teaspoon baking soda

1 tablespoon cinnamon

1 tablespoon sugar

Preheat oven to 400°F (204°C) and grease cookie sheet(s). Mix together flour, wheat germ, flaxseed, baking powder, baking soda, cinnamon and sugar. Work softened butter or margarine into flour with your fingers or hand-held pastry mixer until dough is pea-sized. Pour in milk and mix until well blended. Flour your fingers and knead dough with upward motions. Transfer to floured board and lightly roll the dough ½" (1.3cm) thick by hand or with floured rolling pin. Dip cutter into flour to prevent sticking and cut biscuits. Place on cookie sheet and bake for 8 to 10 minutes. To freeze, place pan in freezer until biscuits are frozen, then remove biscuits to freezer boxes or bags. Dough keeps fresh in refrigerator for up to one week.

"Reciprocal Dining": Not a Dinner Party

I stumbled upon an excellent variation of the group cooking idea that's a bit smaller in scope when our "Simple Living" crew visited Denmark to interview Gitte Jorgensen, a Danish simplicity expert and author. I call her idea "reciprocal dining." Gitte is a single mother who lives with her young son in an apartment complex in Copenhagen. A good friend of Gitte's — another single mother with a young son named Pouline Middleton — lives in the same complex. The two organized a meal-sharing system whereby the two families eat two meals a week together. When it's Gitte's turn to cook, she simply doubles her recipe to feed four mouths instead of two.

The two women have established a few ground rules, including: the "guest" does not regard the meal as a dinner party; no gifts such as wine, flowers or dessert are expected or accepted; the "guest" makes no contribution to the dinner; and she's not allowed to assist with the cleanup afterward. The guests come over at the appointed dinner hour, eat, and run. They also can choose to eat and stay for a visit, but would not harbor hurt feelings if the "host" says, "Not tonight."

The system allows each busy single mother to get a "free night" where she doesn't have to worry about what's for dinner; it's better than eating out at a restaurant — she doesn't lift a finger; she doesn't have to pay restaurant prices; and she is certain to enjoy a healthful meal. The "price" for this is simply making a reciprocal dinner another night that week. This same idea could be applied four nights a week, with Gitte and Pouline each taking on two nights. Or you could extend the circle to three parties of two, each to accommodate three nights eating out with a circle of six diners. The possibilities are endless. In addition to helping with cooking, you are knitting close social ties by breaking bread together. Give this lovely idea from Denmark a try!

Reclaim Hunger

A few summers ago at the community pool here in town, Henry and I met his friends, Andrew and Peter Balogh, whom we were entertaining for the afternoon. It was approaching the noon hour, and I was anticipating my daily swim. Just as I was about to dive in, the three boys ganged up on me. "We're hungry!" For most American mothers, the hunger plea trumps everything else. If your child is hungry, you'll drop everything to feed him. Tamas Balogh, the boys' father, was in earshot. A native of Hungary who has established a successful cardiology practice in North Carolina, he immediately came to my defense: "You boys can wait to eat. Henry's mother needs her swim."

You can wait to eat. How long has it been since you've heard that one? In our instant-gratification era, waiting to eat is about as dated as making a call on a rotary-dial phone. Dr. Balogh's simple comment cuts against the American grain. If someone is hungry — especially a child — he deserves to be fed. *That minute.* In our snack-food culture, waiting for meals simply doesn't occur. When I'm hungry, feed me.

But I appreciated Dr. Balogh's intervention. He is of the old school, like me. So I swam. And the boys waited with long faces — not so patiently — for me. But I am hopeful that with that noon swim a larger lesson was learned. *Hunger is not necessarily a bad thing.* Not occasional hunger in a culture where the danger of starvation is minimal. Hunger should be experienced by all of us; it makes eating better, just as patience is a virtue that we can learn by having to wait our turn.

Reflecting on that moment in Mount Airy, I am reminded of the passages in Laura Ingalls Wilder's book, "Farmer Boy," about the childhood of her husband, Almanzo Wilder. Anyone who reads the book can't help but remember his strong account of hunger. The farmer boy works in the fields feeding livestock, cleaning barn stalls, milking cows and bringing in crops. And through it all, the growing, working boy lives to eat. His hunger grows large. When he sits down at the family table with all his siblings, every meal is a great feast. When his hunger is satisfied by his mother's home cooking, all's right with the world. Even if you don't want to go on a full-fledged fast, try letting your stomach's hunger gage dip down to a full zero before filling up again.

Ritual of the Meal

Once you've decided that at-home, sit-down meals are important, you can set the stage for a successful dining experience. Think of your meal as a "slow food" experience, in which you slow the pace in order to savor your food, your company, and your time together. In order to make your nightly (or regular) meals truly magical, approach your meals as you would a theatrical production, where the stage is set, the curtain goes up at a certain time and the action unfolds.

Setting the table: If your child is 5 or older, she is probably mature enough to help set the dinner table. Teach her how to properly position the utensils and fold the napkins. If you use cloth napkins more than once before laundering, ask your child to pull them out of the napkin ring to check to be sure they're clean enough to use for a second (or third) outing. Using the same dinner service night after night adds predictability to your ritual. Children crave predictability and routine, so establish regular chairs for each member of the family.

Ornamental touches. I like to take a cue from the ritual of communion at the Episcopal Church, in which the silver chalice is polished before and after the offering of sacramental wine and bread. Candles are lit and snuffed out. After use, the chalice is covered with ornamental cloths. While I wouldn't ritualize my meals to this degree, most of us could do with a bit more ceremony in our meals. Put some thought into the rituals, staging, and regular features you'd like to create in your dinner table. If flowers are in season and available in my yard, I cut some and add a vase to the table. Henry loves candles, so most evenings, part of our ritual is lighting the candle. (He does the honors.)

Disconnect and reconnect. If the television or radio is on, turn it off. If cell phones are likely to interrupt, turn them off, as well. If your landline rings during dinner, let the answering machine pick up a message. Remember, you're setting the mood for conversation and connection; this is no time to be available to the outside world.

Say grace. Every night at dinner, Henry and I say grace at the table. Say it, and as you do so, allow the words to sink deeply into your consciousness. (See "Graceful Simplicity," page 188.)

Engage in conversation. Teach your children basic conversational skills such as asking questions, listening politely and offering their own opinions. If your child is not doing so, I prompt such basics as maintaining eye contact while another person is speaking. Try to hold one conversation all around the table, with each person having his or her turn to speak. Henry knows he is supposed to ask questions of others, including elders. If he doesn't come up with a question when his grandmother comes over, I'll prompt him with suggestions such as, "How has your day been?" Or, "Did you get a good night's sleep?"

Assign jobs. A sure way to engage your family is to get them to pitch in and help. If your spouse or child helps with meal prep, wonderful. Assign tasks such as chopping carrots, making a salad, or assembling the ingredients for fruit salad. If you want to handle the cooking, assign tasks around the meal, such as putting away items. Henry always clears the table and puts our yogurt spread and salad dressing back in the refrigerator.

Invite guests. A wonderful way to expand your hospitality is to invite guests over from time to time. This models the concept of hospitality and service to your children. Guests always come first. For example, if there's just one biscuit left on the plate, be sure to show by example that your guest gets first dibs on it.

Graceful Simplicity

"Consider the act of saying grace before a meal. Here the core is an attitude of thanksgiving, of appreciation. The focus is on recognizing the full value of what one has rather than lamenting what one does not. While one can mouth the words, one cannot authentically begin a meal with a benediction of grace and at the same time maintain a sense of dissatisfaction with what one has. There is a certain peaceful contentment that is part of genuine thankfulness. ...

"Saying grace is not necessary for graceful living, nor as I understand it, does saying grace require any religious belief. But in its authentic form, making the dinner table a place of grace can be an important constitutive element of the aesthetic life of Simplicity."

— *Jerome Segal*

You know from personal experience how much better you feel when you eat a meal that was lovingly prepared at home — even better, when you've had the chance to savor it over time without feeling rushed. Once you decide to make mealtime a priority rather than a rarity in your life, you're making a wise decision that will bear fruit for you, your children and your family.

Chapter Six

Beating a Path to the Garden

Plant a new victory garden and allow its growth to spur on your own. Grow flowers for your body and soul.

Reclaim the pleasure — and multiple benefits — of gardening, especially the fruits of your labor. Once you make the commitment, site your garden for maximum sun exposure, enhance your soil fertility, begin composting and start growing nourishing fruits, herbs and vegetables. But don't stop there. While you're at it, cultivate places of beauty with flowers and plantings to adorn your yard and home. Finally, overcome "nature-deficit disorder" and establish an ongoing connection with the outdoors through your new "home outside."

Beating a Path to the Garden

Beating a path to the garden is a sure way to extend the good life in your world. In fact, there is no single better method of connecting with the source of your sustenance than growing fruits and vegetables in your own garden. Establishing a personal connection with the plant world offers a vital relationship with the source of life itself. And nothing quite compares to celebrating the present moment in your home — not to mention introducing beauteous sights and uplifting aromas — than by festooning it with flowers. Just gazing at a beautiful plant can calm your mind and boost your spirits.

When you take time to create a garden, you are not only nurturing plant life, but providing habitat and cover for birds and animals, butterflies and fireflies and other winged creatures. Even small patio or balcony gardens — pockets of green — create healing sanctuaries for you and wildlife and allow you to do your small part to improve air quality in your community. In our hurry-up world, gardening forces a slower pace. Nature will simply not be rushed. What is more, when you provide the foundation, space, and energy to support the growth of plants, you are magically nurturing your own inner growth — the development of your soul.

Gardening "is nothing short of miraculous," writes Peg Streep, author of "Spiritual Gardening: Creating Sacred Space Outdoors" (Time-Life: 1999). "You kneel, dig a bit, drop in a seed, add water and wait. In time the miracle unveils itself, beginning with an ever-so-tentative shoot of green: Life!" Gardening is a vehicle for spiritual and emotional connection, she writes, which allows us to "participate in the process that is life, from the greening of the shoot to the dying-off of the flower."

Like so many simple living choices, gardening extends multiple and overlapping benefits. By growing your own edibles, you eat healthier, you save money, and you become a better steward of the environment. When you're cultivating flowers and ornamentals, you're adding an ephemeral, mood-lifting beauty to your home, the value of which is impossible to measure. Because you're more connected to the life force by having a stake in nature's workings — its ebbs and flows; its magic and ferocity; its stunning products — you become a more grounded and compassionate human being. Placing the fate of your garden in the hands of Mother Nature quickly unravels humanity's anthropomorphic arrogance, which means, gardening is the best medicine for recovering control freaks.

> *"The first gatherings of the garden in May of salads, radishes and herbs made me feel like a mother about her baby — how could anything so beautiful be mine. And this emotion of wonder filled me for each vegetable as it was gathered every year. There is nothing that is comparable to it, as satisfactory or as thrilling, as gathering the vegetables one has grown."*
>
> — Alice B. Toklas

Save on Your Grocery Bill

Interest in home-scale gardening has skyrocketed during our recent economic downturn. Indications pointed to seven million more households growing their own fruits, vegetables, herbs or berries in 2009 than the year before, according to a National Gardening Association (NGA) survey. This is up fully 19 percent from 2008 and anticipated to nearly double the 10 percent growth already seen in this area from 2007 to 2008.

A few other noteworthy statistics from the NGA survey:
- 43 million U.S. households plan to grow their own fruits, vegetables, herbs and berries in 2009, up 19 percent from 36 million households in 2008.
- 21 percent of households said they plan to start a food garden in 2009.
- 11 percent of households already active in food gardening plan to increase both the amount and variety of vegetables they will grow in 2009.
- 10 percent also said they will spend more time food gardening this year.

The reasons cited for the heightened interest in food gardening:

● 58 percent — better-tasting food.

● 54 percent — to save money on food bills.

● 51 percent — for better-quality food.

● 48 percent — to grow food they know is safe.

"As in previous recessions, we've seen increased participation in and spending on food gardening as people look for ways to economize," explained Bruce Butterfield, research director for the NGA. George Ball of Burpee Seeds, the nation's largest mail-order seed company, reported a dramatic increase in demand for his firm's vegetable seeds in 2009. According to a report appearing on the Web site, *www.NaturalNews.com,* Ball said that his company sold out of seeds for some popular varieties of tomatoes, peppers and onions. Estimates vary, but depending on the scope of one's effort and dedication, home gardeners can save anywhere from $500 to $1,000 on their grocery bills in a season from an investment of just $50 or less in gardening materials. For more information on this or subsequent surveys go to *www.gardenresearch.com.*

In 2009, my neighbor, Joe Lamp'l, set out to grow a summer's worth of produce for his family of four on $15. This passionate and personable gardener, who lives with his wife and two young daughters a few houses down the street from me in Mount Airy, as of this writing on July 23, has produced over 50 pounds of cucumbers, tomatoes, squash, beans, lettuce, baby bok choi and Swiss chard. "I am shooting for a total harvest in excess of 100 pounds before the summer is over," writes Joe, whose Web site is *www.joegardener.com.* "Not bad for a total investment of 15 bucks. That will put the cost per pound at less than 15 cents!"

This uptick in interest in gardening is neither surprising nor unprecedented, though. When times get tough, people traditionally take up hoe and plow. Think Victory Gardens during World War II; think back-to-the-landers during the economic downturns of the early to mid '70s and late

'80s. The good news about these recent developments is that most experts project that even if the economy stages a comeback, most of these new gardeners have gotten the bug and will stay with it.

The Good Earth

Ever since I was a child growing up in various houses around the country, my memories of summer were equally divided between gardening and outdoor play. When my family lived in Buffalo, New York, summertime action centered on the backyard grape arbor — an impressive piece of outdoor furniture equipped with built-in bench seats and held together by connective latticework with thick grape vines snaking through. Nothing was quite as magical as sitting in that arbor with ripening fruit to my side and overhead, bees buzzing in and out — a hive of activity. I would nibble on a few of the thick-skinned bluish-black Concord grapes off the vine (though most were turned by Mother into jam and jelly). I have lived in many more places since then, and, at a minimum, I always put a few tomato plants in the ground — or into pots, as was the case when I lived in Los Angeles and my only space for growing was on the patio or deck.

Since moving into the Sunflower House in 2007, my passion for gardening has quickened. Here, in my manageable-sized backyard plot, I have come to love nothing more than puttering among my plants, pulling up weeds, checking daily on the progress of my plants. The summer of this writing, I'm as nervous as an expectant parent over the development of our Sugar Baby watermelons — a crop that eluded us before. (The joke was on Henry and me the previous year when we mistakenly watched a volunteer from the compost pile that we believed to be a watermelon morph into a pumpkin.)

Something about being out in nature connects me to the seasons, puts my own professional (and personal) challenges in perspective. When I'm in need of a quick break from the computer screen, I dash from my chair in the study, step through the sunroom and head outside for just a moment

— to pull up a weed or score a ripe blackberry or two. These simple acts of connection with my pet plants suggest that all's right with the world.

My first spring and summer in the Sunflower House, we had to break some new ground for the garden. Though two rapidly maturing black-berry plants set out by the previous owners were going strong, I could find no evidence of a vegetable garden. I selected a spot, tilled and improved the soil, and set out my first plants. For guidance, I studied back issues of Mother Earth News, a publication with which I feel a special affinity as a long-time reader and for having shot a "Simple Living" segment on organic gardening in Kansas with Editor-in-Chief Cheryl Long. (I'll never forget the remarkable garden that Cheryl tends just outside of Topeka, nor the mud through which we slogged on the day of our shoot, after a three-inch downpour the night before.)

That first summer in my garden, I planted tomatoes, zucchini, squash, cucumbers and beets. I set out rhubarb and lemon verbena along the fence as perennials to complement the blackberry bushes. I used newspapers weighted down with rocks and sticks for mulch. (The newsprint served its purpose, though it was a bit unsightly, especially when occasional pages would break loose and fly about the lawn.) This year, taking a page from Cheryl Long's garden book, I've turned to grass clippings for mulch, which carry the added benefit of fixing nitrogen into the soil. When the skies don't supply adequate rainfall, Henry's job is to water the plants every several days. He also takes special care of the Japanese maple tree that was planted at the periphery of our yard during our open house ceremony in May 2008.

Start Gardening

Gardening is actually pretty simple stuff. I'm no expert, and if *I* can do it, anyone can. You don't need a lot to get started — just a few basics: soil, water, sunlight, and, of course, seeds or plants. With those primary elements, you can get busy.

- *Sun*: Siting your garden is extremely important. Be sure to select the place in your yard that receives maximum sunlight. Eight hours a day — or more — is best. Although bearing plants can produce with fewer hours of sun beating down on them, you won't enjoy the same quality or quantity of yield. If you have so much mature vegetation in your yard that you can't find a spot providing that much sun, consider growing leafy vegetables such as collards, kale, spinach and lettuce. Or place your vegetable garden in the front yard where there may be more available sun. Remember, even if your neighbors don't do it this way, be the first. All movements call for pioneers! If they ask what you're doing, tell them that edibles are the latest landscaping trend.

- *Water*: My neighbor and gardening mentor Joe Lamp'l recommends an inch of water per week for healthy plant growth. "Supplying water every two to three days, so that a total of an inch is delivered each week works well," he writes in his book, "Over the Fence with Joe Gardener" (Cool Springs: 2006). Joe also recommends watering at night or in the early morning in order to work within the natural "dew cycle," therefore not prolonging the time your plants remain moist, which can lead to disease. If you travel a lot in the summer or can't find the time to keep up a watering regimen during a busy work week, consider using soaker hoses, connected to battery operated timers. This puts your garden irrigation needs on autopilot while you're away.

- *Soil*: Without good soil, your garden dreams are not likely to materialize. Soil not only provides the base for your plants to take root, but soil is a repository for your plants' nutrients, minerals, oxygen, organic matter and water. All but the most pristine soil calls for amendment with compost material, manure, and other improvements. Be sure it is rich with a range of nutrients but that it is aerated. You may want to consider containing your garden soil in raised beds held in place by wooden railings. (But be sure the wood is not treated with toxic chemicals.) This method helps prevent erosion and promote intensive gardening. Delineating and elevating one's garden makes your plants more accessible, and lessens back strain.

• *Seeds/plants*: You can start your garden by growing plants from seed or by purchasing young plants from a nursery or garden center. Either way, you'll want to set them out in the ground when the danger of frost has passed. Most gardeners go for warm-season crops such as tomatoes, squash, cucumbers, peppers and beans. But the beauty of gardening is that *you* get to choose; this way, over the years, you can tilt toward what works in your space. Saving seed from year to year adds another level of excitement and self-sufficiency to your efforts. This year, I'm paying special attention to my Brandywine tomato plants, grown from seed saved from last year's plants. My spaghetti squash plants are also the product of seed delivered to me the previous September by my Fairfax, Virginia cousins, Tad and Aleksandra Tuliszka. Both the tomatoes and spaghetti squash are thriving.

• *Pest control:* Call it preventative maintenance for plants. If you grow healthy plants, they're less likely to be plagued by bugs and diseases. But if you do see something like a tomato hornworm, the first line of defense should not be an application of pesticide but rather mechanical methods of removal. (Read: picking them off by hand.) Also, when you encourage the presence of natural predators (such as birds, toads, bats and others), your pest-abatement job is likely to be smaller.

Seed Savers Exchange

If you're just starting out and are interested in procuring heirloom seeds, you need to know about Seed Savers Exchange in Decorah, Iowa, *www.seedsavers.org*. Seed Savers Exchange is a non-profit, member-supported organization that has been distributing rare heirloom garden seeds since 1975. The organization was co-founded by Diane Ott Whealy, after her ailing grandfather passed on the seeds of two heirloom tomato varieties that had been brought to Iowa from Bavaria when his own parents migrated there in the 1870s.

Our "Simple Living" crew shot footage of Diane in Decorah, and I have been a fan of her ground-breaking role in saving our plant heritage ever since. Today, Heritage Farm is the largest non-governmental seed repository in America, holding over 25,000 endangered vegetable varieties.

Visitors are welcome at the farm, which is open weekdays from 9 a.m. to 5 p.m., and weekends from 10 a.m. to 5 p.m. Guided tours and bus tours are available for $3 a person by calling 563-382-6104 in season.

Gardening and Your Health

I'm a lifelong journal writer. After moving into the Sunflower House, I decided to keep two journals: an all-around life journal and a second one that was more specific, devoted to my health and my garden. In my mind, the two issues are integrally linked. The health/garden journal is one in which I record such things as cholesterol readings, blood pressure, weight and other vitals, along with the emotional information that accompanies them. Likewise, the garden section is loaded with data, such as the dates when seeds were put to soil, dates when young shoots first appeared, date of first bearing, as well as my thrill at seeing the miracle of growth. There's an aspect of scrapbooking to this journal as well, as I tape empty seed packets into the pages for future reference.

I feel healthy when I'm out strolling in my garden, gazing at my plants, celebrating the success of each new fruit or vegetable. (My spirits can also fall when I find a plant branch that has succumbed to the forces of gravity, or I spot evidence of pests.) And while you may not burn as many calories pulling weeds as, say, running a marathon, every bit of exertion adds up. And, when working outside, your skin is absorbing all-important vitamin D. In my case, there is no question that a vital link exists between my health and well-being, positive sleep and dream patterns, and my work in the garden. To all of those folks who seek to improve their health through exercise and improved diet, take note. There is yet another way! Consider gardening as a route to a healthier self.

Sample Health/Garden diary entry — this one from April 17, 2009:

"Something remarkable is happening and taking root inside of me. I'm getting healthier. All the signs are moving in a positive direction — the vitals like cholesterol, etc. Also, I'm starting to (better) tolerate my biweekly allergy shots. It makes me happy to know that even though I'm aging, I'm getting better and stronger and taking hold of my life."

Eco-Friendly Ideas for Your Garden

• *Use hand tools* whenever possible. Rakes, hoes and shovels are preferable to power tools that emit gas fumes.

• *Let muscle-powered machines replace their gas-powered equivalents.* Cold shoulder the leaf-blower in favor of the rake and broom, and replace the conventional lawn mower with the hand-push variety. Remember the multiple and overlapping benefits I've been touting? When you let your muscles do the work, you're burning calories, maintaining quiet, not contributing carbon emissions into our fragile atmosphere, and you're saving gas money.

• *Start or join up with a neighborhood tool exchange,* so you don't have to purchase (or rent) every implement you may need to use.

• If you can't borrow a seldom-used tool, such as a rototiller, for your job, *rent rather than purchase.*

• *Start or join a plant or seed swap* with neighbors and friends or in your garden club. Exchange information about how to care for your plants.

• *Trade time.* Help your neighbor put his garden in one week in exchange for him helping you with yours the next.

• *Share compost* or leaves with others, if you have a surplus.

• *Share the bounty of your labors* with others in your neighborhood or community. Little opens doors more quickly than sharing vegetables with friends and neighbors.

I am fortunate to live in a single-family home on a one-third acre plot. Not everyone is so blessed. The good news is you don't have to own or rent a house with a yard to garden. Options abound. Generally found in cities, community gardens are wonderful meccas for growing produce and building community. If your area doesn't have one, consider getting a group together to start one. Work with a religious institution, school or community group to get one off the ground.

Some progressive businesses encourage their employees to start community gardens at work. TS Designs, the eco-friendly T-shirt printing and dyeing company in Burlington, North Carolina, does just this with its "square foot garden" located on company grounds, just outside its plant. When our "Simple Living" crew shot a segment at the facility, I was struck by the harvested organic vegetables available for snacking in the employee lunch room, free for the taking. Supporting a company garden is one element of TS Designs' pursuit of the "triple-bottom-line" business model: for people, the planet, and profits. It is an inexpensive way to add value to your employees' lives, and by extension, your business.

Common Garden at a Charlotte Condo

Robb Webb, a program officer for the Duke Endowment's Rural Church Program, lives in a 14-unit condominium complex in bustling Charlotte, North Carolina. Robb's professional and personal interest in the transformative powers of gardening led him to try an experiment on his home turf. Several years back, he obtained permission from the condominium association (luckily, he sits on the board) to plant a garden. "Their first reaction," Robb recalls, "was that they didn't want something that would hurt resale or cost too much to maintain." (He offered persuasive assurances on both counts.)

Robb identified an area in the back common courtyard with a fair amount of sun, dug up ivy, and carved out a 12- by 15-foot plot. There he put in tomatoes, squash, cucumbers, carrots, bell peppers and basil. In the garden's first year, Robb planted more than he needed for his personal use, guessing that neighbors would emerge and engage. "The presence of a garden stirs curiosity, and volunteers appeared," he says. "Someone walked by with a dog; he pulled a weed and picked a tomato." That first garden year proved to be a remarkable success — not only with the garden's bounty but in generating fellowship among neighbors who had previously been too busy to speak.

Among the greatest accomplishments of the garden was helping engage two elderly Charlotte natives, now living in the complex, in conversation. "I knew them only in passing prior to the garden — a hello at the mailbox or a brief word at our yearly homeowners' meeting," says Robb. "In the garden, I learned stories about them and our city that I would have never known. For example, there is a beautiful building about a block from our complex that used to be a grocery store. It turns out that in their youth, the building was a place folks from Myers Park gathered to dance on Friday and Saturday nights."

Unfortunately, the garden was brought to its knees in its second year from a severe early-June storm that beat the young, tender plants to the ground. But Robb feels that his mission of building community around plant life at the condo has been accomplished. "While we didn't harvest much food in 2009, the experience provided a great lesson on the fragility of farming: farmers take risks every spring. We replanted a few tomato plants along with some cilantro and basil and will try again next year." While the plants may not have provided a yield, the connections amongst and between the condo residents are enjoying a full flowering.

The Joy of Composting

I've previously mentioned my personal pet peeve about the excessive waste in our country, along with my desire to reduce my personal waste stream. While it's clear that disposable diapers, dishware, and packaging bulk up our trash cans and landfills, "organic waste" — that is, decomposable kitchen waste — is also a big contributor. According to statistics provided by the North Carolina Extension Service, *fully 20 percent solid waste that's landfilled* comes from yard and garden waste. Reducing (or eliminating) this part of our American waste stream constitutes what I call the "low hanging fruit" of lifestyle change. That is, with relatively little effort, you can have a big impact.

Along these lines, one of my greatest pleasures with gardening has been establishing a compost pit in the backyard that diverts a sizable portion of my garbage directly into my backyard. This compost pit feeds my passion for waste reduction, especially by putting kitchen and table scraps to work. How silly to throw something like a banana peel into your trash-headed-for-the-landfill rather than plunking it down in your own backyard where it will perform miracles and turn into "black gold." Composting your organic waste carries multiple and overlapping benefits: it helps improve your soil quality while providing on-site recycling; it reduces the "yuck factor" in your garbage can, while helping create healthy, disease-resistant plants; and you're making your home more sustainable by using every part of what you bring into it — even the waste. So let it rot!

Why Compost?

According to "The Complete Compost Gardening Guide" (Storey: 2008) by Barbara Pleasant and Deborah L. Martin, composting:
• Increases the organic content of the soil, which improves its texture, drainage, fertility, and ability to anchor plants.
• Invigorates the soil's food web by providing nutrients, moisture and habitat for a huge range of beneficial life forms.
• Enhances plants' resistance to pests, diseases and weather challenges.

"Making the most of compost," Pleasant and Martin write, "means understanding and using its dynamic powers to enhance the growth of your plants and the many other living beings with which you share your landscape."

When I began composting in earnest at the Sunflower House, I knew I didn't want to buy a pricey compost tumbler or bin. My friend, Judit Balogh, told me that in her native Hungary people dig holes in the ground and add fruit peelings, coffee grounds, eggshells and the like, and turn them with a shovel whenever the spirit moves them. (You don't want to add meat scraps or bones that will attract rodents and other undesirables.) That made sense to me, so not long after moving in, I dug a hole in the backyard a few feet from my main vegetable garden. It has thrilled me to no end to watch the soil develop in richness and complexity, to watch the earthworms weave through the decomposing matter, to see how quickly and sturdily plants like pumpkins and cantaloupes sprang forth from my leavings. As I've developed my composting skill, I've learned that adding dried leaves, shredded newspaper and sawdust enhances your heap.

In fact, the compost pit has worked its way into my unconscious as my main diary entry from April 5, 2009 reads: "My dream life has been extraordinarily rich lately — like the soil emerging from the compost pile, with heat flairs and worms moving through. Perhaps it is my subconscious mind trying to work through letting go of the past and garnering the courage to advance with confidence into the future."

My Future Rain Barrel

Another no-brainer when setting up your garden is to install a rain barrel to take advantage of the gallons of "free water" tumbling from your roof. Though as of this writing in the Summer of 2009, we've been blessed with abundant rain in our section of the Southeast, having suffered through droughts for several years now and hearing increasingly alarming reports about the coming global water shortage, I'm not about to be lulled into complacency by the rains of the moment.

Not only does harvesting the rain off your roof make environmental sense — why let a finite resource run through your fingers when all you have to do is capture it? — it makes economic sense in communities like mine where you pay for water by the gallon. And it makes sense to be prepared for future shortages while resting assured that when the next drought comes — as surely it will — the city's water restrictions will not cause your prized tomatoes, squash, and sunflowers to wither and die.

I already have my barrel — a RainPro™ barrel made by Rainwater Harvesting Specialists — it's black and made here in North Carolina of 100-percent recycled plastic. It holds 100 gallons of water and looks like it would withstand an invasion of the body snatchers. Though I've not yet installed it — my fledgling barrel rests in my carport alongside, well, my flimsy-by-comparison city-issued trash can — its day in the sun (and rain) is coming. My future plants don't know it yet, but it's said that rainwater is sweeter for plants than the treated stuff flowing from the tap. Give it a try. Get a rain barrel of your own.

Plant a Tree: Lower Your Carbon Footprint

A great way to reduce your carbon footprint is to plant — and maintain — a tree. (More, if you can swing it.) The way it works is this: Trees absorb carbon dioxide from the atmosphere and return oxygen back into it. As long as the tree is alive, it continues absorbing carbon dioxide from the atmosphere, retaining carbon in its cells and spewing out oxygen. Once the tree is cut down and turned into framing for a house, for instance, or a frame for your picture, the sequestered carbon stays in place — until the wood either rots or burns. According to The Washington Post, three common trees that store carbon efficiently include the American elm (159 pounds of CO_2 per year); hickory (159 pounds per year); red maple (108 pounds per year). (These calculations are based on trees that are five to 10 years old with a six-inch trunk width.)

Flower Gardening

Though vegetable gardening contributes to the health, economy and overall well-being of your home, flower gardening brings something less tangible, but no less important: happiness. In our rushed-up world, what could be better than your own simple, at-home prescription for bliss? Flowers and floral displays in the garden improve your yard, and cut flowers and potted plants in the home lift spirits and contribute color and beauty. Certain ones are thought to improve indoor air quality.

One simple way to reclaim the good life is by focusing your attention on creating a paradise *outside* your home. Think of your yard and garden as that transition zone between the controlled environment of your interior and the uncontrolled world at large. At the Sunflower House, I must admit to devoting more attention to cultivating my vegetables rather than my flower garden. In part, this is because the previous owners had done a fine — if none too original — job with the landscaping, thus leaving less work in this department. Landscaping around the Sunflower House features mature plantings, including evergreen boxwoods circling the front, a giant, fragrant magnolia tree dominating the front lawn, and lovely spring-blooming azaleas dotted around the house. The mature plantings help shade the house in the summer, reducing energy bills. The back wall of the house is lined with a column of hearty, mature aucubas, and hostas fringe the side of the house adjacent to the driveway.

"Banks of azaleas, ruddy, white, and purple, bloomed in one place; roses of every hue turned their lovely faces to the sun; ranks of delicate ferns and heaths with their waxen bells, were close by; glowing geraniums and stately lilies side by side. ... All manner of beautiful and curious plants were there; and Christie walked among them, as happy as a child who finds its playmates again."
— Louisa May Alcott

In terms of flowers, I can't resist sunflowers, which I start from seed and plant alongside the back fence; begonias and geraniums live in planters in the front and back. I started a lilac on the back fence from a cutting but it succumbed to the monsoons of June 2009 and drowned as a result. My pussy willow — rooted from a part of Mother's birthday bouquet — has taken root in my yard and promises a great profusion in the future.

If you're just getting started with flower gardening, my best advice is to start with simple perennials and annuals that are easy to grow and favor the sun. Bulbed flowers like daffodils, tulips, irises and the like are wonderful to work with once you've figured how you'd like to lay out your yard. Even if you make a misstep, nothing's really lost since you can always transplant them. In addition to Web site research, ask your green-thumbed neighbors what grows best in your neighborhood. You may want to visit your local nurseries and ask every question that comes to mind.

Local extension agents, who sometimes offer seminars to the public for a small fee or for free, are another valuable resource.

"Flower Power"

A couple of nights before my presentation about how libraries can go green at the 2009 American Library Association's annual meeting in Chicago, I had the privilege of meeting a remarkable memoirist named Wesley Adamczyk. The author of "When God Looked the Other Way: An Odyssey of War, Exile and Redemption" (University of Chicago: 2004). Wesley was a 7-year-old, upper-class boy living in Eastern Poland when Soviet troops stormed his home and deported Wesley, along with his mother, sister and brother to an existence of slavery and starvation in Siberia. His story is without a doubt one of the most exquisitely rendered among the vast literature of World War II — an especially impressive feat given that Adamczyk wrote in his second language (English) and had no previous training in writing or literature.

A remarkable and resilient human being who has risen above unspeakable suffering to bear witness to the atrocity of war, Wesley is not bitter, but rather a driven, intense and courtly gentleman. When we met for dinner at a restaurant in Millennium Park, he presented me with a lovely bouquet of lilies. I carried the bouquet — which originated in the garden of a Polish allergist friend of his — to the Renaissance Hotel. On the morning of my ALA presentation, on the spur of the moment, I decided to bring the bouquet with me into the auditorium in McCormick Place. I placed it on the podium and began my speech. Voila: magic!

Though I've spoken frequently during the 23 years since publishing my first book, I can honestly say that I've never felt better about a presentation. Maybe it was the subject, for which the time has finally arrived. I'm sure my audience of forward-thinking, eco-friendly librarians played a part. Maybe the stars were lined up because we were in Chicago — a city working overtime to make its name as a "green" metropolis. Or maybe the "X" factor in hitting my home run came from the presence of that bouquet of lilies — their sweet aroma and even sweeter well-wishes wafting my way throughout my talk. Forget Power Point. After this, I may never again agree to speak in public without benefit of "Flower Power" or lovingly given flowers.

Create a "Room Outside"

During her three decades of landscape design work, acclaimed, Vermont-based landscape designer, Julie Moir Messervy, has observed that Americans are not only spending less time outdoors, but they're devoting fewer resources to landscaping. In many new housing developments, she says, generally there are almost no plantings around the house, except perhaps a spindly tree or two, and maybe a few bushes. As for exterior built features, at most, there may be a patio or deck. Seemingly every resource in new home construction is earmarked for grooming and perfecting interior spaces at the expense of those outside. "The McMansions turn their back and front and sides on the landscapes," she says, "and the landscapes serve as doormats around the throne of a house."

Messervy's expertise calls for creating outdoor spaces that beckon: front, back and side yards; contemplative retreats; and areas for play, entertainment, and escape. In her book, "Home Outside: Creating the Landscape You Love" (Taunton: 2009), she presents a plan to tap into your intuition to create or expand your living space outdoors. She also addresses the issue of enhancing flow from indoors to outdoors and back again. In our new downsized era, spending relaxed time at home on a "staycation" has become more popular than ever before.

Ironically, creating defined spaces or rooms outside is not only innately satisfying, but can be one of the least expensive — and most impactful — improvements you can make to a home. If resources are limited, she says, the first order of business is for the family to create a space to congregate out-of-doors, she says. If your home is utterly barren, you'll probably want to do at least a minimal amount of landscaping in the front first, but Messervy recommends putting the majority of resources into creating at least one comfortable, inviting "family place to be."

If your primary outside space is a deck, make it a deck you want to live in. Container gardens and outdoor furniture go a long way toward accomplishing this. If you are building or rebuilding steps on a deck, incorporate a lower landing "so you're not tripping down stairs with a tray of food." If mosquitoes are a problem, screen the deck, and be sure to screen the underside as well, so the mosquitoes can't get in that way.

If you decide to create an outdoor room in the yard, it's essential to give it definition. The cheapest way to go, she says, is to create a room in grass, for instance, "an oval of grass." You might border it with billows, or surround it with vegetables, like a British cottage garden, in which vegetables, roses and shrubs are intermingled. Investing in upgrading your yard and garden will not only enhance your enjoyment of your property but will upgrade its value when you do decide to sell. You'll also find more sustainable ideas for your yard from eco-landscaper and author, Tom Girolamo, "Your Eco-Friendly Yard: Sustainable Ideas to Save you Time, Money and the Earth" (Krause Publications: 2009).

Pointers for Creating a "Home Outside"

1. Select a focal point for your outdoor room, such as an arbor or fountain or a compelling statue. Those with a wabi-sabi bent often designate found objects such as an antique trellis or playful vintage bicycle with planter basket in this role.

2. Frame your space with fencing, stone walls or plantings. Walkways work in this capacity.

3. Balance the energy in how you compose your landscapes through the interaction of focal points and frames.

4. Consider incorporating a water feature, such as a man-made waterfall, fountain or ornamental pond. Even a birdbath works here, but never allow the water to stagnate and breed mosquitoes!

5. Incorporate walkways into your outdoor space. Always opt for permeable surfaces which allow water to perk down into the ground. Use brick, gravel pea stone, or flagstone or some equivalent for stepping stones. Leave room

(continued)

for grass to grow between the stones. Consider laying out the path in S-curves, which create a poetic sense of flow.

6. Include comfortable weatherproof furniture, including tables on which to place beverages, snacks and candles.

7. If you have children, let your imagination — and theirs — loose and give them a playhouse. Tree houses also work magic and give your child a unique perspective on the world below.

Wildlife and Bird-Friendly Outdoor Spaces

As you're working to make your outdoor world more appealing, consider the needs of wildlife. Look into submitting your yard (or even your apartment balcony) into the Certified Wildlife Habitat program through the National Wildlife Federation (*www.nwf.org*) or 800-822-9919. The program gives guidelines for creating a wildlife sanctuary while restoring habitat in commercial and residential areas. By providing appropriate food, water, cover and a place for wildlife to raise their young — and by incorporating sustainable gardening practices — you not only help wildlife, but you also qualify to become an official Certified Wildlife Habitat™. (Application fee: $20.) Many participants like to display the Certified Wildlife Habitat™ sign in their yards to help spread the word — and educational message.

My friend, Karen Bearden in Raleigh, who is passionate about birds, offered the following suggestions about drawing winged friends into our worlds.

Make Your Garden Bird-Friendly With Water, Food and Shelter

"Loss of habitat is affecting birds tremendously, so by offering an inviting landscape, you'll be helping our feathered friends. Like humans, birds need water, food and shelter. Following are tips to help make your yard and garden bird-friendly:

• *Plant with native plants* as much as possible. Check resources to see which plants are native to your region.

• *Birds need food,* so include a variety of plants that offer berries and seeds. (Dogwoods, viburnums, spruce and black-eyed-Susans work well.)

• *Make sure to include tubular plants* such as pineapple sage, coral honeysuckle and cardinal flower that provide nectar for the hummingbirds.

• *Different size shrubs* provide opportunities for nests and cover.

• *Don't cut down dead trees* (unless they threaten to fall on your home or people)! Woodpeckers and nuthatches use dead trees to create cavities for their nests.

• *Offer a different variety of bird seed* that you buy from your local bird store (the seed is fresher than from big-box stores and supermarkets.)

• *Sunflower seed* is the most popular with the majority of birds.

• *Niger seed (thistle)* attracts goldfinches and pine siskins.

• *Millet* is a favorite of ground birds such as sparrows and juncos.

• *Suet* is a hit with many birds. You can make your own by mixing peanut butter and corn meal, or buy suet cakes at the bird store.

• *Offer a different variety of feeders.* Make sure they're placed near some cover, but not too close, so squirrels can't jump from the tree or bush onto the feeder. Include tube feeders, ground feeders (hummingbird feeders), a tray or log on which to put out suet or mealworms. Clean your feeders periodically to ensure your offerings are safe and healthful.

• *Make your own hummingbird nectar* and omit the red food coloring added in the store-bought kinds. Mix ¼ cup (100g) of sugar to each 1 cup (240ml) of boiling water. Cool, then fill up your feeder. Make sure you clean your hummingbird feeders at least twice a week to prevent spoilage.

(continued)

• *Install bird houses.* Your local bird store can help you decide which ones will work in your yard so you can hope to attract cavity-nesting birds like chickadees, wrens, bluebirds and owls.

• *Create brush piles with downed limbs* in your yard. Wrens and other birds will find food and shelter there.

• *Keep cats indoors.* Cats kill millions of birds each year! Check out *www.abcbirds.org/abcprograms/policy/cats/index.html.*

• *Provide water.* If you don't have a creek or pond in your yard, add a bird bath on the ground or pedestal. While moving water is an attractant, birds also enjoy water misters that can be found at bird stores.

• Once birds start coming to your yard, consider becoming a "Citizen Scientist" by counting them! Links below.

1. Project FeederWatch: *www.birds.cornell.edu/pfw/*
2. Great Backyard Bird County: *www.birdsource.org/gbbc/*
3. Audubon's Christmas Bird Count: *www.audubon.org/bird/cbc/index.html*

— *Karen Bearden*

No doubt about it, gardening is great therapy — good exercise, and a powerful way of overcoming our culture's prevailing "nature deficit disorder" by connecting to the seasons and to a universe larger than yourself. It's also a great way of minimizing the distance from farm to plate, and from farm to vase. Vegetable and flower gardens can help introduce wonder back into your world. So get busy and get going. A bountiful garden is one of the best gifts you can give yourself — and your family.

Chapter Seven

Reclaiming Ritual and Community for Life

Design the rituals of your life for meaning. Engage in community life for health and well-being.

Bring consciousness to your daily rituals, reflecting on the significance of each one. Consider these rituals as beads on the necklace of your life; select them carefully, honoring their significance and place in the lineup. Remove the ones that no longer resonate with you. Engage in community organizations and activities as a primary life ritual. Infuse your important celebrations — such as birthdays, graduations, weddings and funerals — with meaning. Save money with advance planning and by giving original thought to your annual and rite-of-passage celebrations.

The Rituals of My Life

The seventh path to simplicity involves choreographing the rhythms and rituals of your life to ensure greater structure, stability and contentment. Our society's prefab version of "the good life" leans on haste, convenience and improvisation while accommodating the driving force of commercial interests. This version of the "good life" comes at the expense of carefully constructed, self-generated ritual and routine. Here's how it works: You make no provision for lunch so you pick up fast food on the fly, or you fail to prepare for a child's birthday, so you rush out at the last minute to a big-box store to pick up all the pricey themed trimmings. By pressing this commercial default button for the celebration of life, the activity itself not only rings hollow, but carries out-sized financial and environmental costs.

Since moving into the Sunflower House in 2007 and launching full-bore into my life as a single mother, I have devoted a great deal of attention to the role of rituals in my life. I'm not talking so much about religious ceremonies or annual celebrations around birthdays and holidays (though these are important and I'll address them in this chapter) as life's little routines — the choreography of my daily life. I have applied my own mantra, "Nothing's too small to make a difference," to my daily routine, focusing my attention on the minutia that make up the day. As a result, I have taken a hard look at every act: from my wake-up-in-the-morning routine, to my exercise regimen, work habits, meal prep and meal time, to the way I prepare for sleep. I believe that the structure of each day — which is composed of hundreds of tiny decisions — is vitally important for my well-being and that of my son.

Without this structure and ritual, life threatens to become pattern-less, unproductive and chaotic, with no sense of progression or flow. These small decisions, when made in advance and adhered to, have led to greater control over my life, allowing me to set large goals and steer my life — by increments — in whichever direction I choose.

My Morning Rituals

Without going through every single ritual of my day, let me give you insight into how I infuse meaning into my "top-of-the-morning" routine. In bed, before I get going for the day, I repeat the mantra of the moment to focus my mind on what I plan to accomplish that day. Sometimes, I repeat affirmations around my larger life goals, such as my long-standing desire to learn the Polish language or to live more fully in the present. Sometimes, I say affirmations to wrestle down fears, financial and otherwise.

When I get up, generally around 7 a.m., the first thing I do is draw up the hemp Roman shades in my bedroom to let the light in, then make my bed. Moving into the kitchen, I turn on the heat under the tea kettle to start the water boiling for coffee. I mix two ounces of pomegranate juice with an equal amount of orange or grapefruit juice and swallow my vitamins, including calcium and capsules of flaxseed and fish oil. With each vitamin, I say a little prayer to support the pill's purpose, such as "for better bones," when swallowing the calcium. I make my way through the dining and living rooms and my den, opening all the curtains and blinds, offering thanks for a new morning and for the lovely quarters I inhabit. I move into the sunroom where my activity has roused Whiskers; his meows signal a readiness for human attention. I check his food and water bowls.

As I move through the day, going for my morning swim, stopping by the post office to pick up and send out mail, coming back to work in my home office, all of my activities incorporate a similar level of ritual. Because I work on myriad projects, I set a list of priorities daily and weekly and divide the day into blocks of time with specific goals attached to each block. Introducing this level of structure into my day is tremendously helpful and allows me to achieve my goals.

You, too, would be wise to pay specific attention to your rituals and to the arc of your day. Once you design rituals and routines for your life, you can start to gain mastery through conscious choice and affirmation. When tackling major life changes, for example, instead of going on a crash diet to lose 60 pounds, try building self-reinforcing prompts that may come at your habit of overeating from more indirect acts. Cheer on positive decisions around food choices, for instance, such as reaching for a kiwi fruit instead of, say, a chocolate chip cookie. When you bite into the kiwi, run through the list of benefits: you're protecting your eyes from macular degeneration and lowering your risk for blood clots, you're consuming significant amounts of vitamin C and potassium; and accelerating the healing of your wounds. Similarly, expressing gratitude for the "little things" in life (your heated home in the winter or the security provided by your job each time you deposit a paycheck) effectively moves your mental framework from negative or teetering to positive.

Examine your own daily rituals and find ways to create new ones — or tweak existing ones — to help improve your body, mind and spirit. No doubt about it, these routines are vitally important not only to you but to the significant others in your lives. I've found that Henry relishes our mealtime and bedtime routines. My elderly mother has come to count on frequent invitations to family dinners at my home. While shared mealtime is without question the gold standard of family rituals (see discussion in Chapter 5), take a hard look at your other personal rituals to advance change in your life, to make your way toward a satisfying and balanced life.

Raising Your Consciousness Through Life Themes

Crafting the important rituals of your daily life may well be the best way of introducing consciousness — and intentionality — to your existence. But other tools exist toward the same end. My remarkable writer friend of a quarter of a century, Holly Stevens, who lives at Glenagape, a 40-acre retreat center near Greensboro, North Carolina, has developed another way of raising awareness in life: *by training her attention and con-*

sciousness on life themes. If you need to be more forgiving, for example, set forgiveness as your theme for a month, a season, or a year. Holly selects new themes for herself on an annual basis and shares her perspective in the following reflection.

Out With Resolutions and In With Themes

"Several years ago, I gave up the practice of setting New Year's resolutions, most of which were forgotten by February anyway, in favor of establishing a New Year's theme. Instead of focusing on a personal deficiency as resolutions often do, each theme establishes a single word that serves as a filter, helping me to find novel meanings in ordinary experience and to make better choices about how I spend my time.

My first such theme, for 2002, was gratitude. At the time, my 1992 breast cancer had recurred, lodging in my hips, ribs, spine, jaw and skull. I wanted to hold onto awareness of the small and large mercies given me. Little did I know how well gratitude would serve me that year, as my back fractured at the site of a tumor, paralyzing me from the waist down. By cultivating gratitude, I could frame these setbacks as an adventure, if not one of my choosing.

In 2003, my theme became transition, as I moved back to my beloved North Carolina after an absence of 19 years. I focused on embracing a new faith community in Greensboro, North Carolina, and establishing new patterns with my husband, Bill, which include a daily meditation after breakfast and reading aloud to each other in the evenings.

Storytelling and its counterpart, listening, became my separate themes for 2004 and 2005. In the first year, I recorded my life stories for loved ones and led a spiritual autobiography course for adults. In the next, I designed a three-day listening retreat in which I could read or listen to others but could not write or speak aloud. I began to realize that even with my physical limitations, I could make a difference by serving as a conduit for stories, both in sharing my own and in eliciting the stories of others.

(continued)

Each year since has brought new threads of insight and options via carefully selected themes: stillness in 2006, benediction in 2007, gentleness in 2008. Gently, these themes have reminded me to slow down and be mindful of the present; to use language, as a benediction does, to raise up the good in others; to use forms of leadership that embrace consensus-building and patience.

For 2009, I have chosen handicraft. As with all New Year's themes, only hindsight will reveal how it will play out, but I see the effects of its persistent nudges: I'm writing more handwritten notes rather than emails or word-processed letters; I'm saying "yes" to some invitations because they contain a hand-spun element; I've even taken up re-teaching myself algebra after 35 years, which, if nothing else, is reintroducing me to pencils and erasers!

About the only quality New Year's themes share with New Year's resolutions is their timing: I do begin reflecting on possible themes for the coming year as winter approaches, turning the candidates over in my mind and during meditation, listening or reading with an alertness to possibilities. Early winter also becomes a time for taking stock of the quality of my life, as I review the year to identify the ways that the chosen theme played out. Unlike a resolution, too often broken and forgotten just weeks after it is set, my themes are my friends, always there, nudging and beckoning, and bending even when I don't always respond as soon as I should."

— *Holly Stevens*

Ritualizing Community Involvement

Aside from the important rituals established inside your home, heart and head, when constructing "the good life" for yourself, little else ranks as high as community engagement. The reality, though, is that Americans have been gradually *disengaging* from organized groups, clubs and societies since the late 1960s, in general terms, abandoning the public realm for private, cloistered lives. As we work longer hours to make money to ratchet up our materially based, financially indexed "standard of living," in reality, our satisfaction-based, people-oriented "standard of life" has been rapidly declining.

When I refer to "community involvement," I'm talking about regular attendance at such religious organizations as churches, synagogues and mosques, as well as committed participation in clubs, societies and civic groups like Rotary, Lions Club, Toastmasters, the PTA, the NAACP, the AAUW, bowling leagues, garden clubs, professional societies and the like. Robert Putnam's landmark book, "Bowling Alone: The Collapse and Revival of American Community" (Simon & Schuster: 2000), identified a national crisis of plummeting social engagement, which translates into reduced social capital. ("Social capital" refers to the social networks and relationships among and between individuals who cooperate and share values and behaviors; it is a powerful asset that carries economic benefit.) Putnam makes the case that America has become a nation of isolated loners — we now literally and metaphorically "bowl alone" rather than in leagues with others — and offers solutions to reverse the trend. (With the popular Wii™ sports video game, you can now literally bowl alone in the privacy of your own rec room.)

"For the first two-thirds of the twentieth century, a powerful tide bore Americans into ever deeper engagement in the life of their communities," he writes, "but a few decades ago — silently, without warning — that tide reversed and we were overtaken by a treacherous rip current. Without at first noticing, we have been pulled apart from one another and from our communities over the last third of the century." Putnam goes on to say that civic engagement may be hard to see but serves to build a kind of "civic infrastructure" that is as crucial to the society it serves as the roads, and the water and sewer lines. "Our schools and neighborhoods don't work so well when community bonds slacken … our economy, our democracy, and even our health and happiness depend on adequate stocks of social capital."

Though Putnam's work has received enormous attention, it is not the only alarm bell ringing from the social sciences showing that our community life is at peril. Another troubling study — based on research from a 2006 poll commissioned by the National Science Foundation — demonstrates without a doubt that *social isolation is growing rapidly in America.* The number of people who say that they have no one in whom they can confide *has more than doubled since 1985.* "Overall, the number of people Americans have in their closest circle of confidants has dropped from around three to about two," The Washington Post reported in June 2006. "The comprehensive new study paints a sobering picture of an increasingly fragmented America, where intimate social ties — once seen as an integral part of daily life and associated with a host of psychological and civic benefits — are shrinking or nonexistent. In bad times, far more people appear to suffer alone. ... If close social relationships support people in the same way that beams hold up buildings, more and more Americans appear to be dependent on a single beam."

> *"Whereas nearly three-quarters of people in 1985 reported they had a friend in whom they could confide, only half in 2004 said they could count on such support. ... The number of people who said they counted a neighbor as a confidant dropped by more than half, from about 19 percent to about 8 percent."*
>
> — The Washington Post, June 23, 2006

Get Involved

So what's to be done about this erosion of bonds among and between us?

The answer is community involvement, which is central to one's health and well-being. Indeed, Lewis M. Feldstein, president of the New Hampshire Community Foundation and coauthor with Putnam of "Better Together: Restoring the American Community" (Simon & Schuster: 2003), during a taping for "Simple Living," cited data indicating if you're not a member of a single social, civic, religious or fraternal organization and you join one, your chances of dying that year will drop by half. "If you join another organization that year," he said, "your chances of dying drop another 25 percent." In other words, engaging with others is as vital to your health and well-being as eating healthfully, exercising regularly, and quitting smoking.

Going forward, as you examine your commitments and priorities, I urge you to find the time in your life for community. Bear in mind that community, like love, doesn't happen overnight. It takes concerted effort and long-haul commitment to pull off. When thinking of ways to construct community in your realm, remember, you don't have to invent the wheel. What matters is joining a group and throwing yourself into it.

Each of our lives is unique, of course, so without knowing the specific perimeters of yours, it's hard to prescribe precisely how you can manage this. But, in general terms, in order to carve out time for community life, you may need to cut back on something else: too many hours at work; computer or television time; even privatized recreational activities like boating, weight lifting or exercising on Wii™. If you spend two hours a day commuting, consider moving closer to where you work, which would allow you to reduce your commute and engage in community life.

I can attest to the fact that my attendance at church and my Rotary Club each Tuesday for lunch has proven, year in and year out, to be an almost universally uplifting experience. If I am stuck on a professional or personal problem, going to Trinity Episcopal Church in Mount Airy, in which congregants are reminded weekly about the universality of human foibles and God's compassion, transports me to another place. Just walking into the room where Rotary lunch is served and seeing the smiling faces of my many friends takes me out of myself. I've been a member of the club for 17 years now and that longevity adds depth and meaning to the experience.

Following are ways to create community in your world:

• *Join a group and take your membership seriously.* Find meaning in your own Rotary. For my sister, that would be Toastmasters, in which members develop public speaking and leadership skills. Once you find a good fit, attend the group's meetings and take its mission and goals to heart. If it's a book club, read the book before you go, so you can fully engage in discussion. If your group is looking for volunteers, find a way to pitch in.

• *Donate to worthy causes.* Give blood (if you're able), money, books, or whip up a peach cobbler for the neighborhood bake sale. These generous gestures will help out worthy causes while building bonds with members of your community. As my friend, Peggy Payne, relates in the book she coauthored with Allan Luks, "The Healing Power of Doing Good" (Fawcett Columbine: 1991), "generosity invariably circles round to bless the donor more than anyone else."

• *Break bread together.* Eating together on a regular basis is one of the best ways to create community. Start or join a dinner club. Make it potluck, or get 12 individuals or couples together and let each feed the group one month of the year. You may organize a diverse group or gather around common interests. Schedule regular dinners, but at least once a month. You'll be amazed to see how community flourishes in this setting.

• *Start a simplicity circle.* Simplicity circles are an ideal way to build community while creating support for the scaled-back life. According to my friend and colleague, Cecile Andrews, author of "The Circle of Simplicity" (Harper: 1997), the ideal group size is 10 to 12. Rotate meetings at different people's homes, or establish the meeting at a community center. Let the circle run for at least 10 weeks (longer if you like). Ask each participant to commit to one action step per meeting (even something simple like contacting an old mentor to express appreciation, or cleaning out a shelf in the garage), then report back to the whole group later about the results of her action step.

• *Learn names.* This may sound trivial, but it's well worth the effort. Learning someone's name is a simple but meaningful good-will gesture that is guaranteed to build bonds. When you first meet someone, ask the person's name and then repeat it as many times as you can in conversation (and later privately) until you've got it down pat. Then, next time you see that person, say, "Chad, I'm happy to see you!" Or, "Shirley, you do a great job keeping the locker room clean." People feel significant — and cared for — when you take the trouble to learn their names.

• *Practice the art of listening.* Deep listening goes a long way toward crossing the bridge to another soul. Hearing about someone else's life, struggles and triumphs will bring perspective to your own — as well as offer ideas and inspiration. Really listening — being in the present moment with another person — represents a profound act of love.

• *Take control of your time.* If you're like most Americans, you may need to recast your approach to time. In general, slowing your pace will bring more pleasure to your life while making room for others — especially community connections. While you're at it, honor the time of others by keeping appointments and being punctual.

Female Friendship: A Life-Saver!

A landmark UCLA study shows that women can chemically relieve stress by bonding with other women. New research shows "that women have a larger behavioral repertoire than just fight or flight," explains Laura Cousin Klein, Ph.D., an Assistant Professor of Bio-behavioral Health at Penn State University and one of the study's authors. "It seems that when the hormone oxytocin is released as part of the stress responses in a woman, it buffers the fight or flight response and encourages her to tend children and gather with other women instead." When a woman is either "tending or befriending," studies suggest that more oxytocin is released, which mitigates stress and creates a calming effect. Unfortunately, this calming effect does not extend

(continued)

to males, due to the effects of testosterone which is produced under stress and effectively tamps down the effects of oxytocin. Estrogen, Klein states, appears to enhance it. Clearly this study opens the door for new work and even the possibility that the female tendency to "tend and befriend" may explain why women outlive men. Studies confirm that social ties lower our risk for disease by reducing blood pressure, cholesterol and heart rate.

Are You "Game" for a Good Laugh?

Board games are enjoying a resurgence of late as folks look for diversions that don't break the bank. Chess, checkers, cards, jigsaw puzzles and board games are making a big comeback, often in group settings.

"Many times we've commented about how hard it is to be there on a Friday night after a long week of work," Shirley Ferguson, a member of a board game group called the Game Dames, recently told the Winston-Salem Journal about the monthly get-together. "But we always feel energized after eating, talking, laughing and playing games. It's a good deal all around." The Game Dames — a group of women in their early 60s who have been playing together for 12 years — enjoy the intellectual challenge of games such as Trivial Pursuit®, Cranium® and Pictionary®. "Sometimes it humiliates us," she says. "Other times, it gives us a chance to shine. Most of the time, it just gives us a good laugh."

Board games offer adults, like Ferguson, the chance to play — a casualty of the modern age. Adults, as it turns out, need play, just as children do. We all thrive on the twists and turns of fate, the element of surprise; we need the opportunity to exercise our skill and sharpen our wits in the real-time company of others.

A couple of years back, I met an entrepreneur named Tony Kvale at a green living show in Chicago and, before we knew it, we found ourselves on the subject of board games. Turns out, Tony has channeled his life-long passion for tabletop games into the creation of a four- to eight-player game called Head1liners. "The players write headlines relating to photos on the front page of a newspaper. The game is played by submitting all of these headlines anonymously," Tony explains. "Each player votes for the one he likes best, and no one can choose his own." Turns out, it's reminiscent of the game of Fictionary that was the hit of a recent Thanksgiving at my home (see below). "The inspiration came from my friends and me writing wacky captions to ads," he explains. "The fun is in putting together short, succinct phrases about an image — seeing who can come up with the most imaginative one."

So how do games such as his, along with the old standbys like Monopoly™, Scrabble™ and Clue™, compare to the new electronic games that my son and others of his generation seem to prefer? "Instead of one person being in front of the computer, you have face-to-face interaction and eye contact," explains the Twin Cities-based Kvale. "This is not going to occur with a computer game." Board games, he says, allow people to "reconnect in the company of others." Another benefit: zero carbon cost to play. When constructing his game, Kvale worked overtime to make it eco-friendly. The cards are printed on recycled paper printed with vegetable-based inks, and the tiles made from recycled glass; to keep score, biodegradable pencils, commonly called golf pencils, are tucked into the box. (Head1liners can be ordered from *www.headlinegame.com* or by calling 651-204-6781.)

Thanksgiving Fun With Fictionary

"Have you ever played Fictionary?" asked my friend Krysia, her trademark impish look flooding her face. It was Thanksgiving in North Carolina a few years back and my California visitor was determined to introduce us to a simple party game that she assured us was a barrel of laughs. How could I object? No quicker than the dishes were in the kitchen, we all were on the couch, learning a game that requires nothing other than a dictionary, some paper, pencils and a vivid imagination.

The game goes like this: For each round, a designated player scans the dictionary for a word for which no one knows the definition. She reads it out loud. If no one knows what it means, then she writes down one of the

(continued)

definitions from the dictionary listings and all players concoct definitions that are meant to sound real and fool the other players. The designated player then scrambles the papers and reads out all the definitions. Players vote on which one they believe to be real. Players win points for selecting the correct one as well as for having their false definitions selected.

The night we played, some of the words selected were "welter," "revenant," "fleche," "patonce," "wegotism" and "vellication."

For "vellication," for instance, one player wrote, "vellication: proof that someone is 'vell' or 'well' as spoken by someone with a German accent." Another concocted: "a condition of acute inflammation of the vericose veins in mammals other than humans." Still another wrote of "vellication": "a medical condition indicating hardening of the veins." (The correct answer: twitching.)

On the final round, Henry selected the term "clinker-built" — which elicited a range of fake definitions for something that was poorly constructed. One false definition that elicited several rounds of laughter was this: "a temporary and often substandard method of building, primarily seen in sub-Saharan Africa developed by Sir Francis Clinker."

Belly laughs were the ideal final course after our Thanksgiving feast. This game was perfect for our range of ages from 9 to 84. Our wallets were not lightened one bit by trying the game. Henry loved Fictionary so much that he kept begging for additional rounds — and never once the entire evening did the word "Gameboy®" cross his lips.

Co-Housing Gives You Your Village

If you're ready to take the plunge into community life in a big way, consider co-housing. Co-housing communities offer individual residences — from free-standing houses to town houses to condo-apartments — along with common areas that foster bonding and community life. A small but rapidly growing segment of residential housing in America and worldwide, co-housing provides an ideal foundation for creating familial bonds amongst people who may not be related by blood or marriage. The approach of most co-housing projects is eco-friendly: including clustered housing and construction from green building materials. Co-housing offers "traditional forms of social and economic support that people once took for granted: family, community, and a sense of belonging" according to Charles Durrett, author of "The Senior Cohousing Handbook" (New Society: 2009), "which must now be actively sought out."

"Stop and Chat": Simplicity in One Seattle Neighborhood

"Walking home from the "think tank" the other day, I thought about the fun we'd just had, laughing and talking. The "think tank" is a group of us who meet regularly every Wednesday at 12:30 p.m. at Mae's Café in Seattle. Our purpose? Just getting together; everyone is welcome.

My husband and I started the group as part of our Phinney EcoVillage program — a neighborhood project to encourage sustainability and community. (Phinney is a neighborhood in Seattle.) We're looking for ways to encourage people to live more simply and sustainably, and the research points to the importance of relationships. When people have friends and community, they're happier, healthier, and live longer! Further, they save money because they lose their desire to be consumers — consumerism is often a desire to fill an emptiness that comes from loneliness and isolation.

Phinney EcoVillage is part of the growing localization movement. All over the country neighbors are coming together to garden together, share tools, create emergency watch programs, and encourage people to live more sustainably. Each neighborhood group comes together to find ways to help people reduce their use of energy, to eat local food, to drive less, to walk and cycle more, to support their local businesses, and to revive old-fashioned skills like canning and preserving foods. But most of all, it's about the joys of getting together. The research is very clear: The best thing you can do for yourself is spend time with others in warm, supportive conversation or activities.

Many of the sustainable neighborhood programs help people live more simply — something we really need these days as the economy continues to slip and slide. We help people figure out the best thrift and consignment

(continued)

stores, the best techniques for garage sale-ing, or how to get free things from Free Cycle (www.freecycle.org). A lot of people hardly buy anything new at all! It's amazing what you can learn from your neighbors when you take time to talk with them.

There are lots of different groups you can form. We have a voluntary simplicity circle, a climate change group, and a group we call "Democracy Conversations," where we read political books. These are organized events that meet regularly, but more informal activities work, as well. For instance, one of my favorite programs is our "stop and chat" project. It encourages people to get out of their houses, walk around the neighborhood, and chat! This doesn't have to be hard. Try it, and you'll see how wonderful it is to walk through your neighborhood and strike up conversation. If you want to taste the joys of this new movement, see if there's a cafe in your neighborhood where you can hang out. Don't take your laptop, but chat with the person at the next table.

Neighborhood programs encourage people to shop at farmers markets where you not only get great produce, but mingle with others. Eat local, buy local, live local! A few years ago, a neighborhood in a South American country reduced its crime rate just by having the neighbors take the time to greet each other every morning. You bring new satisfaction to your life by just saying hello. (And it doesn't cost a thing.)"

— Cecile Andrews

Celebrations and Rites of Passage

Just as you need to put thought and effort into crafting daily rituals, and time and commitment into building community bonds, annual celebrations and lifetime rites of passage likewise require an active rather than passive approach. As with so many areas of our lives, we have detached ourselves from involvement and full participation in such events as christenings, birthday parties, weddings and retirement parties. Our arms-length approach to these important celebrations prevents us from experiencing the full component of emotions associated with them. For instance, the "convenience" of picking up the fixings for a child's birthday party at a big-box retailer, all paper and plastic and throwaway all the time — making it a "no-fuss, no-muss" affair — actually detracts from participating fully in this festivity. This method is costly, impersonal, and leaves a large waste stream in its aftermath.

Choosing instead to infuse rituals and celebrations with original thought and meaning allows you to creatively construct such events, making them heartfelt. For example, instead of calling the wedding planner and choosing between packages A, B and C and letting her take care of the rest, when you put forethought — and original thinking — into this important rite of passage, you're likely to wind up with a far more meaningful event, one that honors your values.

When you take ownership of all the important celebrations in your life, you can enjoy the multiple and overlapping benefits which simple living choices provide. You can not only personalize the event and put your own (or your loved one's) stamp on it, but you can save money, be more eco-friendly — a more thoughtful consumer — all at the same time.

Percilla Sue Counts did exactly this when planning a "green retirement event" to celebrate her career with the North Carolina Extension Service, from which she retired in October 2008 as extension director for Watauga County. Instead of holding a ho-hum event in a rented room, with yellow layer cake, balloons and perhaps a gold watch, Sue allowed her passion for the environment to direct the action. She orchestrated an outdoor party, held at a farm near Boone, North Carolina. The festivity featured local foods, local mountain music, solar-generated electricity and, best of all, it generated zero waste. For the children, puppets were on hand along with a learning center focused on water quality. Instead of presents, Sue requested $25 donations be made to the Sue Counts Family and Community Development Foundation. But even this was optional, and children were free. "I wanted to celebrate the end of my official working career with an event that signified my commitment to education and environmental stewardship," Sue told me. Sue wanted her celebration to be memorable and resonate with her values. She succeeded — on all counts!

Thanksgiving, Christmas, Hanukkah and Kwanzaa

As we get older, the major holidays — Thanksgiving, Christmas, New Year's, etc. — seem to roll around more frequently; a new one is here before the last one ends. For women especially, the holidays add the pressure of increased family obligations, including organizing parties, cooking, decorating, buying presents — checking items off an endless "to-do" list. When money is tight, some may feel disheartened, especially when they have long focused on expensive gifts and parties rather than entering into the spiritual meaning of the holiday at hand.

"Simplifying and celebrating really do go together, especially at Christmas," states Alternatives' "Simplify & Celebrate: Embracing the Soul of Christmas" (Northstone: 1997). When you view streamlined celebrations as an opportunity rather than a deprivation, you may start to catch the holiday spirit ... once again. Indeed, with our recent economic downturn, many more Americans have taken up the baton for pared-down holiday celebrations — not only for Christmas, Hanukkah and Kwanzaa — in keeping with the desire to live more frugally, within our budgets, and more lightly on the earth. So rethink your holidays this year. When you focus on the meaning of the big day and are able to live in the present moment, you may be amazed by the happiness and meaning the holiday will bring to you and your loved ones.

Twelve Tips for Creating a Simpler Holiday

1. Make conscious choices: You decide what constitutes a meaningful holiday for you and your family rather than shifting into autopilot and following our consumer culture's pre-scripted plan for what you should do, be and buy.

2. Be true to yourself: Try not to compare yourself, your celebration, your gifts or activities against some "ideal," real or imagined.

3. Feel free to change: Just because you've always "done it that way" doesn't mean you have to do it that way forever. Remember that the most constant reality of life is change, and you will feel more active and alive when you're creating something new.

4. Plan ahead for the holiday: Whenever possible, involve your immediate and extended family, and anyone with whom you plan to share the holidays. For instance, if you decide to reduce spending this year, call or email family members in advance, telling them you plan to lower spending, for example, from $100 per recipient to $50 this year.

5. Avoid spending beyond your means: Do not be pressured by the culture around you — or even your closest friends — to compete dollar for dollar, bow for bow. When you're selecting a gift, or throwing a party, arrive at the dollar amount at which you feel comfortable and stick with it.

6. Consider buying gifts year-round: If gift-giving continues to be part of your holiday celebration, shop year-round. This will extend the holiday fun and take financial and shopping pressure off during the holiday season. Also, you can snap up something on sale and buy the perfect gift when you see it, rather than engaging in frantic, last-minute shopping excursions.

7. Shop inside your own home: Face it, most of us have more than we need, or even know we have. Find something of significance and give it to someone you care for with a history attached.

8. Give gifts of time and talent: Give gift certificates for your services: a home-cooked meal for four delivered to your friend's home; a massage to your significant other, redeemable when he needs it most; house cleaning or baby-sitting for an evening.

9. Give experiential gifts: That is vanishing gifts — gifts that don't add clutter. Tickets to the Nutcracker, an art show, the theater or a movie. If you cook or bake, give a loaf of bread, a jar of apricot preserves, or some heart-healthy oatmeal-granola cookies!

10. Wrap your gifts in comic strips: This is the method suggested by Billy Romp in the book we co-wrote, "Christmas on Jane Street" (Morrow: 1998). Or use second- (or third-) run gift wrap. Another eco-friendly option: those wonderful reusable cloth bags!

(continued)

> *11. Give to a worthwhile cause:* Make a donation in someone's name. Write him or her and tell what inspired you to make this gift. Just as with a material gift, the best donation comes when you tune into the recipient's philanthropic interests rather than giving to something that you support.
>
> *12. Focus on spiritual matters:* Capture the spiritual side of the holiday by reading religious scripture, prayer, study and reflection. Attend religious services.

Try some or all of these ideas out this year. Then take stock: Were your holidays more satisfying and meaningful? Jot down some notes. How can you improve it next year?

A Progressive "Green Wedding"

As a research associate for the World Watch Institute, Erik Assadourian has been studying the impact of environmental crises on the health of people and the planet since 2001. So when he and Aynabat Yaylymova, a native of Turkmenistan, decided to marry in September 2008, they planned nuptials that would minimize the carbon and financial cost and maximize the involvement of family, friends and their local Washington DC neighborhood in the planning and festivities.

The couple's approach was both practical and thoughtful. Because their friends and families were scattered along the East Coast (DC, Connecticut, and Atlanta), they decided to stage three separate parties and do the traveling rather than asking guests to do so. As a result, Erik and Aynabat were able to keep the total number of air travelers to 16, not counting their own travel. "This still added up to three metric tons of CO_2, or 6,600 pounds," Erik says, "but it would have been much more if we had had the wedding in one centralized location." Not only did this arrangement translate into reduced total carbon emissions, but it saved money for guests and enabled the nuptial couple to use smaller venues for two of their three parties. (Both of these smaller venues were free.) Erik estimates that they spent between $5,000 and $6,000 on the wedding, depending on what is included — or roughly a fifth of the cost of the average American wedding today. In the future, "progressive weddings" like Erik and Aynabat's may become the norm, with the bride and groom doing the traveling rather than the guests, comparable to the "progressive dinners" held in many communities in which diners move from house to house, taking their salad course in one home, the entree in the next, and so on.

Among the other eco-friendly ideas that Erik and Aynabat incorporated into their wedding:

• Inherited rings.

• Minimal flowers (and the ones they bought were organically grown).

• Vegetarian food at all parties.

• Bride's dress was locally tailored.

• The creation of a wedding Web site and electronic invitations to reduce the ecological and monetary cost of mailings.

• Erik's sister baked the wedding cake as a wedding gift.

• Local destination for honeymoon (no additional flights).

• Two photographer friends took photos and video of the Connecticut party as a gift.

• Guests volunteered to help set up and clean up at the parties, also saving expense.

Looking back on it now, Erik views his wedding to Aynabat as almost a textbook example of how social capital — family and friends pitching in — can replace financial capital in the creation of an amazing event. "Of course I'm biased but I can't imagine it being more wonderful any other way!"

Erik and Aynabat are among a growing number of couples in America who want to start their married life off without incurring significant debt or extracting a pound of planetary flesh. A progressive minister in Mount Airy, North Carolina, Steve Lindsley, who has officiated numerous weddings, offers the following insights into making getting hitched come off without a hitch. As a minister, musician and happily married father of two young boys, Lindsley devotes a lot of time to weddings — and sees a need to simplify, streamline and de-stress the big event — to keep, he says, "what should be a joyous ceremony from morphing into a Broadway production."

Getting Hitched Without a Hitch: A Minister Speaks

"Following is a list of suggestions about how to simplify your big day without feeling shortchanged.

• *Plan ahead:* Start early by talking to friends and finding out what they did for their weddings. Choose what feels right for you and only you, because it's your wedding. Plan a budget and stick to it.

• *When possible, have a longer engagement:* I suggest around a year in length, no less than nine months. This is a huge life transition that takes time to make. Shorter engagements make for a frantic time that is not as enjoyable as it could be.

• *Tame the guest list:* Most folks intend on having a "small wedding" until the guest list rears its ugly head. And by the time you've invited your friends, your fiancé's friends, your parents' friends, and your third-grade teacher, it's all over. The cost of your wedding is directly proportional to how many people you invite. Consider a smaller reception for families only. You can ask a few friends to host a larger covered-dish dinner a week after the wedding at someone's house or a fellowship hall.

• *Invite family members to help with various tasks:* Weddings are not just about a husband and wife getting married but about two families coming together. Often there are family members who want to be involved. Rather than resist and create hurt feelings, let 'em help! Just make sure you are direct with them about what *you* want and how you want it done.

• *Take a break once a week — together:* Put down the planning book once a week. Yeah, you can do it. Go out to dinner and a movie, take a walk through town, curl up on the couch together and watch your favorite TV show. Talk about anything and everything, even being married — but not the wedding. This is a time for the two of you to remind yourselves why you're doing this in the first place.

• *Rethink the "where" and "when" of the honeymoon:* Most folks bolt for their honeymoon right after the reception. But think about it: when else in life do we plan for a huge event and then go straight into a week away from home? Consider delaying your honeymoon a few weeks — or better yet, take a few "mini-honeymoons" over the first six months. Instead of a 10-day trip to the Bahamas, do two or three weekend excursions to a cabin in the mountains.

• *Oh, and one last thing: it's your wedding:* Enjoy the first few moments of your new life together!"

Steve Lindsley is a minister, singer/songwriter, college instructor, and blogger. For more visit www.stevelindsley.com.

Green Burial: Redefining the American Way of Death

Though weddings represent blissful beginnings for couples tying the knot and vicarious renewal for the rest of us, funerals also present us the opportunity for meaningful ritual in how we orchestrate the farewells to those significant others in our lives. The simplicity approach invites those preparing for their own deaths — and those handling funeral arrangements for their loved ones — with the opportunity to become better funeral consumers by taking back the preparation of the dead from institutional providers. The growing home funeral movement offers individuals and religious congregations with models for tending and burying the dead.

The (Toxic) American Way of Death

Earlier this year, I had the privilege of hearing one of America's foremost advocates of green burial, the writer Mark Harris, speak to a large, engaged audience at First Lutheran Church in Greensboro, North Carolina. Harris told us that in America today, cemeteries are less "bucolic resting grounds for the dead" than toxic dumps. The standard body preparation and burial process is a grisly, resource-intensive practice that extracts bodily fluids from the deceased and pumps into the cadaver a formaldehyde-based formula for preservation. After the embalming, the corpse is dressed, made up, and laid out for public viewing. Then it's placed into a casket, which is usually constructed of chemically treated wood and metal, which itself is secured in an outer liner. The whole process is meant to preserve the cadaver for as long as possible with negligible concern for the environmental impact on the land on which cemeteries are located. When this process is multiplied by the millions, the overall environmental impact is enormous, an infrequently mentioned culprit in our rapidly warming world.

I've long been aware of the terrible financial strain that the American way of death imposes on families. All but the most affluent among us are hit hard by the high cost of a conventional burial, including embalming, viewing, pricey coffins, headstone and the burial plot. A price tag averaging around $10,000 is daunting to families — coming at a time when they're least prepared to explore alternative arrangements or engage in financial negotiations. Many families are made to feel that the amount they spend on the deceased is somehow a reflection of the regard they had for that person, a public statement of their concern for the deceased, as well as an indicator of the family's position in the world.

I had always assumed that cremation was the most eco-friendly (and lowest-cost) option. But in his presentation and book, "Grave Matters: A Journey Through the Modern Funeral Industry to a Natural Way of Burial" (Scribner: 2007), Harris makes it clear that a "natural burial" is superior to cremation (though cremation is better than a conventional burial). Natural green burial can involve a ritualistic cleaning and wrapping the body in a shroud, cloth or simple, untreated wooden (or cardboard) box and laying it into a shallow grave where the body can return to the elements that gave it life. It's the way Americans were buried in the past.

My friend, Holly Stevens, who has been battling cancer since 1992, has taken on the role of "funeral consumer advocate." In her work advocating for natural burial, she hears time and again from families "who have no idea that embalming is rarely required by law, that they can indeed buy a low-cost casket from a source other than the funeral home, or even construct their own, or that in all but six states a family may care for its own dead until burial or cremation with no involvement of a licensed funeral director."

Adding insult to injury is the fact that the cost of a funeral places a disproportionate burden on the poor. In a 2008 survey conducted by Stevens, of funeral homes and crematories in Greensboro, she "discovered the median cost of a funeral represents 15 percent of the average income of a resident in the most affluent zip code area and a whopping 44 percent of the average income of a resident in the least affluent. Like the regular surveys of the National Funeral Directors Associations, those figures didn't even factor in the costs of a grave liner, plot, marker, flowers or obituaries."

Stevens calls on religious bodies to reclaim their traditional role of helping minister final rites. Stevens' own Quaker congregation, New Garden Friends in Greensboro, recently formed a small committee "that is learning what used to be common knowledge — how to bathe, dress and lay out a body for a vigil in the home and then transport it to its final destination," she says. "While a family can independently acquire the simple skills and legal knowledge to care for its own dead, caring groups add consistency and acquired wisdom to the mix. Most importantly, they invite the role of the faithful community in sanctioning a funeral etiquette that is simpler, more affordable, and ultimately more sacred than before."

My Journey to the Good Life

The last two years of my life have been about continuing to improve and refine the life for my down-sized family of two, plus Whiskers, our beloved gray cat. I know that when I am following my own rituals and routines, I am happier and more effective with my work. I am convinced that Henry relishes our routine as well — despite the fact that he rolls his eyes and tries to poke holes in whatever I construct. (What else would you expect from a 12-year-old, a newly minted tweenager!) I know this because when life's inevitable stresses erupt, he is the first to reach out for the comfort of our rituals.

I remain engaged in community life — here in Mount Airy, but also with friends and colleagues nationally and internationally. Little is as satisfying to me as connecting with others, helping them whenever I can, advancing my agenda of promoting simple, sustainable living wherever I can. Luckily, there have been no funerals for my close family since my father passed away in 1996. However, I have incorporated the directive in my own will for a natural burial, if possible, or the most eco-friendly option available when my time comes.

I have also made a conscious effort to bring special meaning to birthday celebrations and other holidays and events over the last two years. My mother's most recent birthday this past March was one of the best ever. My dear cousin, Scott Kelley, traveled from Springfield, Missouri to celebrate. I prepared a special dinner for Mama, and along with Scott and Henry, entertained two lovely friends from Mount Airy and a special friend from Winston-Salem that night. I joke, that my cousin, Scott, was the "girl in the cake" of the evening. His outsize effort to attend the party will not soon be forgotten.

Your Journey to the Good Life

Your journey to the "good life" is now nearly complete. I'm not suggesting that you've learned every lesson or taken it all in. Guess what! I haven't either. Achieving simplicity in this lifetime is not an easy thing. It does not happen overnight, nor does anyone ever really "arrive." Like life itself, the progression toward simplicity is a continuous process. Two steps forward, one step back. We've covered a lot of ground in these pages — perhaps much of it is new to you. We've examined ways to achieve financial independence through frugality and the wise management of money; we've looked at ways to find meaningful work and bring meaning to the work you have. I've shared my ideas with you about finding happiness by rethinking your housing choices, urging you to reach for decorating choices that reflect your inner self, as well as incorporating green cleaning and clothing choices into your home. I've led you back into the kitchen to reclaim home cooking and the old-fashioned sit-down meal and out into the garden to grow some of your own food while reconnecting with nature.

On the final path to the good life, I have invited you to closely examine the daily rituals of your life and make conscious choices around them. One of the most valuable but under-heralded components of the good life is ritualized community involvement. We as human beings vitally need connection with others, yet forces in our contemporary society — such as automation, the accelerated pace of life, and the Internet age — are conspiring to separate us from each other more rapidly than ever before. Connecting with community adds value to your life, your health, and your worth as a human being. Reclaiming the good life cannot be accomplished without finding your place at the fire, the circle of life in the company of fellow human beings. Finally, bringing attention to important rituals — whether they are annual holiday or birthday celebrations — or once-in-a-life rite of passage events such as births, weddings and funerals

— can help bring special and unique meaning to your life. So take it all in; then make your choices. The simple life awaits you, around the corner and off on the horizon.

Resources

Books:

- "Your Eco-Friendly Yard: Sustainable Ideas to Save You Time, Money and the Earth" by Tom Girolamo (Krause Publications: 2009).

- "Natural Alternatives for You and Your Home: 175 Recipes to Make Eco-friendly Products" by Casey Kellar (Krause Publications: 2009).

- "Grow Your Own Tree Hugger: 101 Activities to Teach Your Child How to Live Green" by Wendy Rosenoff (Krause Publications: 2009).

- "Quick-Fix Healthy Mix: 225 Healthy and Affordable Mix Recipes to Stock Your Kitchen" by Casey Kellar and Nicole Kellar-Munoz (Krause Publications: 2009).

- "Get Satisfied: How Twenty People Like You Found the Satisfaction of Enough" edited by Carol Holst (Easton Studio Press: 2007).

- "Less is More: Embracing Simplicity for a Healthy Planet, a Caring Economy & Lasting Happiness" edited by Cecile Andrews & Wanda Urbanska (New Society: 2009).

- "Nothing's too Small to Make a Difference" by Wanda Urbanska & Frank Levering (Blair: 2004).

- "Simple Living: One Couple's Search for a Better Life" by Frank Levering & Wanda Urbanska (Viking/Blair: 1992; 2004).

- "Affluenza: The All-Consuming Epidemic" by John de Graaf, David Wann & Thomas H. Naylor (Berrett-Koehler: 2005).

- "The High Price of Materialism" by Tim Kasser (MIT Press: 2003).

- "Take Back Your Time: Fighting Overwork & Time Poverty in America" edited by John de Graaf (Berrett-Koehler: 2003).

- "A Circle of Simplicity: Return to the Good Life" by Cecile Andrews (HarperCollins: 1997).

- "Slow is Beautiful: New Visions of Community, Leisure & Joie de Vivre" by Cecile Andrews (New Society: 2006).

- "The Overworked American: The Unexpected Decline of Leisure" by Juliet B. Schor (Basic Books: 1993).

- "The Wabi-Sabi House: The Japanese Art of Imperfect Beauty" by Robyn Griggs Lawrence (Clarkson Potter: 2004).

- "Green from the Ground Up: Sustainable, Healthy & Energy-efficient Home Construction" by David Johnston & Scott Gibson (Taunton: 2008).

- "Green Remodeling: Changing the World One Room at a Time" by David Johnston & Kim Master (New Society: 2004).

- "The Not So Big House: A Blueprint for the Way We Really Live" by Sarah Susanka (Taunton: 1998).

- "Home By Design: Transforming Your House into Home" by Sarah Susanka (Taunton: 2004).

- "Not So Big Remodeling: Tailoring Your Home for the Way You Really Live" by Sarah Susanka (Taunton: 2009).

- "Ecopreneuring: Putting Purpose and the Planet Before Profits" by John Ivanko & Lisa Kivirist (New Society: 2008).

- "Rural Renaissance: Renewing the Quest for the Good Life" by Lisa Kivirist & John Ivanko (New Society: 2004).

- "Moving to a Small Town: A Guidebook for Moving from Urban to Rural America" by Wanda Urbanska & Frank Levering (Simon & Schuster: 1996).

- "Natural Remodeling for the Not-So-Green House: Bringing Your Home into Harmony with Nature" by Carol Venolia with Kelly Lerner (Lark Books: 2006).

- "Economics of Happiness: Building Genuine Wealth" by Mark Anielski (New Society Publishers: 2008).

- "Green Restorations: Sustainable Building & Historic Homes" by Aaron Lubeck (New Society Publishers: 2010).

- "Voluntary Simplicity: Toward a Way of Life that is Outwardly Simple, Inwardly Rich" by Duane Elgin (Quill: 1981).

- "The Living Universe: Where Are We? Who Are We? Where Are We Going?" by Duane Elgin (Berrett Koehler: 2009).

- "Small Is Beautiful: Economics as if People Mattered" by E.F. Schumacher (Harper & Row: 1973).

- "On Light Alone: A Guru Meditation on the Good Death of Helen Nearing" by Ellen LaConte (Loose Leaf Press: 1996).

- "Living the Good Life" by Helen & Scott Nearing (Schocken: 1954).

- "Gift from the Sea" by Anne Morrow Lindbergh (Random House: 1955).

- "State of the World" annual books (World Watch Institute).

Web Sites:

Krause Publications
www.krausebooks.com

Simple Living With Wanda Urbanska
www.simplelivingtv.net

Alternatives for Simple Living
www.simpleliving.org

Center for the New American Dream
www.newdream.org

Begley's Best
www.begleysbest.com

Green America
www.coopamerica.org

Not So Big Life
www.notsobig.com

Post Consumers
www.postconsumers.com

Share Save Spend
www.sharesavespend.com

Sierra Club Sustainable Consumption Committee
www.sierraclub.org/sustainable_consumption

Simple Living Network
www.simpleliving.net

Take Back Your Time
www.timeday.org
www.right2vacation.org

Index

A

Advocacy, 46, 50, 63, 174

Affirmations, 27

Affluenza, 24, 62

Ahluwalia, Gopal, 90

Alexander, Lamar, 72

American Libraries magazine, 73

American Library Association, 73, 205

Andrews, Cecile, 6, 14, 220, 226, 239-240

Authenticity, 41, 144

B

Balance, 22, 27, 37, 39, 56 64, 66, 81, 97, 207

Barbour, Elizabeth, 70

Barrington Village, 82-84

Begley Jr., Ed, 1, 113, 155

Behavior, 25, 48, 77

Benefits, 33, 45, 47, 61-63, 79, 83, 94, 100, 102, 150, 161, 170, 176, 180-181, 189-190, 198, 201

Blair, Gary Ryan, 70

Blogs, 25

Brintle, Hattie, 38, 40, 42-43, 75, 115-117, 133

Blair, Nick, 6

Brodnick, Bonni, 99, 157

Brody, Liz, 6

Bruzas, Laura, 6

K

L

M

S

About the Author

Wanda Urbanska is the author or coauthor of eight books, including "Simple Living; Nothing's Too Small to Make a Difference"; "Christmas on Jane Street" and "Less is More." She is the host/producer of the first nationally syndicated public television series advocating sustainable living, "Simple Living With Wanda Urbanska," which debuted on PBS stations in 2004. The series has produced four broadcast seasons (*www.simplelivingtv.net*). She has been published in The Washington Post, Los Angeles Times, Chicago Tribune, Mother Earth News, American Libraries and Natural Home. The New York Times described her as "a spokesperson for a phenomenon known as the simplicity movement," and O, The Oprah Magazine called her "the Martha Stewart of the voluntary simplicity movement." A graduate of Harvard University, Wanda is a speaker, consultant and blogger. She makes her home in North Carolina with her son, Henry, and cat, Whiskers.

Also by Wanda Urbanska:

- "Moving to a Small Town: A Guidebook for Moving from Urban to Rural America" (with Frank Levering)
- "Simple Living: One Couple's Search for a Better Life" (with Frank Levering)
- "The Singular Generation: Young Americans in the 1980s"